FRENCH ROCK

About the author

Bill Birkett, climber, author and photojournalist, has climbed exten-sively in Europe, USA and Japan. Author and photographer of a dozen books on the subjects of climbing and the great outdoors, his work is widely known and appears regularly in *Climber and Hillwalker*. Born in the Lake District, son of one of Britain's foremost rock climbers, climbing and the hills have been his passion from an early age.

Responsible for many new and hard climbs in the Lake District and Scotland, in 1985 he foresook his career as a Chartered Civil Engineer to write about and photograph his favourite subject. Bill still lives in his beloved Lake District but tours extensively, working from his Camper Van. He is a member of the Climbers' Club and Fell and Rock Climbing Club.

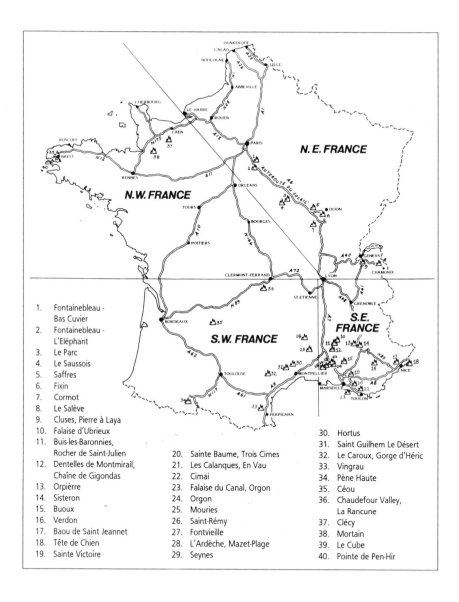

N. E. FRANCE

N. W. FRANCE

S. W. FRANCE

S. E. FRANCE

1. Fontainebleau -
    Bas Cuvier
2. Fontainebleau -
    L'Eléphant
3. Le Parc
4. Le Saussois
5. Saffres
6. Fixin
7. Cormot
8. Le Salève
9. Cluses, Pierre à Laya
10. Falaise d'Ubrieux
11. Buis-les-Baronnies,
    Rocher de Saint-Julien
12. Dentelles de Montmirail,
    Chaîne de Gigondas
13. Orpièrre
14. Sisteron
15. Buoux
16. Verdon
17. Baou de Saint Jeannet
18. Tête de Chien
19. Sainte Victoire
20. Sainte Baume, Trois Cimes
21. Les Calanques, En Vau
22. Cimai
23. Falaise du Canal, Orgon
24. Orgon
25. Mouries
26. Saint-Rémy
27. Fontvieille
28. L'Ardèche, Mazet-Plage
29. Seynes
30. Hortus
31. Saint Guilhem Le Désert
32. Le Caroux, Gorge d'Héric
33. Vingrau
34. Pène Haute
35. Céou
36. Chaudefour Valley,
    La Rancune
37. Clécy
38. Mortain
39. Le Cube
40. Pointe de Pen-Hir

Front cover: Martin Bagness on the belay ledge of La Voie Normale (6a+), La Rancune, Chaudefour Valley.

Back cover: Dave Birkett on Rodéo (7a+), Cimai

FRENCH ROCK

by Bill Birkett

CICERONE PRESS

MILNTHORPE, CUMBRIA, ENGLAND

ISBN 1 85284 113 3
British Library Cataloguing-in-Publication Data.
A catalogue record for this book is available from the British Library.

ACKNOWLEDGEMENTS

Many have helped and assisted in the production of this book, by climbing with me, posing for my photographs, offering advice and sharing their knowledge. I would like to take this opportunity to thank them all - although to produce a detailed list would be virtually impossible and grossly unfair to any that I may have inadvertently missed. However, the following I feel I must single out as being especially influential and helpful: Catherine Destivelle for showing me the Fontainebleau boulders and a freedom of movement that was breathtaking to watch, Cherry Harrop of the Green Parrot at La Palud for information on Verdon, Martin Bagness who shared a more than hectic trip in my camper van, Trevor Jones, not for capacity to consume wine or power up routes but for his meticulous proofreading, Claudie and Ian Dunn for their in-depth knowledge of France and their own contribution in words and photographs to the Brittany section, Dave Birkett for proving Darwin's theory of evolution by showing he has inherited his grandfather's climbing genius, similarly Chris Hamper who powered up many hard routes upfront and provided a million laughs.

Thanks are also due to North Sea Ferries, sailing from Hull to Zeebrugge, for their service and assistance on my many trips over the Channel. Likewise to Karrimor International whose rucksacks, clothing, footwear and camera bags have elegantly and functionally withstood my merciless pounding.

Finally very special thanks must go to my companion for the last ten years, for changing draft to final copy, for keeping the show going when all threatened to fall apart, for bearing Rowan our beautiful daughter - Susan my wife.

CONTENTS

Advice to Readers

Readers are advised that whilst every effort is taken by the author to ensure the accuracy of this guidebook, changes can occur which may affect the contents. It is advisable to check locally on transport, accommodation, shops etc but even rights-of-way can be altered and, more especially overseas, paths can be eradicated by landslip, forest fires or changes of ownership.

The publisher would welcome notes of any such changes

INTRODUCTION

As a land which is rich in rock for climbing, France offers cliffs of excellence stretching from one end of the country to the other: a staggering variety of quality rock with fair weather and sunshine to match. Its development has made France nothing short of a sport climber's paradise. From the 300-metre sheer white walls of Verdon, the pocket pulling perfection of Buoux, to the sandstone bouldering circuits of Fontainebleau can be found some of the finest free rock climbing in the world.

Intense development along with the widespread use and acceptance of bolt protection has revolutionised the art of climbing rock. Particularly so in France where today the hardest technical climbs in the world are to be found. Yet whilst for the élite few this may be everything, for most the climbing experience here is actually much deeper and broader. You don't have to be at the leading edge of technical performance to enjoy French rock.

Far from it, for with a wealth of rock climbing at all grades of difficulty, it can be very much a family affair. Take the beautiful Fontainebleau Forest where the boulders rise from a soft sandy base to provide a whole spectrum of interest. On any one day here, honed rock athletes tackle the most desperate moves possible side by side with toddlers making their very first rocky steps. A naturalism and freedom of movement combine to provide an intensity of pleasure thought by many to be the ultimate rock climbing experience.

On these crags quality climbing is coupled with a wonderful ambiance that can only be described as French - there is much to discover and enjoy. This book is both a guide to and an exploration of the best experiences to be found on forty quality crags. In keeping with the popular modern idiom that rock climbing should be fun in the sun, with easy car to rock access, the selection in this book excludes crags with a mountain seriousness, predominantly poor rock or generally unsound gear. It selects crags where the ultimate challenge is that of the upward movement itself. For those that thrill to the purity of movement on rock few will find this challenge lacking.

THE CONCEPT

French Rock selects crags throughout the country, dividing it into four geographical areas - NE, SE, SW and NW. Whilst undoubtedly the greatest concentration of climbing is to be found in the sunny south, crags of quality exist in each region. It is no longer necessary to charge headlong into the popular honeypots of the deep south. With the use of this book you can plan an itinerary of crags on the way.

Primarily the book serves as a guide. Firstly it locates and identifies the CRAG and its best routes. Secondly it describes something of the experience and character to be found (CRAG CHAT). On many of the crags selected it then goes further and selects one or more routes of particularly outstanding quality (SELECTED CLIMBS) - often this is regarded as the classic of the region. A concise description (ROUTE FACTS) is then followed by comment on the climb (ROUTE CHAT).

It will be appreciated that this book is not only a selected guide to the whole of France but also provides informative comment on both area and specific route character. In this way it is hoped that those planning a visit to a particular area can have some beneficial pre-knowledge of its flavour and quality. Additionally, back in the less temperate climate of England, some reference will remain to invoke pleasant memories of those far distant days on French rock.

I have always been a keen advocate of the principle that a single picture is worth a thousand words. This book has been designed to give a highly visual representation of the climbs available. The many photo-topos form the heart of the description and should be used in conjunction with the brief text to determine quickly the line of any particular climb. The book is meant to be carried in the rucksack and brought out at the base of the crag to identify the routes. Massive in its coverage of France, the guide must obviously be highly selective in its choice of routes (HIT LIST). Whilst I have carefully chosen and detailed each crag from personal experience the names of most of the routes are written at the base of the climb and this should always be used as a check against the photo-topo. However, each SELECTED ROUTE has been carefully detailed (with full route description given in traditional British style) and should serve as a reliable introduction to any crag. In almost all instances once the climb has been correctly identified at its base, climbing the route is simply a matter of following the line of bolts.

At present this is the most comprehensive guide to French rock climbing in any language, though a project such as this must be finite. Every crag, every route cannot be included, and development continues at a tremendous pace. New crags and new routes constantly emerge. In due course *French Rock 2* will be published offering an additional selection of great crags and climbs.

CLIMBING STYLE - SPORT AND ADVENTURE

"Sport Climbing" is fully protected by modern bolts spaced at regular intervals (fully equipped). "Adventure Climbing" is not fully protected by bolts; protection may consists of old insitu pegs or bolts randomly placed, or no insitu gear at all. Details on how to use this guide are to follow, but firstly there are some general points worth highlighting for those who may not yet have climbed in France.

French rock climbing falls basically into the two above categories. The former relies solely on bolt protection and in this category of climbing the routes are fully equipped by modern bolt protection. Generally the climb will finish at a lower-off point consisting of a fixed chain and crab. Depending on your rope length the crab can be clipped and the leader lowered to the ground, or an abseil can be made. Carefully note that in France it is usual to sport climb with a single full-weight rope (ranging from 10mm to 11mm in diameter), the most common length of which is 55m (they may range up to 65m). THIS MEANS THAT IN MANY INSTANCES THE STANDARD BRITISH ROPE OF 50M WILL NOT REACH THE GROUND. Many serious accidents have resulted, with the end of the rope running through the second's belay plate. If in doubt knot the ends of the rope in a lower-off situation, or if abseiling ensure that the ends of the rope touch the ground. A common location for this kind of mishap is on the Styx wall at Buoux - particularly on the popular route "Nombril de Venus".

On sport climbs only quick draws need be carried for protection. Adventure climbs are more akin to British routes and it will be necessary to place nuts etc. If in doubt as to the status of a route, particularly on a long route, at Verdon for example, carrying a small selection of nuts is a sensible precaution. The usual British tradition of double half-weight ropes are the best policy for these climbs.

The philosophy and style of French sport climbing differs drastically from that of traditional British free rock climbing. With bolt protection it is quite safe, even enjoyable and exhilarating, to push yourself to your own personal limit to the point of falling off. Once it is realised that falling is safe and part and parcel of the game, most people surprise themselves at just how much they can achieve.

If a route can't be climbed free on the first attempt it is usual to hang from the bolts - an ascent made in this manner is classed as having been "dogged". Hard routes are practised in this fashion until, often every move rehearsed, they can be led from the ground up without hanging from the gear. Particularly on the longer routes it is quite usual for a party to climb a route normally higher than their standard of difficultly, utilising some aid. At the higher standards of difficulty the ultimate objective is known as "the on-sight flash" - that is to climb a route free on first acquaintance. If this can't be achieved a climber will work on a route, practising the moves from a rest on the bolt, until a point where he pulls down the rope (leaving the quick draws insitu). If he/she then manages to lead the route without hanging or pulling on the bolts the ascent is known as a "red point". Leading the route free without any pre-placed quick draws, but with prior knowledge, is known as a "flash" - the second most prestigious form of ascent.

GRADING

The unspecified grades given in this guide are always the French Technical Pitch Grades. As a rule of thumb the French grade minus two, equals the British pitch grade, ie. French 6a = British 5b. Only for the SELECTED ROUTES is a comparison made, here an equivalent British grading is given in brackets. This is important for those new to French grading but will become less useful after a few routes have been climbed and an appreciation of the French system begins to materialise. At this stage forget about comparison - think French. Below is a table comparing French technical pitch grades with British and other international grading systems.

TABLE A

France	GB	USA	UIAA	Australia
3a (3-)	2b	5.2	3+	11
3b (3)	2c		4-	12
3c (3+)	3a	5.3	4	13
4a (4-)	3b	5.4	4+	
4b (4)	3c	5.5	5-	14
4c (4+)	4a	5.6	5	15
5a (5-)	4b	5.7	5+	
5b (5)	4c	5.8	6-	16
5c (5+)	5a	5.9	6	17
6a	5b	5.10a		18
6a+		5.10b	6+	19
6b	5c	5.10c	7-	20
6b+		5.10d	7	21
6c	6a	5.11a		22
6c+		5.11b	7+	23
7a	6b	5.11c	8-	24
7a+		5.11d	8	25
7b	6c	5.12a	8+	26
		5.12b		
7b+		5.12c	9-	27
7c	7a			28
7c+		5.12d	9	29
8a	7b	5.13b	9+	30
8a+		5.13c	10-	31
8b		5.13d	10	32
8b+		5.14a	10+	33
8c		5.14b		34

The British overall grading system was constructed with the element of danger as a vital constituent. There is a fundamental difference between safe, bolt protected sport climbing and traditional British climbing because the former has no element of danger inherent in a leader fall. There can be no direct comparison and it is important to realise that awarding sport climbs a British overall grade is a complete nonsense. The only common link between the British and French grading is the technical pitch grade. If in doubt, subtract two grades from the French to determine the approximate British technical grade, then equate this to an overall British grading if you must. For those who require to know the relationship between British overall grade and British technical (pitch) grade please consult TABLE B below.

TABLE B

Used Together		
British Overall Grade	British Technical Grade	
Moderate		1a
Difficult		2a
Very Difficult		2b
Severe (Mild)		2c, 3a
Severe		3a, 3b
Severe (Hard)		3b, 3c
Very Severe (Mild)		4a, 4b
Very Severe		4b, 4c
Very Severe (Hard)		4c, 5a
Extremely Severe	E1	5a, 5b
	E2	5b, 5c
	E3	5c, 6a
	E4	6a, 6b
	E5	6a, 6b
	E6	6b, 6c
	E7	6c, 7a
	E8	7b, 7c

One should also note, that as in every country, there is often a marked regional variation/interpretation of grading difficulty.

Particularly for the SELECTED ROUTES I have attempted to standardise grading, but regional variation may be judged to exist elsewhere. Certain routes have some permanent aid sections or utilise a point or two of aid to lower the grade of a classic route that would otherwise be impossible for the majority of climbers.

If aid occurs its difficulty is indicated by the universally accepted system of grading aid climbing - A0 to A4: a system where use of an insitu bolt at some point would be classed as A0 and the most technical and serious form of placing aid to achieve an ascent would be A4.

NOTES ON USE OF THE GUIDE

Areas

This guide is split into four geographical regions. A map illustrates these and another shows the postal areas or "Départements" referred to in the text. Within the four areas are maps showing the relative positions of the crags. The areas are dealt with in a clockwise order of rotation within the book: the North East, the South East, the South West and finally the North West. Within each area the crags are dealt with similarly in a clockwise manner. It is recommended that this book be used in conjunction with the *Michelin Motoring Atlas of France* (Scale

DÉPARTEMENTS

01 Ain	41 Loir-et-Cher	53 Mayenne	72 Sarthe
02 Aisne	42 Loire	54 Meurthe-et-Moselle	73 Savoie
03 Allier	43 Haute-Loire	55 Meuse	74 Haute-Savoie
04 Alpes-de-Haute-Provence	44 Loire-Atlantique	56 Morbihan	75 Paris
05 Hautes Alpes	45 Loiret	57 Moselle	76 Seine-Maritime
06 Alpes Maritimes	46 Lot	58 Nièvre	77 Seine-et-Marne
07 Ardèche	47 Lot-et-Garonne	59 Nord	78 Yvelines
08 Ardennes	48 Lozère	60 Oise	79 Deux-Sèvres
09 Ariège	49 Maine-et-Loire	61 Orne	80 Somme
10 Aube	50 Manche	62 Pas-de-Calais	81 Tarn
11 Aude	51 Marne	63 Puy-de-Dôme	82 Tarn-et-Garonne
12 Aveyron	52 Haute-Marne	64 Pyrénées-Atlantiques	83 Var
13 Bouches-du-Rhône			
14 Calvados			
15 Cantal			
16 Charente			
17 Charente-Maritime			
18 Cher			
19 Corrèze			
2A Corse-du-Sud			
2B Haute-Corse			
21 Côte-d'Or			
22 Côtes-du-Nord			
23 Creuse			
24 Dordogne			
25 Doubs			
26 Drôme			
27 Dure			
28 Eure-et-Loir			
29 Finistère			
30 Gard			
31 Haute-Garonne			
32 Gers			
33 Gironde			
34 Hérault			
35 Ille-et-Vilaine			
36 Indre			
37 Indre-et-Loire			
38 Isère			
39 Jura			
40 Landes			

65 Hautes-Pyrénées	84 Vaucluse
66 Pyrénées-Orientales	85 Vendée
67 Bas-Rhin	86 Vienne
68 Haut-Rhin	87 Haute-Vienne
69 Rhône	88 Vosges
70 Haute-Saône	89 Yonne
71 Saône-et-Loire	90 Territoire-de-Belfort
	91 Essonne
	92 Hauts-de-Seine
	93 Swine-St-Denis
	94 Val-de-Marne
	95 Val-d'Oise

1:20,000); for each crag a page and grid reference to the 1987 edition has been given. Additional reference has generally been made to the detailed IGN area maps (roughly equivalent to our Ordnance Survey) and to the Michelin maps.

The Text

A number of abbreviations are used for words that constantly re-occur; R = Right, L = Left, N, E, S and W indicate the points of the compass. A module of information is presented for each separate crag. The sub-titles are mostly self explanatory. Each module ends with a HIT LIST of routes chosen for that particular crag. Following many of the crags will be found a similar module detailing a SELECTED ROUTE or ROUTES.

The Climate/Climbing Season notes are best appreciated when comparing one area with another.

HIT LIST AND THE PHOTO-TOPOS

The **Hit List** of routes lists all the climbs that have been chosen for any particular crag. The photo-topos and routes are all uniquely referenced. "LP 4 Alea Jacta Est 30m, 6b" - can therefore be found on the photo-topo labelled LP (1-5). The LP (1-5) label indicates the crag is Le Parc and illustrates lines of routes LP1 to LP5. This is a simple but very effective system which means easy cross-reference can always be made between the route (in the **Hit List**) and photo-topo (a system I have adopted after many frustrating years attempting to match route and illustrated line of ascent).

When relevant, mainly where the climb is longer than one rope length to a lower-off point, the overall length of the route is detailed. Multi-pitch routes are usually given individual pitch gradings as follows: L1:6a, L2:5c - which means that pitch 1 is 6a, pitch 2 is 5c etc. When a SELECTED ROUTE is highlighted this means that this route will be exclusively detailed.

THE ENVIRONMENT

France is an outstandingly beautiful country but it should be appreciated that its often wild and rugged face is in reality quite fragile. In the dry south the risk of fire is especially potent, the consequences devastating. As climbers we are in a privileged position. We visit its most scenic areas, see more of its wildlife, play closer to nature than possibly any other group. Of course, for many this is a great part of our fascination with climbing. Have fun, enjoy it, but remember it is our own personal responsibility to ensure the areas we touch remain as we found them. Whenever possible leave no trace of your visit - take only photographs and the memory of your climbing day.

13

Fontainebleau, Bas Cuvier, White No 6 - 'La Défroquée (Graded 6b) - a popular slab problem on the white circuit.

AREA 1 NORTH EASTERN FRANCE

Roughly defined by a line drawn between Lyon and Paris and another due east from Lyon I have detailed some nine crags and seven selected climbs for this important region. Crags stretch south from Paris to Genève and further to the edge of the high Alps. In many respects this is the most traditional rock climbing area of France with Parisians developing Fontainebleau and the crags of the Saussois since the turn of the century. Likewise the Swiss of Genève have long developed the impressively large Salève as an alternative to alpine climbing. The crags at Cluses form a popular day alternative for those based in Chamonix. Recently many climbs in the charming Dijonnais region have been developed.

Including the crags of Saffres, Fixin and Cormot there is a fine array of climbing available. The classic tour to the sunny south should include Fontainebleau and the Saussois, the rainswept exit from the high Alps, Salève and Saffres. Although climbing may be possible all year round, the rain most certainly does fall in this area.

FONTAINEBLEAU BAS CUVIER

Map Ref: *Michelin Motoring Atlas, page 54, B2.*

Area Maps: IGN 2416w, L=(1082.9, 622.3), additionally there is a 1:25,000 scale map specifically covering the forest - sheet number 401. MICH 61.2/12

Guidebook: *Fontainebleau escalades et randonnées.*

Climate/Climbing Season: Precipitation (rain/snow) 600mm on 110 days of the year. Driest months are April and September/October. Climbing is possible all the year round although it can be both cold and wet from November to March inclusive.

Restrictions: Open all year round. Wild camping/bivouacking amongst the boulders and adjacent forest is strictly forbidden (no problem - free campsite a few hundred metres down the road). Widespread and liberal use of chalk frowned upon. Only use chalk on the harder problems or better still use a *pof* or resin bag as the French do.

Rock and Protection: Fine grained sandstone boulders with many of the problems somewhat polished, all the problems are soloed.

Situation: 8km NW of Fontainebleau, lying just N of the N7 and 3km SW of Chailly-en-Bière. The town of Fontainebleau is situated 65km NE of Paris. Département Seine-et-Marne (No.77).

Access: There are large car parks on either side of the N7. The car parks are connected by a pedestrian tunnel crossing under the busy road and the first rocks lie a mere 100 metres from the edge of the car park (1 minute).

Camping etc: There is an attractive free camping area 1.5km NW along the N7 (heading towards Paris).

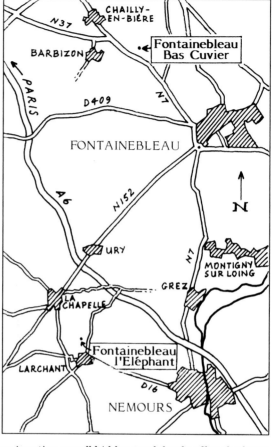

Virtually opposite the Barbizon junction a well hidden track leads off to the busy N7, past a house, to the campsite. Although the area is unwardened there is a fixed water supply, constructed barbecue sites and litter baskets. Supplies are best purchased in Fontainebleau (there is a kind of supermarket) and here will be found many cafés, a cinema, etc. Fontainebleau is the upmarket holiday escape from nearby Paris and is therefore expensive. At weekend a *Cordonnier des Falaises* mobile-van boot repairer and equipment seller operates from the car park. He does an excellent re-sole at a very reasonable price.

Crag Facts: The famous sandstone boulders scattered throughout the beautiful Fontainebleau Forest provide perhaps the finest concentration of bouldering in the world. There are around 60 distinct groups throughout the forest which vary enormously in quality, height and quantity. At Bas Cuvier there are some 147 individually numbered problems, from 3m to 7m in length, within the four main circuits. The circuits are colour coded to represent distinct groups of difficulty and within each group the problems are individually numbered. The ORANGE circuit is the easiest and consists of 50 numbered problems ranging in difficulty from 3c- to 5c- (British technical grade 3a to 5a). Then comes the BLUE circuit with 48 problems from 5c to 6a+ (British technical grade 5a to 5b+). The RED circuit consists of 42 problems from 6a to 6c (British technical grade 5b to 6a-) and is followed by the most difficult: the famous elite Bas Cuvier WHITE circuit with 27 numbered problems from 6c+ to 7c (British technical grade 6a to 6c). Bas Cuvier represents the best of Fontainebleau bouldering. Additionally it is simple to find, access couldn't be quicker and a campsite lies within a few hundred metres. On the debit side it is very popular (particularly at weekends) and many problems are rather polished.

CRAG CHAT

Arguably at its most devastatingly beautiful in autumn, when the leaves are falling from mid to late October, the *forêts de Fontainebleau* with their broad-leaved mixed deciduous trees and natural pines provides the rock climber with an unparalleled bouldering area. Beneath the canopy which shelters its white sandy base, a soft landing, lie a vast array of fine grained hard sandstone boulders sculpted perfectly for the rock climber. Resembling the tough rumpled grey skins of ancient elephants and fissured by cracks, flakes and pockets there is climbing here to nurture and entertain the climber from cradle to grave.

Long popular with Parisian-based climbers (serious climbing started here prior to the First World War), the area is affectionately known as the Bleau. Whilst each individual problem is capable of being totally absorbing, the variety, the range of technical difficulty and nature of

Fontainebleau, Bas Cuvier, White No 6t - 'Le Carnage' (Graded 7b) - one of the hardest. To the L is the famous White No 6b - 'L'Abattoir (Graded 7a).

Fontainebleau, Bas Cuvier, a popular boulder named Authenac with Red Nos 14, 15 & 16. The delectable Red No 17 (Graded 5b) is round the corner to the R.

the climbing is staggering. This combined with the pleasant ambiance of the area, green filtered light dappling rock, warm sand between toes, sweet heady smell of pine resin and bracken, makes it a unique area. It is enjoyable at all levels from the family day out, where all can participate, to those that seek the most technically demanding challenge and here are many very hard problems indeed. Pierre Allain, who developed the PA modern rubber rock shoe specifically for the boulders of the Bleau, so shaping the future of modern free rock climbing around the world, aptly summed up the technical fascination when he commented to Robert Leininger after their successful ascent of the North Face of the Dru: "It's been a long time since we've done any serious climbing. I suggest we get back to the Bleau" (Bob French, "Fontainebleau - a commentary" *Mountain* 89 [January-February 1983]).

Catherine Destivelle first introduced me to the Bleau in the mid 1980s. It left a lasting impression of pure freedom of movement and self-expression on rock. We visited many areas and I have returned to explore the *forêts de Fontainebleau* many times since. But even so Bas Cuvier remains my favourite. Not only does it provide the premier technically difficult bouldering circuit in Europe - the famous Bas Cuvier White circuit - but also a whole spectrum of climbing throughout the range of difficulty. Add to this its level floor, relative ease of locating the problems sequentially and great natural beauty. A remarkable climbing ground.

On a practical level, from the car park on the northern side of the N7 the *carrefour de l'Epine* - stroll directly to the first boulder. Here will be found White No.1, Red No.1, Orange No.7 and on the slabby face of the boulder to the right Blue No.1 with Orange No.6 on its other side. A tremendous start: rather than attempt to detail the complex maze of boulders that span mainly north and west from here, I will leave it up to you to discover them. To identify the problems the colour of the circuit is painted on the rock with the number of the problem superimposed on this. A white square with a number in black on it is a white problem - the number itself may by necessity not be the same colour as the circuit but the background it is painted on is!

Having tackled and identified individual problems and got to know the layout of the boulders a little, you may wish to string together the circuit: another dimension which adds longevity and stamina to the pure technical difficulty. It is a worthy exercise and whether completing the Orange circuit (no little accomplishment), or like Jerry Moffat fully completing the White circuit twice in a morning (incredible but true), you will be physically and mentally satisfied. Of course there are problems not numbered on the circuits. Jerry Moffat has an unnumbered problem up the blunt arête of the boulder to the left of White No.6b (the latter being **L'abattoir,** grade 7b, one of the most classic white problems). There is also a Black circuit (rather faded and hard to find) with some excellent problems at a standard slightly easier than the White, though harder than the Red circuit. For those that manage to raise their level to the Red circuit it is fascinating to note that many of these were climbed by Pierre Allain and his group of Bleausards in the 1930s and 40s - before sticky rubber was invented!

On a tour of France there are two reasons why you should not visit Bas Cuvier or the Bleau first. The style of climbing, similar to British gritstone climbing, can be physically shattering, savage on the skin and finger ends. An intense period here can wreck you for a week. The second reason is simply that having experienced the magic of the Bleau you may not want to climb anywhere else.

FONTAINEBLEAU L'ELÉPHANT

Map Ref: *Michelin Motoring Atlas, page 54, B3.*

Area Maps: IGN 2417w, L=(1065.9, 619.0), additionally there is a 1:25,000 scale map specifically covering the forest - sheet number 401. MICH 61.11

Guidebook: *Fontainebleau escalades et randonnées.*

Climate/Climbing Season: Precipitation (rain/snow) 600mm on 110 days of the year. Driest months are April and September/October. Climbing is possible all the year round although it can be both cold and wet from November to March inclusive.

Restrictions: Wild camping/bivouacking is strictly forbidden. Widespread and liberal use of chalk frowned upon. Only use chalk on the harder problems or better still use a *pof* or resin bag as the French do.

Rock and Protection: Fine grained sandstone boulders with many of the problems somewhat polished, all the routes are soloed.

Situation: Some 2km NNW of Larchant, 14km NW of Nemours, one of the most distant areas to Fontainebleau itself on the very SW corner of the forest (strictly speaking a separate forest known as Forêt De Larchant). Département Seine-et-Marne (No.77).

Access: Located just off (S of) the A6 *Autoroute du Soleil* access is simple. Heading along the A6 from Paris turn off at Ury to follow the N152 S to La Chapelle, then follow the D16 to Larchant. Alternatively if heading N up the A6 quit the motorway at Nemours to head W along the D16 to enter Larchant in 8km. A minor road leads due N from the village of Larchant to find in 2km, on entering the woods, a small pull-off on the L side of the road. A barrier gate prevents vehicular access into the woods. Pass this on foot to follow a path/track leading due W through the forest to reach a clearing and the rocks in 200m (3 minutes).

Camping etc: There is a campsite in Nemours and all facilities can be found here. Some 2km N along the road is bunkhouse accommodation at the Auberge Chez Jobert, a restaurant and café, placed beneath the traditional bouldering area of Dame-Jouanne - a good place for a coffee, beer or snacks and a famous meeting ground for climbers.

Crag Facts: Rising from a sandy base, the boulders are located in a naturally open clearing in the forest. It is one of the most pleasant areas and offers a wide spread of climbing; enough to occupy both novice and expert. In all some 400 routes from 4m to 7m in length range in difficulty from 3b to 7a (British technical grading 2c to 6b). There are five main coloured circuits and in ascending order of difficulty these are: ORANGE (the easiest circuit with 44 numbered problems - considered to contain some of the greatest classic problems at Fontainebleau), BLUE (a superb and long circuit with 84 numbered problems and 34 variations), RED, GREEN (30 numbered problems), and finally the BLACK circuit (40 numbered routes, 2 variations - the most technically difficult circuit). Additionally located at the periphery of the boulders, there is a white circuit designed for children - very useful for those unable to manage the Orange circuit!

CRAG CHAT

As the trees part to reveal an open prairie of sand the first rock to be encountered, standing alone at the head of the group, is the distinctively shaped boulder of L'Eléphant. A boulder offering a variety of problems; from those of some strenuousness - swinging round the overhang formed by its neck - to the precarious and bold up the trunk, and to those of more amenable nature up its flanks. Descent is by its SW rump and the high polish makes this something less than straightforward.

From here boulders tumble W and spread gently N up the easy flanks of Rocher

Fontainebleau, L'Eléphant, the boulder, after which the area itself is named, provides a feast of problems both easy and hard

de la Justice, a veritable maze of boulders that will take more than one visit to unravel. Even if the locally popular *pof* or resin bag is not carried, a mat (rubber car mat ideal) and towel, to whack the rock and clean the sand from the boots, are essential. The sharp crack, as a whipped rag or towel strikes rock, in addition to the careful dusting of resin on the holds, is the distinctive ritual of the experienced Fontainebleau boulderer intent on ascending the hardest problems. In this sandy environment even those tackling more modest courses may be well advised to adopt the procedure.

It may be wondered how all these boulders came to rest so contentedly on a flat and sandy base? Well, the sand forming the boulders once lay on the bed of an ocean and above this was deposited the sediment of living creatures. The sediment became limestone and the sand beneath, sandstone. Then around 30 million years ago the sea departed. Rainwater dissolved passages in the limestone and seeped through to the sandstone below. Here chemical action further hardened and cemented the sandstone. Subsequently, over the eons of time, the limestone was worn away (although it remains in certain locations). Once the protective limestone cap disappeared the forces of wind and weather removed the softest areas of sandstone leaving only the most resilient. It is the hard rock that forms the fantastic boulders as seen today.

At least the sand provides an excellent landing surface and generally the problems can be jumped-off with little ill effect. Of course there are exceptions: if rocks lie below, a spotter should be employed, but nobody here uses a rope unlike the neighbouring rocks of Dame-Jouanne, just 2km N (continue along the road).

The boulders of this traditional area lie just beyond the chalet-restaurant of Chez Jobert (a popular and fashionable meeting place for Parisiens and climbers). Dame-Jouanne offers one of the highest faces in the area, some 15m high, highly polished with insitu pegs, where a rope is fairly essential. Despite offering some 500 problems, spread across a steeply inclined hillside, the landings are generally hard and nasty compared with the deliciously soft sand of L'Eléphant.

When you have bouldered, picnicked and bouldered some more, when you think you have explored every nook and cranny and your fingers and arms scream for mercy, then descend to the path (GR 13) and walk a little further W. To the L (S) you will find the largest overhanging wall at L'Eléphant. The holds are reasonably juggy but the overhanging nature makes the routes a strenuous proposition (probably starting around British technical grade 5b). Just the thing for the end of the day when the most difficult move will always be found right at the top - exiting from the overhanging onto the rounded horizontal. It's amazing how much extra reserve of energy you can find when the other option is to take a sickening 7m plunge to the ground below. Before the arms fail you either make the move or retreat to a safe jumping distance; a fall from the top of this particular boulder would invoke serious consequences.

Perhaps the best reason for ending here is because the track beneath leads along the edge of the sandy prairie skirting the boulders, directly back to the car. Through the sweet resin pines, through the dappling sun and shade, over the warm sand interspaced with heather and pine cone. A deliciously scented and relaxed exit, cunningly seducing you away from the one-last-time scenario of pain and defeat. There's always another day to climb at Fontainebleau.

LE PARC

Map Ref: *Michelin Motoring Atlas, page 72, A3.*

Area Maps: IGN 2721w, L=(2286.0, 698.5). MICH 65.5/15.

Guidebook: *Escalades dans le massif du Saussois* by Thierry Fagard and Jean-Paul Lebaleur.

Climate/Climbing Season: Precipitation (rain/snow) 750mm on 115 days of the year, at a maximum between December and January. The driest months are April and September. Climbing is not an attractive proposition all year round for it can be cold and wet from November to March inclusive.

Restrictions: None.

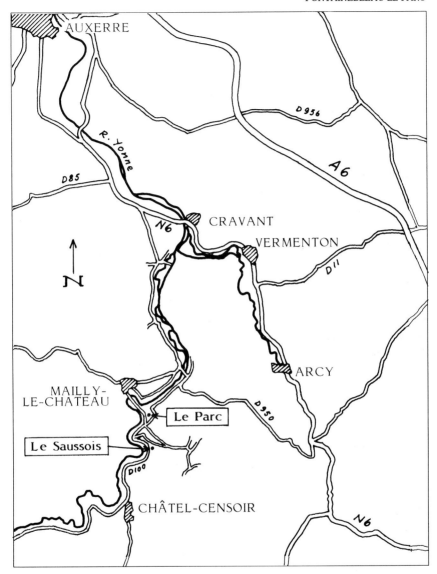

Rock and Protection: Limestone, well equipped with bolts and belay/abseil/ lower-off points. Only quick draws need be carried but nuts can be placed if required.

Situation: Some 27km SSE of Auxerre directly above the E bank of the River Yonne and the D130, 3km SE of Mailly-le-Château. Département Yonne (No.89).

Access: Leave the N6, 15km S of Auxerre and follow the D100 and then the D950 along the W bank of the Yonne to enter the village of Mailly-le-Château. Bear R on the D130 to cross immediately the bridge over the Yonne. Within a further 2km the crag will be spotted immediately above the road in the trees on the L. Parking space by the river immediately below the mid point of the crag (car to crag 20

seconds).

LP (1 - 5) Le Parc

Camping etc: Municipal campsite some 3km S on the other side of the river at Merry-sur-Yonne. Basic provisions there and at Mailly-la-Ville and supermarkets at Auxerre and Avallon (26km SE).

Crag Facts: The most northerly of a group of crags, Le Parc, Le Saussois and Surgy (some 12km S on the opposite bank of the river and not detailed) all situated

LP (6 - 12) Le Parc

on the banks of the Yonne. Whilst Le Saussois is the most extensive and important, Le Parc is an attractive little crag with a lot going for it. It faces W attracting the afternoon sunshine and lies in a notably sheltered position. The most central part of the crag, an obvious prow of rock, lies just a few metres above the road. A wall stretches L from this, passing two eye-like holes/caves and then a distinct crack, to round a corner before deteriorating. Some 50m L again a small barrel-shaped wall of clean, smooth limestone is known as Mur Zappa. The second half of the main crag constitutes the wall stretching R from the central prow. In all there are some 70 routes, 25m in length ranging in difficulty from 4a to 8a.

LP (12 - 23) Le Parc

CRAG CHAT

It could be the shielding trees, or perhaps it's because the road directly beneath is a lot quieter, but whatever the reason the climbing at Le Parc seems much less of a circus show than at Le Saussois. Whilst there isn't the length, or the same spectacular overhanging rock, it may be argued that this crag seems altogether friendlier, more pleasant and in some ways more enjoyable than its famous neighbour. Certainly, without a shadow of a doubt, the rock is nowhere near so highly polished. That alone must be a considerable bonus.

' There are some big numbers here too. On the smooth barrel wall of Mur Zappa (on the far L end) tiny finger holds may allow some to ascend **Joe's Garage 1** (7b) or **You Are What You Is** (8a), but most will settle for the overhanging crack of **Joe's Garage 2** (6c) or **200 Motels** (7a). All *petite* but worthy.

In the area L of the central prow the unmistakable crack, taken with its L start, gives the classic of the crag - **La P.J.** (4b) (British Very Severe - 4a). Or with the R start, **So Sprach Zarathustra** (6c), another quality climb. R of this, though the routes immediately L of the central pillar may be the most popular, the route taking the wall and scalloped recess to the R of the "eyes" - **Alea Jacta Est** (6b) (British E3 5c) - is in many respects one of the finest climbs of the area. Enough routes to satisfy more than one day's cragging and variety to interest those from moderate to extreme capabilities. You can climb here in winter, Parisiens do, I have; it's very similar to being in the Peak District - mostly cold and damp.

HIT LIST (From L to R)

LP 1	Ho-Chi-Minh 30m, 6c		LP 13	Belle Marguerite 30m, 7b
LP 2	La P.J. 30m, 4b		LP 14	Taillot 30m, 6b
LP 3	So Sprach Zarathustra 30m, 6c		LP 15	Mama Roma 30m, 7a
LP 4	Alea Jacta Est 30m, 6b		LP 16	Onirisme 30m 6a
LP 5	Couzy 30m, 7a		LP 17	Pervenche 25m, 6c
LP 6	Yanou 30m 6a		LP 18	Oslo 25m, 6b
LP 7	Dame de Mailly 40m, 4b		LP 19	Tutu 25m, 4c
LP 8	Sodome et Encore 30m, 6a+		LP 20	Les 3 Gorilles 25m, 6c
LP 9	Cerne aux Fesses 30m, 5b		LP 21	Charlouse 25m, 6c
LP 10	Demoiselle la Fouine 30m, 6b		LP 22	Fougère 25m, 4b
LP 11	No Name 30m, 7a		LP 23	L'Orientale 25m, 5c
LP 12	Jules 30m, 6c			

LE SAUSSOIS

Map Ref: *Michelin Motoring Atlas, page 72, A3.*

Area Maps: IGN 2721w, L=(2286.0, 698.5). MICH 65.16.

Guidebook: *Escalades dans le massif du Saussois.*

Climate/Climbing Season: Precipitation (rain/snow) 750mm on 115 days of the year at a maximum between December and January. Driest months are April and September. Climbing is not an attractive proposition all year round for it can be both cold and wet from November to March inclusive.

Restrictions: None.

Rock and Protection: Highly polished limestone, well equipped with bolts and belay/abseil chains. Nuts generally unnecessary.

Situation: 27km SSE of Auxerre above the E bank of the river/canal Yonne and between the villages of Châtel-Censoir and Mailly-le-Château. Département Yonne (No.89).

Access: Leave the N6 15km S of Auxerre to follow the D100 in a SSE direction towards Bazarnes. Bear R through Bazarnes and continue on the D100 to cross the river and enter Mailly-la-Ville. On leaving Mailly-la-Ville turn right immediately and drive through Le Saussois to discover (passing the Café des Roches on the L) the rocks towering unmistakably above on the L. There is a large car park on the opposite side of the road by the canal. Walk across the road to the rocks (1 minute or less!).

Camping etc: Municipal campsite across the other side of the river at Merry-sur-Yonne. Basic provisions are available in Merry-sur-Yonne and Mailly-la-Ville and supermarkets at Auxerre and Avallon.

Crag Facts: The nearest major crag to Paris and consequently extremely popular. There are some 200 routes from 40m to 55m ranging in difficulty from 3a to 8b (British technical grade 2b to 7c). From L to R and starting above the Café the massif consists of a number of buttresses which gradually increase in height and importance. Those on the left which culminate in a large buttress nearest the road are known as La Roche Centrale. Next a large gully provides an easy descent. To the right of this, rising from road level in a series of bulges, is the impressive Grande Roche. Some 0.5km (S) down the road stands an isolated buttress, Le Renard. Generally the crag faces W.

CRAG CHAT

A traditional and popular crag, Le Saussois is situated by the tree-lined banks of the Yonne. A very pleasant and convenient place to climb. On a recent trip, from my camper van in the car park we observed a kingfisher of electric red and blue

fishing from a branch overhanging the river - but this was early morning midweek: at the weekends you may have to queue for your chosen route.

Many of the crag's most notable lines had been climbed prior to the 1940s. The harder, steeper places were first aided and then in the late 1970s were climbed free. Today the crag is very well equipped with modern bolts (although sometimes these feel rather spaced) and abseil chains. Many storm-lashed British Alpinists have found their way here. Allan Austin wrote an article in *Climber* extolling its virtues in the early 1970s.

The price paid for its deserved popularity unfortunately, as a result of the hard and resilient nature of the rock, is its high polish. On some routes this is now close to crisis point with any hint of moisture rendering them quite unclimbable. In 1975 visiting the crag with Ed Cleasby, we completed amongst many other routes, a substantially free ascent of **Super Echelle** now graded 7a. Even without chalk it felt OK. In 1984, climbing **Pilier de l'Echelle** 7a with Catherine Destivelle, the

SS (1 - 10) Le Saussois, Le Grand Gendarme & L'Aiguillette (L side of the crag)

rock was so polished that we decided to retreat. Even holds which would normally be classed as jugs felt unusable. So be warned.

HIT LIST (From L to R).

LE GRAND GENDARME
SS 1   **La Vieille au Doigt Gourmand** 20m, 6c

SS 2   **Super Loco** 20m, 6a. A superb pitch.

SS 3   **Locomotive** 20m, 5c

SS 4   **Vérité Cachée** 20m, 6c

L'AIGUILLETTE
SS 5   **Excalibur** 15m, 6c

SS 6   **La Voie Oubliée** 15m, 4b

SS 7   **Président** 20m, 7b+

SS 8   **Chopinette** 20m, 7b

SS 9   **Spéléo** 20m, 6a

SS 10   **La Voie des Trous** 20m, 6a

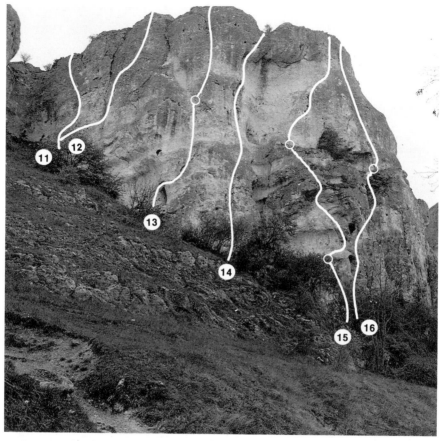

SS (11 - 16) Le Saussois, L side of the Roche Centrale

LA ROCHE CENTRALE

SS 11   La Revanche des Cons Vaincus 25m, 6c

SS 12   Crapaud Volant 25m, 6a

SS 13   La Ouest 35m, L1:6a, L2:7a

SS 14   Sans Nom 35m, 7a

SS 15   Spirale/Diagonale 55m, L1:6b, L2:6c, L3:6b

SS 16   L'I 50m, L1:5c, L2:5c, One of the great classics of the region.

SS 17   LA RECH 60m, L1:5b+, L2:5c, L3:5c. SELECTED ROUTE (see p. 37).

SS 18   L'Amitié 40m, L1:6b, L2:5c

SS 19   La Tricou 30m, 5c+. An excellent line regarded as the finest crack climb of the area. Although there is good fixed protection it is spaced at the top and a selection of nuts makes it easier on the mind.

SS 20   Catastrophe/Penchant Fatal 25m, 6a. A superb crack climb

SS (16 - 20) Le Saussois, R side of La Roche Centrale

31

SS (21 - 28) Le Saussois, L side of La Grande Roche

Catherine Destivelle in action on the rocks of Bas Cuvier, Fontainebleau

Climber on the first pitch of La Rech (5c), La Roche Centrale, Saussois

SS (29 - 30) Le Saussois, R side of La Grande Roche

SS (30 - 34) Le Saussois, R side of La Grande Roche

SS (35 - 39) Le Saussois, R side of La Grande Roche, La Roche Percée

SS (40 - 44) Le Saussois, Le Renard S Face

LA GRANDE ROCHE

SS 21 **Marion** 10m, 6b

SS 22 **Chimpanzodrome** 15m, 7c/8a. A famous desperate, often top roped, seldom lead on sight.

SS 23 **Dudule** 15m, 7a

SS 24 **Fissure Impossible** 15m, 6b+

SS 25 **Fouette Cocher** 15m, 7c

SS 26 **Jardin Suspendu** 50m, L1:5c, L2:6c, L2:5c

SS 27 **Toit du Fix** 10m, 7b. A tremendous problem climbing through the roof on finger pockets to lunge for a huge bucket on the lip.

SS 28 **L'Ange** 55m, L1:6c, L2:7b, L3:6c. First free climbed in the 1980s, a magnificent and difficult outing.

SS 29 **Super Échelle** 55m, L1:7a, L2:6a, L3:6a

SS 30 **Pilier de l'Échelle** 55m, L1:6a, L2:7a, L3:6a

SS 31 **Super Martine** 50m, L1:5b, L2:6b. A very atmospheric chimney climb where a wide bridging technique helps compensate for the negative effects of its high polish.

SS 32 **Je 55m,** L1:5b, L2:5c

SS 33 **Mimosa/Crayons de Couleurs** 50m, L1:6b, L2:7a, L3:6b

SS 34 **Trampoline** 50m, L1:6b, L2:6c, L3:5c

SS 35 **Troyenne** 50m, L1:6a, L2:6c

SS 36 **Jutta** 20m, 6c

SS 37 **Mantra** 25m, 6c

SS 38 **Toufou** 25m, 6c

SS 39 **Ventripote** 25m, 7a

LE RENARD

SS 40 **Directissime** 30m, 6b+

SS 41 **Sisyphe** 30m, 6c

SS 42 **Ancienne Traversée** 40m, 5b

SS 43 **Nouvelle Traversée** 40m, 5b

SS 44 **Carabosse** 30m, 6b

SELECTED CLIMB AT LE SAUSSOIS: La Rech (SS 17)

LA RECH: 60m, L1:5b+, L2:5c. L3:5c (British grading - Hard Very Severe, 4c+, 5a, 5a).

First Ascent: 1940s

Location: Starts from the very base of La Roche Centrale, faces west and south-west.

Route Facts: Start at the base of La Roche Centrale left of the edge, before the wall disappears into the bushes.

L1, 20m, 5b. Climb the wall directly, harder than first appearances suggest, to gain the top of the fin. It is logical to belay here. A traverse leads easily off at this point.

L2, 10m, 5c. Step left and either climb a hanging chimney groove (Cheminée de la Rech) or move left again to gain the top of the flake - very exposed. Step off the flake rightwards and move up the steep wall to gain a large ledge and belay. Deep hidden finger pockets make this easier than it looks.

L3, 30m, 5c. Step right to the rib (polished) and climb this to the bulge. Move right to avoid the bulge, this can be done at two levels both about the same standard of difficulty, then continue directly to gain the large grass ledge. Finish airily up the short wall from the left end of the ledge.

ROUTE CHAT

A remarkably fine route flowing up the highest part of La Roche Centrale. Technically absorbing, airy and exposed but now generally equipped with

SS (17) Le Saussois, 'La Rech' (5c) - the 2nd pitch

excellent protection it justly deserves an ascent whatever grade you may aspire to. However, for those unused to the nature of the rock at Saussois it may seem high in the grade, with a start that could almost be considered bold. If so, take compensation from the fact that reaching the climb from the car must be one of the shortest approaches in France. That's short.

The grade given here takes into account the polished nature of the rock. Surprisingly, this is one route at Le Saussois that can be climbed in the damp. Somehow the holds, pockets and flakes seem a little more positive than elsewhere and the bolt protection is plentiful. For most of the route it feels that a slip would not be too disasterous.

I have described the route in three pitches, which is the most satisfying way to climb it, keeping rope-drag to a minimum and taking comfortable stances. Each section is quite different in character and although the exposure increases with height the interest is fairly evenly maintained throughout. The initial vertical wall shouldn't be missed by traversing in to the top of the fin from the descent gully - it provides an entertaining piece of climbing. On the second pitch the exposure bites dramatically and suddenly. The moves left are undercut and the chimney looks hard if climbed direct. Moving onto the flake beyond and climbing this to swing right up the steep little wall above to gain the belay ledge is the most impressive way of climbing the pitch, though probably the easiest. The final long pitch up the front rib of the buttress is quite superb. At the top you won't dispute the assertion that "La Rech est la classique des classiques".

SAFFRES

Map Ref: *Michelin Motoring Atlas, page 73, E4.*

Area Maps: IGN 2922e, L=(2266.0, 769.0-770.0). MICH 65.19.

Guidebook: *Saffres Escalade en Côte d'Or.*

Climate/Climbing Season: Precipitation (rain/snow) 1,100mm on 120 days of the year. Driest months are April, July and October. Wettest month is December. Climbing possible all year round but can be wet and cold from November to March inclusive.

Restrictions: None.

Rock and Protection: Generally hard grey limestone, polished on the easier popular routes. Some areas appear blocky and rather loose but most loose rock has been removed and the rock is better than first appearances would suggest. All routes are well protected by modern insitu bolts and it is only necessary to carry quick draws and a long sling for the tree belays.

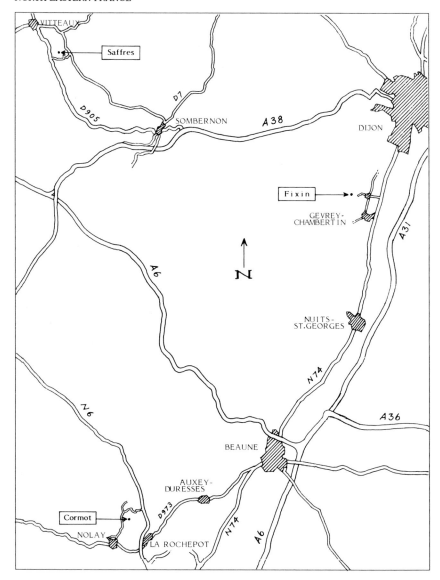

Situation: Some 50km W of Dijon, 4km SE of Vitteaux the crag lies on the hillside just above the village of Saffres. Département Côte d'Or (No.21).

Access: Follow the D905 (ex N5) S from Vitteaux then turn L to drive up through the village. The crag can be approached from either below or above. From the village drive up the road through the woods. To approach from below find a small car park and a track leading up L to the crag (this reaches the R end of the

40

escarpment in a few minutes). To approach the crag from above, proceed up the road - at some hairpin bends the woods thin and the crag can be seen up to the left. Continue to gain the level plateau and a junction with the D9. Turn L and in a short way a dirt track will be found leading off L (a "T" sign marks it as a cul-de-sac). Follow this, crossing a field to approach the edge of a wood. Park here to discover the various access paths leading through the thin band of trees to abseil points above the crag (1 minute).

Camping etc: Wild camping is allowed in the meadow above the crag. Fires contained with stones appear to be permissable. Water and a café will be found in the village of Saffres below. Supplies at Vitteaux.

Crag Facts: Situated on the wooded hillside overlooking the small village of Saffres the crag may not be so impressive as Le Saussois, but offers a greater variety of routes and is a very pleasant place to climb. There are many climbs at a reasonable standard of difficulty in addition to numerous harder routes of excellent quality. There are some 370 routes, all clearly numbered from R to L (the numbers are painted on the rock at the base of each climb). They reach 35m in length and range in difficulty from 3c to 8a (British technical grade 3a to 7a). Even when the crag is approached from above it is easy to locate the routes. The main crag can be regarded as a continuous series of walls and corners stretching for about 400m with a good path traversing beneath allowing easy access. Additionally there are a number of large detached blocks *(Tours)* with the Tour Carrée being the most obvious. Note that the routes on the *Tours* are numbered independently to those on the main crag. To get one's bearings it is useful to walk E along the top of the crag from the campsite/parking meadow to observe, in a few hundred metres, the large rectangular detached block of Tour Carrée. This effectively marks the mid-point of the main cliff. Generally the crag faces S.

CRAG CHAT

Although this is a popular locality at weekends it retains great charm. The ideally sited campsite, fringed by trees, is a wild, flower-strewn meadow and is a great place to picnic or sunbathe. The crags are sited on the hillside generally facing south but the surrounding shroud of trees give a valley feel, shielding them from wind and providing welcome shade in midsummer. Additionally there are enough features to provide walls facing all four directions of the compass - therefore offering a suitable locality for most prevailing conditions.

From a climbing point of view the crag has many virtues, offering good value throughout the range of difficulty. The series of walls that make up the length of the crag provide plenty of variety in climbing technique. In addition to the vertical faces there are lots of corners, cracks, chimneys, overhangs and undercut arêtes. At whatever grade, the most active climbers will find enough to sustain their interest here for a number of days.

TOUR CARREE (EAST FACE)

SF (1 - 344) Saffres, proceeding from R to L the routes are numbered on the rock beneath each climb

The style of climbing is interesting for there are not many pockets and so a greater emphasis on footwork is needed. Those who prefer a natural line of weakness, as opposed to routes possible solely due to the presence of finger pockets, will be happy. Whilst the climbing is invariably steep many routes have frequent blocky ledges and good holds making them a reasonable proposition; approximately 100 of the routes here are up to and including 5c (British Hard Very Severe 5a) and there are at least 30 at or below 4a. Climbing started in 1938 but all the routes were systematically bolt protected and numbered (each number painted on the rock beneath the climb) in 1986 - some feat. Saffres is therefore a relaxing place to climb where it is only necessary to carry a few quick draws to be perfectly safe.

HIT LIST

MAIN CLIFF (From R to L - Photo-topo number corresponds directly with route number as painted on the crag.)

SF 54	**Dièdre à Leblanc** 5b	**SF 84**	**Ondulee** 4b
SF 55	**Floconnerie** 6a	**SF 87**	**Poussière d'Étoile** 6a+
SF 68	**La Hulotte** 7c	**SF 90**	**Dièdre Jaune** 3c
SF 70	**Le Singe** 5c	**SF 102**	**Kir** 7a

SF 104	Top Lisa 7b	SF 214	La Quille 6c
SF 108	Fil à Plomb 6b	SF 226	Le Sens de l'Histoire 6c
SF 111	Rixe 6c+	SF 228	Pivoine 6c
SF 114	Le Pigeon à Odette 5b	SF 230	L'Arrachee 5c
SF 123	Villebrequin 5b	SF 234	Le Mètre-Pliant 5b. Makes
SF 124	Nuits Secrètes 6b		a long traverse to the right
SF 133	Les Jeux des Nuages		beneath the overhangs at
	et de la Pluie 6a		two-thirds height.
SF 135	La Partouze 6b	SF 239	Le Piano à Queue 5a
SF 139	Éclair 5c	SF 243	La Lupa 5b
SF 144	Simone 6b	SF 248	Flambeau 5c
SF 146	La Troyenne 6b+	SF 256	Montagne 4b
SF 154	Guerre des Clans 6b	SF 257	Le Dièdre Sitigier 6a. The
SF 176	Groseiller 4b		steep corner line.
SF 181	Passe Muraille 7a	SF 259	Montreuil 8a. The line up
SF 184	Armir 6b		the impending wall left of
SF 197	Le Boulevard à		Sitigier is the hardest sofar
	Mathieu 7a+		recorded at Saffres.
SF 210	Mondette 6c	SF 260	Calamity Bedi 6c

TOUR CARRÉE
North Face

TC 1   **Batier** 4a. On the gully face.

West Face
TC 12   **Bédoul la Roumoule** 6a
TC 14   **DIRECTISSIME** 5c. SELECTED ROUTE (see below).
TC 16   **Pervers Pépère** 5c
TC 23   **L'Anglais Directe** 6a *South Face*
TC 24   **Voie Allain** 6a
TC 27   **Les Aigles** 5c

East Face
TC 39   **Gus** 6b+. An imposing face route passing through a small overlap.

SELECTED CLIMB AT SAFFRES: Directissime (TC 14)

DIRECTISSIME: 30m, 5c. (British grading - Hard Very Severe, 5a).
First Ascent: Circa 1940s
Location: The west face of the great detached block of Tour Carrée.
Route Facts: Start up the wall just left of centre.

L1, 30m, 5c. Climb to a narrow ledge and continue up the thin crack to gain the left end of a stepped ledge system at about mid height. Move up onto the next step then move across left to find another crack in the wall. Climb this, and through a broken groove to the top. Tree belays.

Descent: Abseil. Double 50m ropes around the tree. Do not attempt to lower off with a single 50m rope as this most probably will not reach the ground.

ROUTE CHAT

A traditional route, and despite a high polish an excellent route to do in the afternoon or evening sunshine so long as you have a plentiful supply of chalk. Nut placements can be found but the frequency and quality of the insitu bolts makes the use of nuts rather superficial. A number of enjoyable routes can be found on either side of Directissime though they are all slightly harder, therefore if you find the going a little tough for the grade you may have strayed. That is not to say that the route isn't fully the grade assigned. It is, and considerably harder, steeper and longer than it looks from below.

SELECTED CLIMB

12

14

16

23

TC (12 - 23) Tour Carrée, W Face

SF (176) Saffres, 'Groseiller' (4b) - Route No. 176, a classic corner which serves as a good introduction to the crag

FIXIN

Map Ref: *Michelin Motoring Atlas, page 88, B1.*

Area Maps: IGN 3123w, L=(2253.3, 798-799). MICH 65.20.

Guidebook: *Escalade en Côte d'Or Fixin - Brochon.*

Climate/Climbing Season: Precipitation (rain/snow) 750mm on 105 days of the year. Despite the fact that the cliff is relatively high in the hills this is the driest area. Additionally the cliffs face south and therefore climbing here is possible throughout the year. However, there is little shade and during the summer months it can be unbearably hot during the middle part of the day.

Restrictions: Strictly no campfires are allowed.

Rock and Protection: Hard flaky limestone, the best in the region. Despite this however, there are some loose flakes and care should be exercised. Generally fixed protection is reasonable (although not all routes have been re-equipped) but a small rack of wires may be found useful.

Situation: 2km WNW of Fixin village, 9km S of Dijon. Département Côte d'Or (No.21).

Access: Drive through the village of Fixin up the hill into the park Noisot (possible to park here). Bear L to take the road rising up the hill - this enters the wood, begins to zigzag and becomes a rough stone-strewn track. The French do drive up this in their family saloons but quite honestly it is extremely rough, involving alternating sections of steep rubble and sizeable rocks (I took my indestructible VW Camper up and was worried!). In about 1km the road levels out to traverse the top of a plateau and in a short way, before the road begins to disappear into the woods and undergrowth again, ample parking spaces can be found (usual to seek the shade of a bush). You are now directly above the crags which form a line along the southern rim of the plateau overlooking the tree-filled valley down below. There are numerous access points leading though the breaks in the cliffs (3 minutes if you drive up onto the plateau, probably 30 minutes otherwise).

Camping etc: Wild camping is allowed on the plateau but only on the crag side of the road/track and fires are strictly prohibited. Water is available in Fixin.

Crag Facts: The crags form the southern rim of a plateau overlooking a wooded valley. The valley penetrates, tongue like, into a limestone upland area from the famous Dijonnais wine growing plains below. There are seven main *secteurs* with 125 numbered routes (numbers painted on the rock) stretching R to L.

From 30m to 35m in length they range in difficulty from 3c to 7c (British technical grade 3a to 6c). The easiest section to identify is Pic Pointu sited roughly centrally. This is accessed by a main walking path marked with red paint (Sentier

Batier which begins in Dijon and continues down into the valley below up the other side and across to Brochon) and consists of the unmistakable pillar (perhaps 15m on its valley face) of Pic Pointu inset with a metal plaque. Looking out, the pillar is down to the left and is surrounded by an amphitheatre - Cirque du Pic Pointu - of short routes of all grades. The climbs on the valley face of Pic Pointu are numbered 47 to 49 and those in the cirque from 50 to 60. The cliffs on the southern rim can be divided into seven areas. Starting from the R and working to the L, the same direction as the routes are numbered, these are: Groupe de la Tour Guet (route numbers from 1 to 17) accessible down scree shoots either side, La Grande Paroi (18 to 40) perhaps the most important section and accessible down a scree path to the right and from the Sentier Batier to the left, Groupe du Pic Pointu (41 to 49) with the routes on and around the pinnacle itself, Cirque du Pic Pointu (50 to 60) a short wall with a mixture of routes from easy to desperate (often top roped), Groupe du Col de la Buche (61-68), Groupe du Château Fort (69 to 114) another important section of the crag and finally hidden in the trees the concave and overhanging Mur des Lamentations (115 to 125). There are some very hard routes on this section but (at the time of writing) many routes are still aided and have not been equipped with modern bolts. (Access to the *secteurs* left of Pic Pointu should be reached by traversing along the base of the crags after descending the Sentier Batier past the pinnacle (alternatively it is possible to abseil if you know the location of your intended route). Above the tree line the south-facing crags can be oppressively hot around midday in summer.

CRAG CHAT

If you do manage to get up onto the plateau and spend some time camping (leave no valuables in the tent) or bivouacking you will discover a serene and beautiful area, wild and unspoilt. That is not so say I recommend taking a car up unless it is a particularly hardy vehicle - mind you 2CVs seem to manage it. Aloof on the rim of the plateau enjoy a commanding view over the tree-filled valley below. On the rim it is hot during the day, at night cold with a big sky wild with stars and silent apart from the noise of crickets and forest animals. On an August evening, when it really is too hot to climb midday, with a bottle of wine from Les Grand Crus, the famous vineyard route which traverses the edge of the plain directly below, shooting stars seem to fly as frequently as sparks from a bonfire.

Escaping the heat of midday is no problem. The woods in the secretive valley below and around its closing rim are cool and inviting. Apart from the path leading past Pic Pointu, steps lead down into the head of the valley from the plateau above and a path plunges through the gorge beneath trees that reach high for the sun. In the cliff at the base of the steps another metal plaque, dented with grape shot, reads "UN SOLDAT DU NAPOLÉON - 29 Juillet 1840".

Chaîne de Gigondas,
Dentelles de Montmirail,
climbing the Arete
Lagarde, on du Turc above
the Brèche de la Pousterle

Climber on Bambino (6c), Grande Dalle -
South Face, Sisteron

FX (27) Fixin, La Grande Paroi, 'Les Colonnes' (5c) Route No. 27 -
Climber (the author) at the halfway ledge

FX (64 - 96) Fixin, from R to L - Groupe du Col de la Buche, Groupe du Chateau Fort

HIT LIST (From R to L - photo-topo numbers correspond with route numbers painted on the crag.

GROUPE DE LA TOUR GUET
FX 12   **L'Arête de la Dalle** 5a and 2 points of aid.

LA GRANDE PAROI
FX 21   **La Voie du Coer** 6a
FX 23   **La Tangentoide** 5b
FX 26   **J.A.Morin** 5c
FX 27   **LES COLONNES** L1:5c, L2:5c. SELECTED ROUTE (see p. 52).
FX 30   **Le Cancer** 7a
FX 36   **Le Kaléidoscope** L1:6c, L2:6a
FX 40   **Le Cerf-Volant** 7a

PIC POINTU
FX 48   **La Gégène** 5b. Climbs the valley face of the pinnacle then steps from the summit onto the short wall behind to finish! A minor classic.

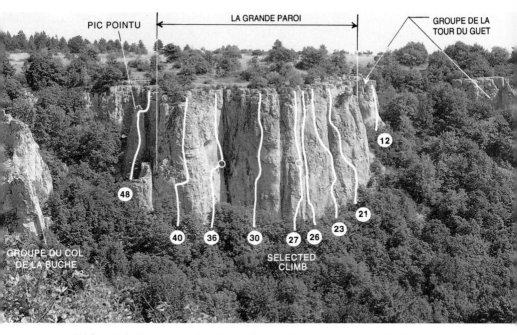

FX (12 - 56) Fixin, From R to L - La Grande Paroi, Groupe du Pic Pointu, Cirque du Pic Pointu

CIRQUE DU PIC POINTU
FX 56   **La Freddy** 3b

GROUPE DU COL DE LA BUCHE
FX 64   **La Voie Dédé** 5c

GROUPE DU CHÂTEAU FORT
FX 71   **La Peil-Plouc** 7a
FX 74   **La Fissure du Château Fort** 5a
FX 82   **La Nikolaievski** 7a. Steep and sustained, one of the best routes hereabouts.
FX 83   **La Voie des Plaques** 4c. A Noted chimney.
FX 91   **La Jacqueline** 6a. A celebrated crack climb.
FX 92   **L'Ophris** 6b
FX 94   **La Batier** 5c
FX 96   **La Toute Bleue** 6b

MUR DES LAMENTATIONS
FX 119   **Coup de Lurne** 7b. Modern equipped but the grade should be treated with caution.

SELECTED CLIMB AT FIXIN: Les Colonnes (FX 27)

LES COLONNES: 35m, L1:5c, L2:5c (British Grading - E1/Hard Very Severe, 5a+, 5a+). (See page 49)

First Ascent: Not known.

Location: Section La Grande Paroi, the obvious pillar up the centre of this crag.

Route Facts: Start round the corner left of the arête and right of a chimney. L1, 20m, 5c. Climb the wall and move right and up to a small ledge on the face of the pillar. Climb the crack just right of the edge to gain a larger ledge and belay. It is possible to continue and climb the route in one long pitch.

L2, 15m, 5c. Move up and pull through an overlap to move left and climb the wall left of the edge. Continue up the centre of the wall passing two further overlaps to reach the top.

ROUTE CHAT

One of the most aesthetic and striking routes at Fixin, Les Colonnes is sustained, and particularly exposed on the second pitch, offering varied climbing that is never less than vertical. It gains momentum once the edge of the pillar is reached and after a ledge progress is made by climbing a steep bottomless crack. The second pitch often looks most improbable and is continually interesting with the moves through the overlaps seeming more strenuous than the rest. Although the rock is generally very good there are one or two flakes that sound hollow and caution should be exercised. A selection of wires would give a feeling of security to the tiring leader though insitu protection is adequate.

My partner had declined to climb, pointing out that whilst mad dogs and Englishmen may go out in the midday sun, the Englishwoman was choosing to forego the pleasure. So I'm afraid I shunted the route on a fixed rope which is why I don't really know if the route equates to E1 or Hard Very Severe. On the upper section it was sometimes difficult just to know how to do the next move but then after balancing up a bit hidden incuts and pockets always appeared when you needed them most.

August without a cloud in the sky and rock that was literally almost too hot to touch didn't detract from the enjoyment of this vertical limestone pillar. In truth I was often glad of the security from the rope above, allowing total concentration on the actual business of climbing, without having to worry about clipping gear.

CORMOT

Map Ref: *Michelin Motoring Atlas, page 88, A3.*

Area Maps: IGN 2925e, L=(2221.8, 775.9-776.4). MICH 69.9.

Guidebook: *Cormot*

Climate/Climbing Season: Precipitation (rain/snow) 900mm on 120 days of the year. Driest months are April and July. Wettest month is December. Climbing possible all year round but can be cold and wet from November to March.

Restrictions: No wild camping on the plateau above the crag.

Rock and Protection: Stratified limestone with numerous horizontal breaks and blocky overhangs. In some areas the rock is acceptably strong, in others apparently loose and crumbly. On the routes I recommend there are modern bolts providing good protection. Routes that are not equipped with modern gear (there are numerous lines) should be left alone.

Situation: Some 50km south of Dijon, 15km SW of Beaune, 4km NNE of Nolay. Département Côte d'Or (No.21).

Access: From Nolay drive N on the D115f in the direction of Vauchignon and Cirque-du-Bout-du-Monde. Go through Vauchignon then turn R (NE) in the direction of Bel-Air. Before the summit of the hill, an area of open ground, turn R (S) along an unsurfaced track to reach a parking area in 400m. Continue along the path (S) on foot to reach the flat top of the crag in a further 500m (5 minutes). An easy descent down the Brèche de Roland can be made at the right end (W) - looking out - of the cliff. The numbered routes go from left to right, therefore this is the best way to identify the areas and climbs. Alternatively numerous abseil points can be located but double 50m ropes should be used to reach the base of the crag. Additionally, the cliff can be reached from below by either: a) following the road rising directly from Cormot-le-Petit which deteriorates to become a rough track before a path bears off L to reach the R end of the crag (limited parking space only); or b) following a path from Vauchignon which leads to the L end of Grande Falaise Partie Ouest.

Camping etc: There is a CAF (Club Alpin Français) hut in Vauchignon - cross a little bridge in the centre of the village and the refuge overlooks a yard by the side of the river. It sleeps twenty and meals are available. Fountain water in Vauchignon. There is a campsite at Nolay but only 7km NE at Auxey-Duresses is a delightfully small and cheap family campsite which must be one of the pleasantest in France. Supplies are best sought in Nolay but the largest town of any size (a tourist area with plenty of banks etc.) is Beaune.

Crag Facts: This is an impressive, large looking cliff rising above the trees

PARTIE OUEST

BRÈCHE DE ROLAND (DESCENT)

CO (17 - 60) Cormot, La Grande Falaise

forming the rim of a plateau above the village of Cormot-le-Petit. The longest face is known as La Grande Falaise and it is divided into three sections - Partie Ouest, Partie Centrale and Partie Est. There are around 80 routes, numbered L to R, from 35m to 45m ranging in difficulty from 4b to 7a (British technical grade 3c to 6b). Although in terms of length and height this is the major cliff of the region, with an imposing array of walls, cracks and corners, the rock is unfortunately poor in many parts. Also many routes are (at the time of writing) not equipped with modern bolts and I would personally stay away from these. The approach described is the easiest but for an approach which allows a better look at the crags it is possible to drive up a little road leading out of Cormot-le-Petit. This rapidly becomes a rough track and it is difficult to find a parking space around the point necessary to follow another smaller track off to the left. Although the crag rises from the trees it does face due S and it dries quickly.

CRAG CHAT

From a distance this crag looks most impressive; by far the most imposing cliff in the whole region of Dijonnais. It is high, long and full of lines just demanding to be climbed. Unfortunately, on closer inspection the rock is found to be quite poor.

One shouldn't be put off by first impressions. There are horrible looking aid pegs and rotting slings festooning the old aid routes but this is a large crag offering sections where the rock is good, modern bolts have been placed and the climbing quite superb.

It is a traditional climbing area and the first climbs done here, mainly aided, were pioneered in the 1930s. Its original importance for this type of climbing is

PARTIE CENTRALE   PARTIE EST

underlined by the presence of the nearby CAF hut in Vauchignon, and in fact a path leads from the S end of the village to the L end of the main section of cliffs.

Whilst one is in the area it is worth driving to the head of the valley into the Cirque-du-Bout-du-Monde, where there are large car parks. It is a scenic tourist area with a waterfall at the head of the cirque. The cliffs on the L of the valley are most impressive but it will be obvious why they are mainly left unclimbed, even should you fight your way through the bushes to reach them. The rock is appalling - real Mick Fowler country!

HIT LIST (From L to R - photo-topo numbers correspond with route numbers painted on the crag.)

LA GRANDE FALAISE - PARTIE OUEST

CO 17   **Le Chant du Cygne** 35m, 5c+. An elegant line taking the face of the slender pillar left of the great corner. The finish taking the crack splitting the neb overhang looks most spectacular.

CO 20   **L'OPPOSITION 35m, 4c.** SELECTED ROUTE (see p.56).

CO 21   **La Kim Directe** 35m, 5c+. Another superb route up the wall from the block and then through the overlaps in the headwall above, there are three bolted variants - the most direct being probably the hardest.

CO 24   **Le Petit Zig** 40m, 7a

CO 25   **La Vertu** 35m, 4c. The distinct corner.

CO 26   **La Bulle** 35m, 5c.

CO 32   **La Panique** 35m, 6a+

CO 33   **L'Androsace** 32m, 5c.

LA GRANDE FALAISE - PARTIE CENTRALE
CO 38   **La Sans Nom** 32m, 5b+
CO 39   **La Dièdre Laurent** 32m, 5b+
CO 45   **L'Arbe** 20m, 5a. Another classic of the crag.
CO 60   **La Batier** 35m, 6b

SELECTED CLIMB AT CORMOT: L'Opposition (CO 20)

L'OPPOSITION: 35m, 4c. (British grading - Mild Very Severe, 4a).

First Ascent: Circa 1940s

Location: On Partie Ouest La Grande Falaise there is a bay formed by a large corner. The right side floor of the bay is marked by a huge boulder and the left by the remains of a narrow rectangular building.

Route Facts: The right wall of the corner holds a magnificent and unmistakable corner line.
L1, 35m, 4c. Climb the corner throughout.

Descent: On foot down the Brèche de Roland or by abseil from the fixed bolts above, carefully noting that double 50m ropes are needed to reach the ground.

CO (20) Cormot, La Grande Falaise Partie Ouest, the classic 'L'Opposition' (4c)

ROUTE CHAT

Whichever of the approach routes has been chosen there is one section of this cliff, a corner bay marked by a huge boulder on its right side, which is unmistakable. A number of attractive lines start from here; as soon as you arrive you feel like unpacking the sac and getting going. L'Opposition is the most reasonably graded, yet offering nevertheless a fine challenge. It couldn't be more obvious: a vertical corner shooting up the right wall of the bay with the name referring to the layback technique best employed in parts to climb it.

Despite simplicity of line the climbing is quite varied. A number of techniques need be employed to guarantee victory on a long and sustained pitch. Whilst the continuity of the crack remains unbroken the stratified nature of the limestone offers a number of blocky overlaps which must be passed. The most strenuous of

these occurs at about two-thirds height just as the vertical nature of the climbing has begun to tell on the arms and the legs. Conversely there are also a number of foot ledges to offer a welcome rest.

Don't be put off by appearances, the overlap at two-thirds height is awkward but the climbing above is not as difficult as it looks. Throughout the climb are good modern bolts, though they do feel quite spaced. If you are unused to the French style of climbing a small rack of medium to large nuts and Friends would complement the insitu gear.

CO (17) Cormot, La Grande Falaise Partie Ouest, 'Le Chant du Cygne' (5c+)

LE SALÈVE

Map Ref: *Michelin Motoring Atlas, page 104, C3.*

Area Maps: IGN 3249w. MICH 74.6.

Guidebook: *Le Guide Du Salève.*

Climate/Climbing Season: Precipitation 1,200mm on 125 days of the year. Climbing doubtful between November and March inclusive.

Restrictions: None

Rock and Protection: The rock is a very hard limestone almost taking on the composition of marble. It is extremely polished. All routes are equipped and it is unusual to carry anything other than quick draws and the odd long sling.

Situation: Only 10km S of Genève (Switzerland), 9km SSW of Annemasse, 1km SE of Collonges. Département Haute-Savoie (No.74).

Access: From Annemasse or Genève head SE for Collonges. From here take the road leading up through the village signposted Col de la Croisette to find, before reaching the village of le Coin, a small track leading up left to a large parking space in front of the café Le Refuge du Salève. The huge cliff (seen from the road) lies directly above and various paths lead to its base (5 minutes).

Camping etc: Bivouacking and wild camping do seem to be permitted on a level area up and right of the car park. There are shops down below in the village of Collonges. Water is available from a fountain in the car park. There is an organised campsite at Neydens, 4km S of St-Julien-en-Genevois.

Crag Facts: This is a huge crag reaching a maximum height of 200m. As a whole the cliffs above the car park of Le Refuge du Salève are known as the Secteur du Coin. They comprise three main sections: a higher wall forming the left side of the main buttress, facing NW; at right angles to this the impressive front of the central buttress which faces SW; right of this and at right angles again, separated by the distinct rift of Le Grand Dièdre, a spur decreasing in height, passing behind a large detached block (15m high) - this is fissured by a large chimney before it finally rounds the corner into the next *secteur*. Because the central buttress area is so dominant it is easy to underestimate the size of the walls on either side of it whereas in actual fact these hold many climbs. On the massif there are 300 routes, between 50m to 200m ranging in difficulty from 2 to 7a (British grading Moderate to 6b). A serious air pervades much of this crag and the length of the routes should not be underestimated.

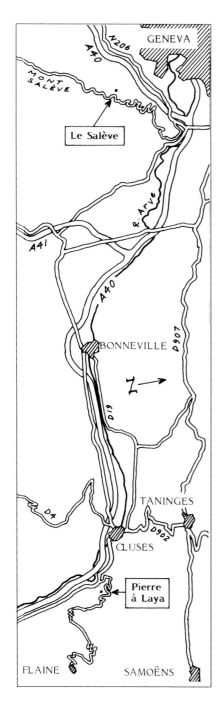

CRAG CHAT

Although geographically in France, this major crag is very much the climbing ground of the Swiss Genève based climbers. Traditionally it provided Alpine training and remarkably the first ascent recorded here, that of la Grande Varappe by Monnier and De Niederhausen, took place in 1880. Its virtues as an Alpine alternative, should the Chamonix Aiguilles be weather bound, were noted by Chris Bonington in the 1960s. Since those days most of the routes have been free climbed, equipped with bolts and many fine hard new routes added. Today it is very much a rock climbing ground in is own right offering a wide variety of routes to suit many different tastes.

Tricouni invented and tested his nailed boots under the influence of the Salève and remarkably many of the early first ascents were made wearing this type of footwear. One tends to suspect that this is why so many of the traditional routes are so highly polished. In fact this can't be the complete answer, for the relatively modern routes seem almost as bad. The solution must lie in the ultra hard nature of the rock which resembles pure marble in certain sections. The character of the climbing takes a little getting used to, for fixed protection can be spaced, the crag is big and invariably steep and the high gloss polish makes a mockery of the grading system.

Bold and brash, the high vertical faces of Le Salève offer many climbs to fill the day and enough scope, should you be able to take the strain, for at least a week's activity. The crag buzzes at weekends and at the end of the Genève

59

SL (1 - 10) Le Salève, Secteur du Coin

working day, with Le Refuge du Salève offering a convivial meeting place. If on your first arrival the crag is seemingly full or time scarce, at the base of the scree, amongst the trees can be found a collection of interesting boulders.

HIT LIST (From L to R)

SECTEUR DU COIN - LEFT WALL

SL 1   **Fissure Paillard** 60m, L1:5b, L2:6a, L3:4c, L4:5b

SL 2   **Ou, d'Angoisse et de Peur, Follement Battra Ton Couer** 60m, L1:6c+, L2:7a, L3:5c, L4:6c. A powerful roof problem in a spectacular position, good bolts.

SL 3   **JAUNE/BALCON/GRANDE ARÊTE/PÂTURAGES** 240m, L1:4c, L2:-, L3:5c, L4:5a, L5:4c, L6:6a, L7:5c, L8:4c. SELECTED ROUTE (see below.

SECTEUR DU COIN - CENTRAL SECTION

SL 4   **L'Arc-en-Ciel** 140m, L1:6b, L2:7a, L3:6a+, L4:6c, L5:6a+, L6:6c

SL 5   **L'Herbe du Diable** 70m, L1:7b, L2:6b. Climbs to L'Arc-en-Ciel in two pitches. Usual to retreat after this.

SL 6   **La Face Ouest** 140m, 6c. L1:5a, L2:6b, L3:6a, L4:5b, L5:6a, L6:4b. Another great multi pitch classic - seriously polished.

SL 7   **Le Grand Dièdre** 100m, L1:4b, L2:4c, L3:5c, L4:6a

SECTEUR DU COIN - RIGHT WALL

SL 8   **Le Tablard/Le Corpuscle** 110m, L1:6a+, L2:6b, L3:6c, L4:5c

SL 9   **la Vieille France** 70m, L1:6b, L2:5c

SL 10   **Les Super-Morgans** 70m, L1:6b, L2:6a, L3:6c. Starts behind the large block of Corne Du Coin, undercut, polished and scary to get going but worth the effort.

       Corne Du Coin. The crag side of the boulder provides a couple of slabby routes.

SELECTED CLIMB AT LE SALÈVE: La Jaune/Balcon/ Grande Arête/Pâturages (combination) (SL 3)

LA JAUNE/BALCON/GRANDE ARÊTE/PÂTURAGES: 240m, L1:4c, L2:-, L3:5c, L4:5a, L5:4c, L6:6a, L7:5c, L8:4c. (British grading - Hard Very Severe, 4a, -, 5a, 4b, 4a, 5b+, 5a, 4a).

First Ascent: Probably first strung together as one route in 1947.

Location: Begins up the obvious corner flake on the left-hand edge of the central buttress of Le Secteur du Coin.

Route Facts: Start by scrambling up to a ledge beneath the flake crack.

L1, 50m, 4c. *La Jaune*. There is a choice; either climb the corner rift direct or make a diversion looping first up left then back right into the final section of chimney. In either case continue to gain the large ledge at the top of the intermediary wall.

L2, 30m. Scramble up and left to take a belay or stance if you can't find one in the crevasse between a large block and the cliff face.

L3, 15m, 5c. *Balcon*. Move up onto the wall with difficulty (easier to step off the block). Move up through the overlap then traverse left until a direct ascent leads to another rift at the foot of the chimney of the great flake.

L4, 40m, 5a. *Grande Arête*. Enter the bowels of the chimney, probably best to keep low initially. After about 8m ascend directly to emerge near the crest of the first flake. A bolt runner can be found on the edge. Squirm along the top for a little way until a bolt and a line of holds leads up the wall (R) above the flake. Climb the wall to enter the next flake crack at a higher level. Make some interesting bridging moves and gain the top of a chockstone hung in the jaws of the rift. Open hook iron spike belay.

L5, 30m, 4c. Continue up the chimney variously bridging and squirming to find the occasional bolt runner. A levelling and stance indicate the end of this Grande Arête section.

L6, 40m, 6a. *Pâturages*. Climb the steep wall above (right of the flake crack). Reach high at the top of the impending flake corner to gain good holds and a rest as soon as a swing right is made. This is the crux but it is possible to reduce the overall standard of the route by using a point of aid. Make an exposed traverse right across the wall to the foot of the cave-like niche. Move right across the base to climb the front of the pillar on its right to stance and belay.

L7, 25m, (5c). Move up the wall then traverse left delicately to gain a leftward diagonal ramp leading to a bush and belay.

L8, 50m, (4c). Climb the wall following the peg runners leftwards. After a few short grooves and ledges the climbing deteriorates and it is best to make an ascending traverse over to the right. A tree marks a ledge and the end of the climb.

Descent: Move across rightwards (looking in) to gain a small scree path traversing through the trees. This soon descends but spirals again right to traverse the edge of the cliff (take great care not to dislodge the scree as it would present a grave danger to those below). The path then contours first right and then back left (once picked up it is obvious) descending the Secteur des Etoillets through a number of rock bluffs where ladders and fixed wire ropes are provided for safety and aid. Allow fifteen minutes to descend to the scree slopes at the foot of the crag.

SL (3 - 7) Le Salève, Secteur du Coin, looking directly onto the W Face, to the L the huge flake marks the line of 'Paturages Combination'.

CENTRAL SECTION

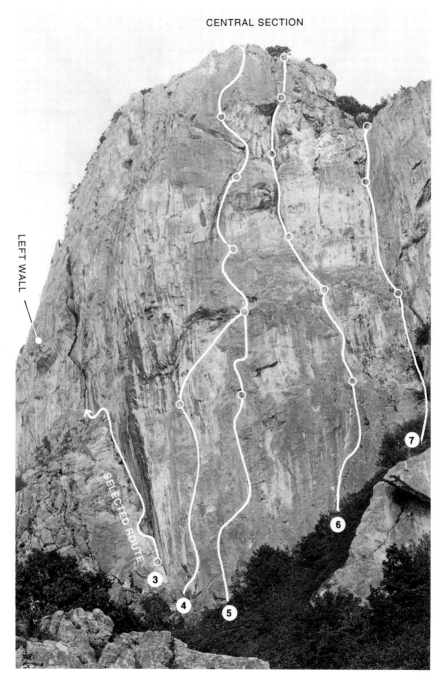

LEFT WALL

SELECTED ROUTE

3

4

5

6

7

ROUTE CHAT

On the left side of the huge Secteur du Coin du Salève an exfoliation flake peels the full length of the vertical wall. It is arguably the most striking line of the crag and its impact is comparable with the Great Flake on the Central Buttress of Scafell: a line therefore that cannot fail to make the climber's heart beat a little faster.

Often referred to simply as Pâturages the line evolved with individual sections climbed over the years. As early as 1876 the small wall of Balcon was descended (how they got above it and just why this date is singled out in the guide I don't know), then in 1905 Félix Genecand (called Tricouni) and Reich climbed La Grande Arête and the initial corner, La Jaune, fell in 1910. Les Pâturages itself was the work of that incredible woman Alpinist who did so much on the great north faces, Loulou Boulaz with Pierre Bonnant (see *Women Climbing* by the author and Bill Peascod published by A. & C.Black 1989). They made two exploratory attempts in 1943 and 1944, linking it together in 1947.

I first visited the Salève as guest on an International Meet organised by the Swiss Alpine Club. With the incredibly powerful Chris Hamper, many hard lines were climbed though we ascended only the top section, the Les Pâturages portion, of this route. For Bill Peascod, also on the meet as Vice President of the BMC and well into his sixties, the Pâturages Combination became an immediate ambition. His satisfaction on successfully completing the ascent with Ian Parsons was unforgettable. Looking up again at the great hanging flake, as we walked back to the car park together, he simply said with a chuckle: "I climbed that?"

I returned to climb the route in 1990 to find out for myself that in every sense this route provides a real feeling of adventure. A long route of some 240m, it has the calibre of a genuine mountain climb - the summit lies at an altitude of 1,200m. The tremendous contrast between the chimney section of Grande Arête and the open wall of Les Pâturages offers varied climbing which is quite unique. If necessary the distinct crux can be aided and this keeps the overall grade at a fairly uniform level.

The great flake above La Jaune is really a continuation of the corner of La Jaune. Climb the rift direct or make a circular deviation out to the left. Both are polished to an intimidating degree and this aspect of Salève takes some getting used to. Either way leads to a finishing chimney so polished that it resembles glass. Fortunately, enough positive holds make it just within reason.

Scrambling leads to a crevasse stance and the surprisingly steep wall of Balcon. I slipped off the bottom move reaching for a high undercut when both my feet simultaneously shot off. Starting off the block, obvious really, makes it much easier. The gear here is quite spaced, and as elsewhere on this climb a serious feel pervades. Perhaps a few wires would make all the difference should you wish to carry them.

The stance below the chimney, uncomfortably sitting on the sharp edge of the rift, belayed to two thick ring bolts, allows you to appreciate the growing exposure. As my partner Martin Bagness led on I had ample opportunity to savour the view. A fine vista stretching from the tiny circular tables outside the café - floating in a pool of shadow they looked for all the world like red lilies in some exotic pond - out across the plains to Genève and its famous fountain. Ironically, for the next section is known as Grande Arête, the route does not aesthetically follow the edge of the flake but escapes into the bowels of the rift.

Not without interest and originality, and if you take the route described, climbing the right wall from one vertical section to the other gives a fair amount of exposure. After the belay on a jammed chockstone carry on bridging the gap for another pitch to reach the next section. On my direction Martin climbed the corner directly above, which is quite hard, leading to a section of very loose rock before the cave niche of Les Pâturages is reached. In the initial corner is one bolt runner to start and a suspect peg sticking out of a crack on the right. Don't make the same mistake.

From the correct stance on Grande Arête moving up the right wall and leaving the flake constitutes the start of Les Pâturages. This and surmounting the flake overlap forms the crux of the route. Steep but short-lived. Immediately you move right the difficulty eases. Traverse right in a fine exposed position to gain the base of the cave, an unmistakable feature easily recognised from the ground. The upper section contrasts totally with what has gone before, so completing the adventure.

CLUSES, PIERRE À LAYA

Map Ref: *Michelin Motoring Atlas, page 105, E4.*

Area Maps: IGN 3530w. MICH 74.

Guidebook: *Les Carroz - Cluses* by Patrick Favières.

Climate/Climbing Season: On the edge of the high Alps but offering climbing from May to October inclusive.

Restrictions: No wild camping.

Rock and Protection: Good quality limestone, all routes modern bolt protected.

Situation: Only 37km W of Chamonix, 36km E of Genève (Switzerland), 10km SE of Cluses, just out of the small village of Araches. Département Haute-Savoie (No. 74).

Access: From Cluses follow the N205 SE until at Balme takes the D6 which winds steeply up the wooded hillside towards Araches and eventually the ski resort of

Flaine. Park in the centre of Araches; there is an open parking area in front of the church. Cross the road (to the W side) and walk up through the narrow streets aiming for the highest point of the village. A sign to La Pierre à Laya and a narrow leafy lane leads out into an open field. Follow the steep path L ascending the hill to a level plateau area. Cross this taking the R path which briefly enters the trees by an outcrop of limestone. Leaving the trees turn L to find the top of the plateau overlooking the Arve Valley (danger sign). Find a path which traverses down L (looking out) underneath some small but very overhanging rocks to pass behind an old broken barrier fence. The first main buttress appears after this (20 minutes).

Camping etc: A café and water are to be found in Araches but the nearest campsite is in Cluses.

Crag Facts: Only 40 minutes drive from either Chamonix or Genève, Cluses is an important alternative to the big mountains should they be out of condition. There are a host of newly developed modern bolt-equipped crags in this region. Pierre à Laya is one of the most pleasant, offering around 70 routes from 5c to 7b and 20m to 25m in length, with easy access. The crag is quite long and divided into nine named *secteurs*. These are from left to right: Secteur Soupçons - this is grossly overhanging; Secteur Six Epines - this is the overhanging section after the iron barrier; Secteur Rosiers Sauvages - the first clean wall set at a reasonable angle (only vertical); Secteur Jump; Secteur Fissure Express - situated about 200 metres right of Fruits du Chêne roughly in the centre of the crag; Secteur Goulette; Secteur Guerier des Ombres; Secteur Tueur; Secteur Ensoleide. The routes are all named and numbered in the guide but only the names are written on the rock. The crag generally faces SW and is quite sheltered. It gets very hot here.

CRAG CHAT

Pierre à Laya is just one of a group of crags in this area covered by the guidebook *Les Carroz - Cluses*. At the time of writing more crags are being developed at nearby St Gras and Les Suets (near Taninges). Given the vast number of limestone cliffs flanking these deep pre-Alp valleys, development will continue for a long time yet. The position of these crags, only forty minutes from Chamonix but noticeably outside the Alpine weather influence of the Aiguilles make them a very useful day alternative to a rain-soaked campsite fester.

With the major ski resort of Flaine just at the top of the road one can imagine that in winter the quaint Alpine village of Araches becomes raped by a steady stream of motor vehicles churning the soft white snow into a dirty slush. Fortunately in summer it is quiet and even if the traditional wooden houses are not quite all they seem - industry lurks within - it feels unspoilt. Leave the conclave of timbered terraces, cow biers and stone water trough to enter a leafy lane underneath a pear tree. Perhaps leaving Chamonix for the Aiguilles once felt like this, wholesome, clean and private.

Pierre à Laya is situated on the crest of the steep wooded side of the Arve Valley where even the narrow access path traversing the hillside feels exposed, though mitigated to some extent by the thick covering of deciduous woods. On first acquaintance the rocks do not appear high or particularly impressive, but this is amply compensated for by the sunny aspect and attractive situation. Having begun to climb you'll realise that the rock is deceptively steep and of excellent quality, with most of the routes noticeably harder than first appearances would suggest.

CL (28) Cluses, Pierre à Laya. Climber on 'Fissure Express' (6b) - the strenuous zigzag crack of the crag

HIT LIST (From L to R - names only written on rock)

SECTEUR ROSIERS SAUVAGES
CL 13   **Rosiers Sauvages** 20m, 6a/6b
CL 14   **Pilier du Lézard** 20m, 6a/b
CL 15   **FRUITS DU CHÊNE** 20m, 6a. SELECTED ROUTE (see below).
CL 16   **Demi-Lune** 20m, 5c

SECTEUR FISSURE EXPRESS
CL 20   **Fantasia** 30m, 6a
CL 21   **Brutus** 30m, 6b/c
CL 22   **Bric à Brac** 30m, 6b/c
CL 28   **FISSURE EXPRESS** 20m, 6b. SELECTED ROUTE (see below).

SECTEUR GOULETTE
CL 35   **Arianne** 30m, 6c/7a
CL 36   **Goulotte** 30m, 6a/b
CL 41   **Le Diable Hautain** 26m, 7b/c
CL 43   **Solitude Oubliée** 26m, 6a

SECTEUR TUEUR
CL 45   **Les Belles Endormies** 40m, L1:6a, L2:7b
CL 46   **Pays de Neige** 40m, L1:6b, L2:7c
CL 51   **Le Couer** 25m, 6a
CL 53   **Le Tueur** 25m, 6c
CL 57   **Clair de Lune** 25m, 6c

SECTEUR ENSOLEÏDE
CL 60   **Coup de Sapi** 20m, 5c
CL 67   **L'Ourson** 15m, 5b

SELECTED CLIMBS AT PIERRE À LAYA:
Fruits du Chêne (CL 15), Fissure Express (CL 28)

FRUITS DU CHÊNE: 20m, 6a. (British grading - E2, 5c).

First Ascent: Not known.

Location: Secteur Rosiers Sauvages, the first clean merely vertical face after the iron barrier fence.

CL (13 - 16) Cluses, Pierre A Laya, Secteur Rosiers Sauvages.
Climber on 'Fruits du Chêne' (6a) - a quality wall climb

Route Facts: Start immediately right of the overhangs - the name is written on the rock.

L1, 20m, 6a. Climb onto the wall and continue directly until a short traverse left can be made. At the end of this pull steeply up the impending wall/groove to gain a sandwiched slab. Step right and move up the next section of bulging wall until an easier finish leads to the tree and lower off chain.

FISSURE EXPRESS: 20m, 6b. (British grading - E3, 5c+).

First Ascent: Not known.

Location: Secteur Fissure Express, approximately 200m right of Fruits du Chêne. The zig-zag crack soaring up the impending wall is unmistakable (name written on rock).

L1, 20m, (6b). Climb the crack laybacking on finger jams and undercuts. It is immediately both strenuous and precarious. At its top pull out of the corner onto a ledge. Do not move right to the short corner groove but make a blind and balancey move left onto the slab. Climb this to gain chain and lower off point in a few metres.

ROUTE CHAT

"Cubby" Cuthbertson first urged me to visit this crag as a worthy alternative should the Chamonix Aiguilles be out of condition. This was backed up by other frustrated Alpinists like Rick Graham and Luke Steer. When I finally made it I certainly wasn't disappointed and would go as so far as to say, given the modern ethic that it is the delight of the individual move that counts, that whilst it is by no means a major crag it is worth a visit in its own right.

Of the routes recommended by "Cubby" the two selected here seem the most representative of the quality of climbing to be found. I found both a good deal harder than they look and hard for the grade. Fruits du Chêne looks about equivalent to British Hard Very Severe at the most. Wrong - it contains four distinctly difficult sections and is sustained throughout.

Fissure Express is easy to find but not so simple to climb. It looks straightforward but proves, from the onset, to be anything but. Not only strenuous but technical too, and not a place you want to linger, because the wall impends and there is absolutely no place to rest. A route that cannot be rushed at first acquaintance - every move makes you think.

For such a well protected and apparently straightforward line it is surprising just how many problems Fissure Express conjures up. Not many whose top limit is E3 will flash this route on sight. Even approaching the top, when you rock out right to take a partial rest from the screaming steepness, all is by no means over. I made the mistake of moving right into the tempting short overhang corner, but you should make one more move up out left to swing onto a slab. You'll have to have faith here because the move is completely blind with the finger holds hidden out of sight. Good value but difficult to grade, for whilst there may be no single move at British 6a there are a whole string of moves at hardish British 5c with no possibility of a rest.

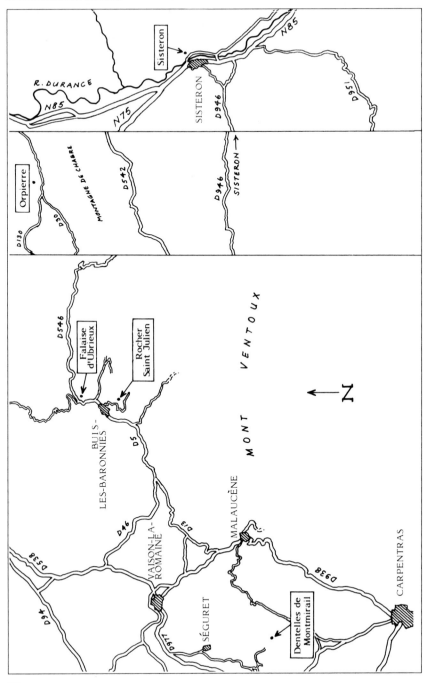

AREA 2 SOUTH EASTERN FRANCE

Defined by a line east from Lyon and due south down the Rhône Valley this may be geographically the smallest but it is by far the most important of the rock climbing areas of France. Containing the magic of Provence, the glamour of the Côte d'Azur, all the sunshine you can handle and the internationally important limestone of Verdon and Buoux, this is a region par-excellence. Naturally it constitutes the largest section of this book and includes eighteen of the best crags and eighteen selected routes.

FALAISE D'UBRIEUX

Map Ref: *Michelin Motoring Atlas, page 145, D3.*

Area Maps: IGN 3140e, L=(3225.5, 835.5). MICH 81.3

Guidebook: *Escalade à Buis-les-Baronnies.*

Climate/Climbing Season: Precipitation (rain/snow) 600mm on 85 days of the year. Driest months are July and August. Lies at a lower level than nearby Rocher de Saint-Julien though climbing between November and March may be unreasonably cold.

Restrictions: No wild camping is allowed.

Rock and Protection: Hard limestone, this is a sport climbing crag so only quick draws need be carried.

Situation: Immediately above the D546 on the E bank of the River L'Ouvèze some 2km NNE of the village of Buis-les-Baronnies, 52km SE of Montélimar, 40km ENE of Orange. Département Drôme (No.26).

Access: From Buis-les-Baronnies (see Buis-les-Baronnies, Rocher de Saint-Julien for details) drive N along the D546 for 2km until, at the point of entry into the confines of Gorges d'Ubrieux, the cliff will be seen on the R. Park directly beneath (allow 30 seconds to 3 minutes).

Crag Facts: This SW-facing crag stretches from those immediately above the road (Roadside Crag) to the slabbier face up to the R. Most routes are single pitch to a lower-off chain. There are some 60 routes, 20m to 40m in length ranging in difficulty from 3b to 7c.

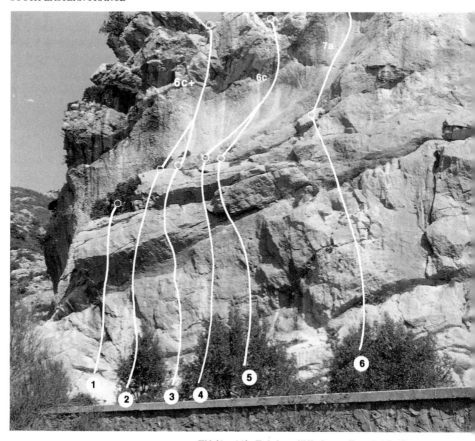

FU (1 - 10) Falaise d'Ubrieux, Roadside Crag

CRAG CHAT

A deservedly popular edge of limestone running up R from the road. The roadside crag offers a number of interesting roof problems and steep face climbs, between 6a and 6c (British technical grade 5b to 6a), whilst the edge to the R provides a feast of technical slab climbing. The rock is excellent hard limestone and the crag offers an attractive low level and easily accessible alternative to the nearby Rocher de Saint-Julien.

HIT LIST (From L to R)

ROADSIDE CRAG

FU 1	Toit Robi 6c	
FU 2	Ça Carton 6b	
FU 3	Sensation 6b	
FU 4	Oh! Con 6b	
FU 5	Ire de la Lune 6a	
FU 6	Aphrodite 4c	
FU 7	Oraison Funèbre 6b+	
FU 8	Passeport Pour l'Enfer 7b	
FU 9	Dernier Soupir 6b	
FU 10	Le Paradis 6a+	

THE SLABS

FU 11   **Psychose** 5b
FU 12   **Turpitude** 6b+
FU 13   **Kesako** 6b
FU 14   **Sex Symbole** 6b+
FU 15   **Entrechat** 6c
FU 16   **Paradoxe** L1:5b, L2:6b
FU 17   **Dévers Gondage** L1:5b, L2:6a+
FU 18   **Symphonie Inachevée** L1:5c, L2:6a
FU 19   **La Diagonale du Fou** 6a

FU (11 - 19) Falaise d'Ubrieux, The Slabs

BUIS-LES-BARONNIES, ROCHER DE SAINT-JULIEN

Map Ref: *Michelin Motoring Atlas, page 145, D3.*

Area Maps: IGN 3140e, L=(3222.9, 834.7-835.6). MICH 81.3.

Guidebook: *Escalade à Buis-les-Baronnies.*

Climate/Climbing Season: Precipitation (rain/snow) 600mm on 85 days of the year. Driest months are July and August. Climbing generally possible from April to November depending on the season although, because of the altitude, it can be snow-bound at Easter.

Restrictions: No wild camping is allowed.

Rock and Protection: Good quality limestone with insitu pegs on the arête and bolts elsewhere but a small selection of nuts and a couple of long slings are useful. Double ropes recommended for abseiling.

Situation: Rocher de Saint-Julien is situated just above the village of Buis-les-Baronnies, 52km SE of Montélimar, 40km ENE of Orange. Département Drôme (No.26).

Access: Heading S on the Autoroute du Soleil (A7) it is usual to turn off at Montélimar Sud and pass through Grigan to Nyons. Take the D538 S in the direction of Vaison-la-Romaine to join the D46 at La Tullière (hardly noticeable - only a couple of houses). Follow this through Mollans (the road now becomes the D5) to reach Buis-les-Baronnies. From Buis-les-Baronnies cross a small bridge to pass the municipal campsite and follow a small winding road. (The road is a cul-de-sac which after passing the crag, continues past a rocky outcrop bearing a ruined church and cross of St Trophime - fine viewpoint over Buis-les-Baronnies below. It ends at La Nibble.) In about 1km reach a stony lay-by and tall transformer building on the right - park here. (If one continues up the road a fine view can be had of the crag.) The base of the rock fin that is Saint-Julien starts just above the road on the opposite side to the transformer tower and is reached by scrambling up steep scree (1 minute). The S-facing flanks of the fin provide many routes and the main area is found by continuing up the steep scree (20 minutes).

Camping etc: There is a municipal campsite in charming Buis-les-Baronnies. Water, cafés, supermarkets, garages and a small climbing shop and climber's *gîte* (self-catering bunkhouse) can also be found.

Crag Facts: A magnificent fin of rock almost Alpine in appearance. Although it lies just above the village the climbing face can't be seen from here - the S face can only be viewed by driving up the road described. On this S face of the fin are some 80 routes from 80m to 120m, ranging in difficulty from 5a to 7a (British technical grade 4b to 6b). Most routes are multi pitch, around 10 quick draws should be carried and double 50m ropes are necessary for the abseil descents.

CRAG CHAT

Cool cruising down the route to the sun (Autoroute du Soleil) this is the first crag to be found with the full South of France flavour. Easily accessible, only 52km SE of Montélimar or 40km NE of Orange it is a logical stopping off point when on the way to Provence or Côte d'Azur. Despite it being one of the more traditional crags with a fifty-year history of rock climbing the village of Buis-les-Baronnies remains totally unspoilt, a charming and beautiful place to be. Even before the Channel Tunnel it is possible to set off from Britain in the afternoon and climb here next morning. I don't recommend it, but it is tempting.

First impressions viewing the elongated S face of the fin from the road far below may suggest that the rocks are broken and vegetated. This is not so, just an illusion brought about by the inevitable presence of the stalwart Mediterranean bushes. These are capable of growing from any slight fissure in an otherwise smooth and vertical section of limestone. Although the arête itself is exposed (and may be snow-clad even in early April) the S face is a sun trap sheltered from the mistral. It can provide an amicable climbing ground in winter depending on the prevailing conditions. In summer don't forget to carry a bottle of water up to the bottom with you. There is none to be found otherwise.

Despite the Alpine appearance of the fin as a whole it is also quite difficult at first to appreciate the scale of the S face. Tiny figures seen on the ridge help bring home the fact that there are routes here up to four pitches and 120m in length. From L to R the fin comprises several towers. The first great tower on the L is separated from the second by a gap filled by the tooth-like presence of the pinnacles. There is a slight notch in the second tower but the third tower (small visible cross on top) is separated by a deep rift *(brèche)*. The bulk of the climbing lies spread along the S face from the first tower to the R end of the second tower. Stonefall, originated by parties on the arête, is unfortunately not unknown and it is a sensible precaution to wear a helmet.

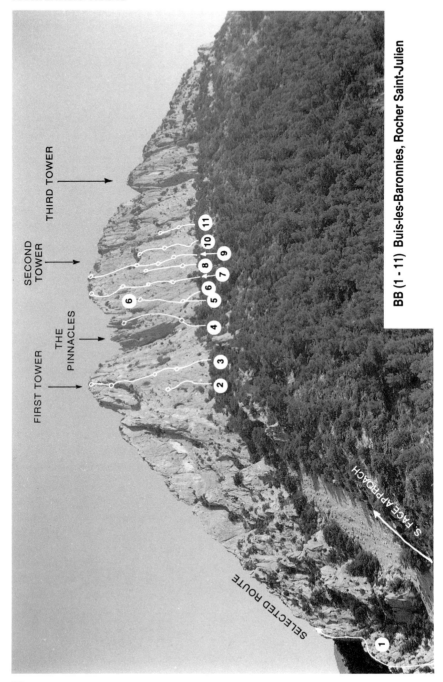

BB (1 - 11) Buis-les-Baronnies, Rocher Saint-Julien

HIT LIST: (From L to R)
SOUTH FACE
BB 1   **TRAVERSÉE DES ARÊTES** 600m, 5a. SELECTED ROUTE (see below).

SOUTH FACE - FIRST TOWER
BB 2   **Love on the Bite** 6b+
BB 3   **Le Gastronome** L1:5b, L2:5b, L3:5b, L4:3b

SOUTH FACE - THE PINNACLES
BB 4   **Les Trois Mousquetons** L1:5c, L2:6a
BB 5   **Force Majeure** 7a
BB 6   **Le Barbarin Fourchu** L1:6c, L2:6a

SOUTH FACE - SECOND TOWER
BB 7   **Bibus** L1:5b, L2:5b, L3:5b, L4:5b. Considered to be the classic of the S face.
BB 8   **Pandémonium** L1:5b, L2:6c
BB 9   **Directissime** L1:5b, L2:6a+, L3:6a, L4:5b
BB 10   **Tannhäuser** L1:6a, L2:6a
BB 11   **Directe des Dalles** L1:6b+, L2:6a+. Another great classic.

SELECTED CLIMB AT ROCHER DE SAINT-JULIEN:
Traversée Des Arêtes (BB 1)

TRAVERSÉE DES ARÊTES: 600m, 5a. (British grading - Very Severe, 4b).
First Ascent: Alfred Couttet, Paul Leroy Edwards, 1946.

Location: The crest of great fin of Rocher de Saint-Julien.

Route Facts: The climb starts just above the road. Allow 7 hours for a party of two.

600m, 5a. Gain and follow the ridge. After 100m or so this becomes knife-edged and considerably exposed. Follow the crest (short section of 4c) until the first horizontal step is reached. Traverse this, then descend a ramp on the right (through a tree) to circumnavigate the first pillar on its south side. Climb up into the gap between the pillar and the buttress beyond and bridge up this until the impressive crack in the headwall can be climbed - insitu pegs (5a). Easily scramble along the top of the first tower until a descent can be made into the *brèche* (gap) between this and the second main tower of the ridge. The gap is filled firstly by a minor and then two major pinnacles. The most enjoyable climbing will be found by sticking to the arêtes. After dropping down the final pinnacle a fine rib leads up the arête to the summit of the second tower. The first 12m constitute the crux (insitu pegs) until climbing deteriorates to scrambling along the easy top of the tower. There is a cleft and afterwards a *brèche* separates this tower from the final tower (cross on the summit). The final tower is not climbed.

Descent: Either (a), find an easy but unlikely looking route on the south face or (b), abseil down the *brèche*. In either case follow the crest until forced down left. For (a) concealed moves around onto the south face of the ridge lead to a line of green paint following across ledges to the first of a series of insitu chains. Descend these and the marked route in between. For (b) continue the descent down a chimney until a large ring marks the first abseil point. Abseil to the neck of the *brèche*. From here a full 50m abseil leads down the chimney (south face) to the

BB (1) Rocher Saint-Julien, 'Traversee des Arêtes' (5a) - Climber on the 2nd Pinnacle between the First and Second Towers

base of the rocks (a half abseil on a single rope leads to a very poor intermediate tree and should be avoided if possible). Continue along beneath the base of the crag until a steep scree descent leads back to the road.

ROUTE CHAT

An expedition of some length and character Traversée des Arêtes of Saint-Julien follows the aesthetic crest of the ridge. It was first climbed in its entirety by Chamonix guide Alfred Couttet and American Paul Leroy Edwards in 1946 although Couttet had climbed sections before. In fact it was Couttet who commenced explorations here as long ago as 1932.

Despite its almost Alpine appearance and exposure the route can happily be climbed over a season extending from April to November (inclusive). But remember that escape can be up to four abseils away and it is a committing climb. Heat from the midday sun can be intense and should not be underestimated.

Mentally the route can be divided into five major obstacles: the initial arête, which rapidly becomes knife-edged; the headwall crack of the first tower, commencing from the gap behind the first pinnacle; the ups and downs of the pinnacle-filled *brèche;* the rib leading from behind the foot of the last pinnacle up the second tower (the balancey crux section); the descent - if you can find the line of chains leading down the south face this is probably the most interesting way. Between these main features most parties will move together or solo large sections which does not detract in any way from the route's interest. This route is the main challenge, pure and simple.

DENTELLES DE MONTMIRAIL, CHAÎNE DE GIGONDAS

Map Ref: *Michelin Motoring Atlas, page 144, C3.*

Area Maps: IGN 3040e and 3140w, L=(3210.8, 815.2). MICH 81.2.

Guidebook: *Dentelles de Montmirail - Escalade by Oliver Gaude.*

Climate/Climbing Season: Precipitation (rain/snow) 750mm on 65 days of the year. Wettest period is autumn and the month of March. Driest month is July. It can often be unpleasantly windy here and climbing is out when the mistral blows.

Restrictions: No wild camping.

Rock and Protection: Many routes have been equipped with modern bolts and generally the limestone is very good on these. Elsewhere, particularly along the tip of the crest itself, there is much loose rock. Only quick draws are really necessary on the re-equipped routes but the rock does run to cracks and a selection of nuts and Friends could be used. Double ropes recommended for abseiling.

Situation: The Chaîne de Gigondas is located beyond the village of Gigondas immediately above the col du Cayron, 15km E of Orange. Département Vaucluse (No.84).

Access: Leave the Autoroute du Soleil (A7) at Orange to follow the D950 SE to Carpentras (23km). Head N on the D7 through Vacqueyras to reach the village of Gigondas. Pass this, without entering the centre, to continue E on the route des Florets. The road turns to a steep rough track and 3km beyond Gigondas the summit of col du Cayron is reached. There is a parking area and plenty of space. The track splits here to drop down NE and rise up to SE but the crag lies directly above the col. Follow the path directly up to the *brèche* marking the L end of the central section of the chain. From here the path traverses R beneath the N face (20 minutes).

Camping etc: There is camping at Vacqueyras and Beaumes-de-Venise. There is a CAF hut close to the Hôtel des Florets (this lies on the left of the road leading to the col du Cayron), accommodation at the Café de la Poste in Gigondas and the *gîte d'étape* at Lafare. Water, café, small shops and two wine cellars in tiny Gigondas.

Crag Facts: The Dentelles de Montmirail are a parallel series of brilliantly white limestone crests running roughly W to E above the village of Montmirail. Situated on high ground above the flat plain of the Rhône Valley they present a striking and highly visible feature. The main crest, that is detailed here, the Chaîne de Gigondas, is a traditional climbing area recently rebolted. The crest, divided by gaps *(brèches),* falls into three obvious sections. Looking upwards from the col du Cayron there is la Pousterle on the L, then a gap known as the Brèche de la Pousterle. Du Turc forms the central and most continuous section of cliff and is separated from the last section, Des Florets, by the Brèche du Turc. Both the Brèche de la Pousterle and Brèche du Turc provide access through the chain. Du Turc is the main area and all the worthwhile climbing lies on its N face (that viewed from the col). There are some 40 routes ranging from 3c to 7b - it is recommended that only the recently rebolted routes are climbed as on others gear is rotten and the rock loose.

CRAG CHAT

Gigondas, raised above the flat plains and backed by hills tiered with vineyards, is a picturesque village with a mountain flavour. The excellence of the local wine is famous and two wine cellars in the one main street bear testimony to its popularity. Beyond the village the Chaîne de Gigondas stretches for almost 2km and approaches some 120m high in places. Whilst there is some climbing on the S face of la Pousterle the best climbing is to be found on the N face of du Turc (the central section). This area is easily accessible and provides a shady venue suitable for the long hot days of summer. It must be remembered however, that it is not a venue for a windy day.

A word of warning; the traverse along the crest of the ridge, although looking appealing from below (viewed from the col du Cayron) and detailed in another English publication (now out of print), is not a worthwhile or enjoyable proposition. Certainly along the middle section it is loose and easily escapable down the short broken, vegetated S face. My experiences suggest that the horizontal section, gained by climbing the arête above the Brèche de la Pousterle or by detouring in beyond this from the S side, is never climbed.

In fact climbing from the Brèche de la Pousterle to the summit of the first pinnacle - Pointe Lagarde - is a route in itself. There are a number of bolted alternatives. The most aesthetic is probably the line following the arête (at a grade of about 5c, English Hard Very Severe) but take care with the rock in the upper regions.

The obvious appeal of this region has long been recognised by climbers and a CAF hut provides bunkhouse-type accommodation. There are many natural lines, chimneys, cracks, ramps and corners leading to the crest of the tooth.˙ Originally climbed with pitons and wedges, most of this equipment is now rotten and untrustworthy. Many lines have however been completely rebolted (these are obvious from below) and provide excellent climbing. Indeed the blank walls, often gently impending, have also been bolted to provide high standard sport-climbing, supplementing the more obvious lines. Nearby the parallel chains of Dent Hadamard and Chaîne du Clapis (best approached from Lafare) both facing S have also been bolted to provide modern sport-climbing venues complimentary to this the traditional crag.

SELECTED CLIMB AT CHAINE DE GIGONDAS:
Dièdre des Parisiens (DM 3)

DIÈDRE DES PARISIENS: 100m, L1:5c, L2:5b. (British grading - Hard Very Severe, 5a).

First Ascent: Unknown

Location: The N face of the central-most crest of the du Turc section.

Route Facts: From the Brèche de la Pousterle take the path traversing R beneath the N face. Pass under Point Lagarde and the largest continuous buttress (capped by Pointe Claire) until the path ascends slightly to traverse beneath a triangular

DM (1 - 4) Dentelles de Montmirail, Chaîne de Gigondas, with Du Turc stretching R from the gap of the Brèche de la Pousterle

HIT LIST (From L to R)

DU TURC

DM 1   **Voie du Surplomb 100m,** L1:6c, L2:6a+

DM 2   **Banana Split** 55m, 7a+

DM 3   **DIÈDRE DES PARISIENS** 100m, L1:5c, L2:5b. SELECTED ROUTE (see p. 83).

DM 4   **Petits Moutons** 90m, L1:6b, L2:6c

DM 5   **La Dulfer** 100m, L1:4c, L2:5b

DES FLORETS

DM 6   **Eperon du Charnier** 100m, L1:6a, L2:6c

DM 7   **La Rattepenade** 100m, L1:4c, L2:5b

buttress. The right side of this buttress is defined by a ramp running the full height of the wall. Ascend through the scrub and bushes to a small bay at its base.

L1, 40m, 5c. Climb the corner to gain the ramp (technical crux). Follow this until a chimney-like stance can be gained (preferable to make this a long pitch in order to reach the top in the next rope length).

L2, 40m, 5b. Climb the chimney and corner, steep and exposed, to take a belay on the knife-edged summit of the crest. The bolts are reasonably spaced although sometimes difficult to spot when you are suspended across the chimney - Friends can be placed.

DM (5 - 7) Dentelles de Montmirail, Chaîne de Gigondas, with Des Florets stretching R from the gap of the Brèche du Turc

Descent: Double 50m ropes should reach the base in two abseils. However, the nature of the top chimney section might cause rope snagging if you are unlucky. An alternative is to make one abseil (double 50m ropes) down the shorter S face then walk back to the Brèche de la Pousterle - if this is done, care must be taken not to snag or dislodge loose rock (which abounds here) particularly when retrieving the rope.

ROUTE CHAT

We discovered this sensational line for ourselves when walking back from the Brèche du Turc. Having already wasted much of the October day making an abortive attempt to traverse the crest, tempers were well blackened. The dark north face towering above the path did nothing to lighten the mood until we spied, shooting aesthetically up to a lighter sky, an immaculate corner ramp - the Overhanging Bastion of France.

A quick look turned into a frantic uncoiling of ropes as Dave Birkett snaked out the line, untroubled by the damp conditions. You start in a shallow corner which splutters out before the ramp proper is reached. Fingery moves are necessary to gain the ramp. Wires could be placed but Dave seemed happy with the new bolts. Solid perhaps, but appearing rather spaced from below. Taking a belay on the left wall somewhere before the main chimney section seemed fine, but leading

85

through on the next pitch left me frustratingly some 10m short of the top. So take note, the line is somewhat foreshortened when standing directly below.

The upper part is predominantly a well formed chimney, steeper than the lower ramp, considerably exposed and offering a constant supply of good handholds. Beginning to feel alarmed on the middle section, having run out perhaps 20m from a bolt (bomb proof as it may have been) I fiddled in an indifferent Friend, not quite the right size. Then infuriatingly saw a bolt 1m below my foot and another one I'd missed 10m below that. Well, it isn't easy to see anything other than your nose when crammed tight in a corner!

On reflection I would say this climb is quite different from lots of limestone in the region; being more flaky than pockety. The two contrasting pitches both offer steep climbing and it is a tremendous line.

When we three, Trevor Jones being the other, all reached the sunshine of the summit crest, it felt ten times better than bursting open a bottle of bubbly. On the ridge again but this time in triumph. Laughter at the ridiculous thought of anyone traversing it. What grade? Who knew. Dave thought MVS. Trevor and I sort of HVS to E1. What length were the pitches? Well we didn't reach the top in two, but who could really re-member. Which way down? A slither into the tangled weave of trees and loose flakes of the S face, enveloped in the intox-icating warmth of the evening sunshine.

DM (3) Chaîne de Gigondas, 'Diedre des Parisienes' (5c) - Climber halfway up the first pitch

ORPIÈRRE

Map Ref: *Michelin Motoring Atlas, page 145, F2.*

Area Maps: IGN 3239e, L=(3229.5, 867.9). MICH 81.5.

Guidebook: *Roc et Falaises* by Régis Mulot.

Climate/Climbing Season: Precipitation (rain/snow) 1,000mm on 80 days of the year. The wettest months are October and November, so much so that much of the remaining winter months are relatively dry. Many of the climbs face S and conversely some shade can be found, making this an all year round venue.

Restrictions: No wild camping.

Rock and Protection: Most routes are well equipped with bolts and generally the limestone is good. Generally ten quick draws meet all requirements. However, on the longer routes on Quiquillon, protection can be spaced and it may be advisable to carry a small selection of nuts.

Situation: Some 23km NW of Sisteron and 10km W of Laragne-Montéglin, 130km S of Grenoble. Département Hautes-Alpes (No.05).

Access: The village of Orpièrre is reached in 8km by leaving the N75 at Eyguians to follow the D30. The horseshoe formation of cliffs is fed by a track rising from the village opposite the church (most routes can be reached within 15 minutes).

Camping etc: The village offers shops, restaurants, plentiful accommodation including a *gîte* and campsite.

Crag Facts: One of the most popular sport-climbing venues of the area. It has easy access, a sunny disposition, and offers a wide range of climbing. There is plenty here for the medium grade climber and routes range from short single pitch to long and involved. In effect the climbing area forms a horseshoe valley scalloped in the hillside immediately to the north of the village. The L flank of this valley is formed by the cliffs of Le Château and the head by the generally slabby wall of Le Belleric (facing due S). The higher R flank is formed, most spectacularly, by the cliffs of Quiquillon. Its W face is hollowed by a huge shallow cave which ends at its S tip in a dramatic pillar - Pilier Sud. There are other routes on this front S face before it turns into the long flat wall of the SE face. Some twenty routes on Le Château range from 35m to 45m in length and from 5a to 7a in difficulty. On Belleric, the most popular face, some twenty-five routes range from 35m to 40m in length and from 3b to 7a in difficulty. As stated Le Quiquillon consists of a number of *secteurs* and offers the longest climbs of the area, some forty routes from 80m to 160m in length range in difficulty from 5a to 7c. Descent from the routes is either by abseil or lower off and, particularly on Le Quiquillon where multi-abseils are necessary (abseil points insitu), double ropes are recommended.

OP (1 - 6) Orpierre, Le Château forms the L side of the valley

CRAG CHAT

The impressive towers of Le Quiquillon may dominate the scene above the small village of Orpièrre, yet the two smaller cliffs of Le Château and Belleric remain the most popular. This despite the poor looking quality of the rock - fortunately a deception, for the rock is generally of good quality - and their ungracious position above a scrubby valley and disused mine tips. Le Château offers afternoon shade, so some respite from the hot sun, and on Belleric there are many climbs to occupy those of average ability. Those climbing British Very Severe and above will be well served on Belleric (whilst a few pulls on the plentiful bolts will open the routes to those who generally don't).

There are easily enough routes to fulfil an energetic week's climbing and many Brits who have stopped off here for the odd day have been enticed to stay longer. The popularity of these cliffs with the French will also be noted, particularly during weekends and holiday periods. Despite their altitude of between 700m and 1,100m cliffs are sheltered from the effects of Le Mistral and climbing remains popular even during the winter months.

It should be remembered that the longer climbs on Le Quiquillon, up to 160m in length, are of a much more serious nature than those on the lesser cliffs. At the time of writing, although re-bolting is being undertaken, some of these routes are rather inadequately protected and it is advisable to carry a small rack of nuts.

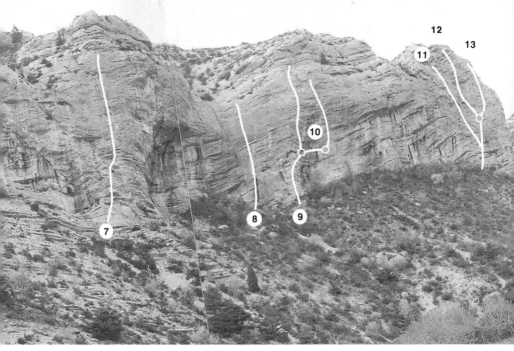

OP (7 - 13)

HIT LIST (From L to R)

LE CHÂTEAU (Generally all these routes are fully equipped and descent is by abseil.)

OP 1	**Directe Canardo-Palmer** 40m, 4c
OP 2	**Les Clochards Célestes** 40m, 5b
OP 3	**Think Punk** 40m, L1:5a, L2:5c
OP 4	**Les Racines du Ciel** 30m, 5c
OP 5	**Le Rou d'Amérique** 25m, L1:4c, L2:5b
OP 6	**Évitons d'Importuner L'Étrangleur** 30m, 6c
OP 7	**La Moulinette Endimanchée** 40m, 6a
OP 8	**Pour un Bébé Robot** 35m, 7a
OP 9	**Améli-Mélo-Die** 40m, L1:4b, L2:6a
OP 10	**Destruction** 25m, 7b
OP 11	**Le Piton Inconnu** 45m, L1:4c, L2:5c
OP 12	**Sauve Qui Peut la Vie** 40m, 5c
OP 13	**Raoul Petite** 45m, L1:4c, L2:5a

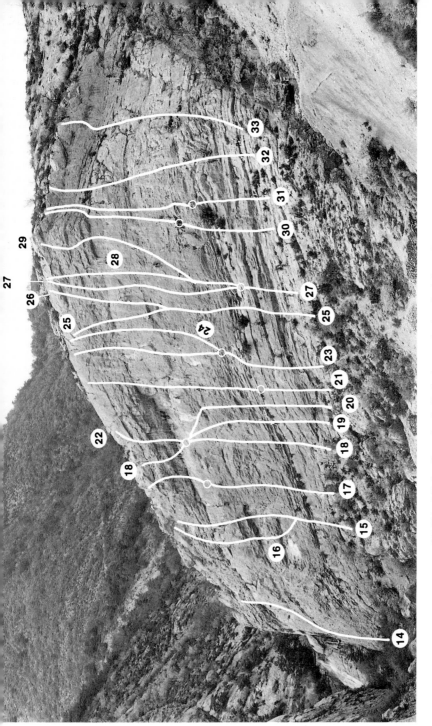

OP (14 - 33) Orpièrre, Le Belleric forms the head of the valley

LE BELLERIC (Generally all these routes are fully equipped and descent is by abseil.)

OP 14   **Parcours Santé** 40m, 6c
OP 15   **Le Petit Toit** 40m, 5c
OP 16   **Bouffons du Flic** 40m, 6c
OP 17   **Jour de Transes** 40m, L1:6a, L2:6c
OP 18   **Le Grand Toit** 40m, L1:6a, L2:
OP 19   **Eh! Super Jules, Tu Craques?** 30m, 6a
OP 20   **La Voie de Son Maître** 30m, 5c
OP 21   **Plus Fort Que Moi Tu Meurs** 45m, L1:4b, L2:6a
OP 22   **La Directe du Grand Toit** 15m, 7a+
OP 23   **Rogntudju** 45m, L1:4c, L2:6b
OP 24   **Rhinocéphale** 45m, 6b
OP 25   **M'Enfin** 50m, L1:4c, L2:6b
OP 26   **Ironie du Sport** 50m, L1:4c, L2:6a
OP 27   **André-Aline Shoot** 45m, L1:4c, L2:6a
OP 28   **Violence et Passion** 50m, L1:4c, L2:6a
OP 29   **Moins Quarante à l'Ombre** 50m, L1:4c, L2:6a+
OP 30   **Tropique du Capricorne** 50m, L1:4b, L2:4c
OP 31   **Balai-Brosse** 45m, L1:3b, L2:4c
OP 32   **Greenpeace** 45m, L1:3b, L2:4c
OP 33   **La Marine** 40m, L1:2b, L2:5c + AO

QUIQUILLON, WEST FACE

OP 34   **La Terreur du Chien Fou** via **Nougat Myope**
170m, L1:5c, L2:7a, L3:4c, L4:5c, L5:4c

QUIQUILLON, SOUTH FACE

OP 35   **Le Pilier Sud** 150m, L1:5c, L2:5b, L3:2b, L4:6a. A magnificent line, a selection of nuts should be carried.

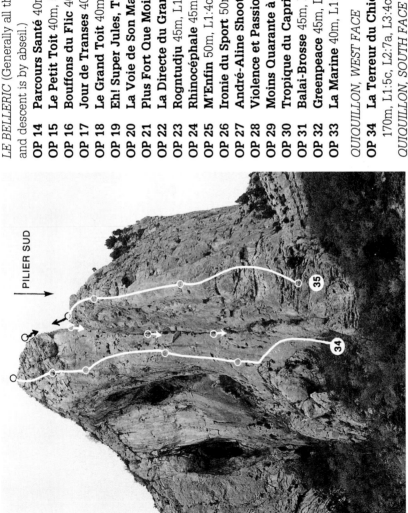

OP (34 - 35) Orpièrre, Quiquillon - W Face

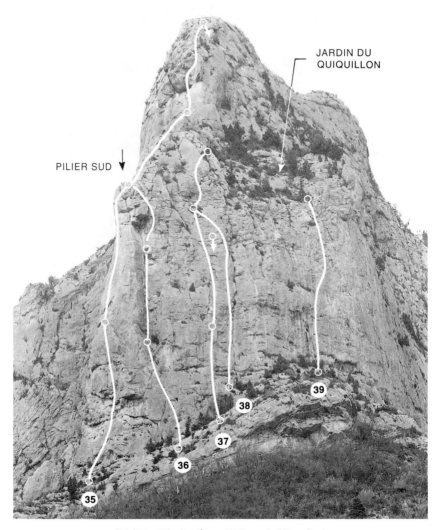

JARDIN DU
QUIQUILLON

PILIER SUD

OP (35 - 39) Orpièrre, W Face & Pilier Sud

QUIQUILLON , SOUTH FACE cont.

OP 36   **Le Dièdre** 80m, L1:5c, L2:5b, L3:4c
OP 37   **Le Mur Bleu** 90m, L1:6c, L2:5b, L3:4c
OP 38   **Mistral Gagnant** 40m, 6a
OP 39   **La Fidélité** 80m, L1:5b & A1, L2:5b

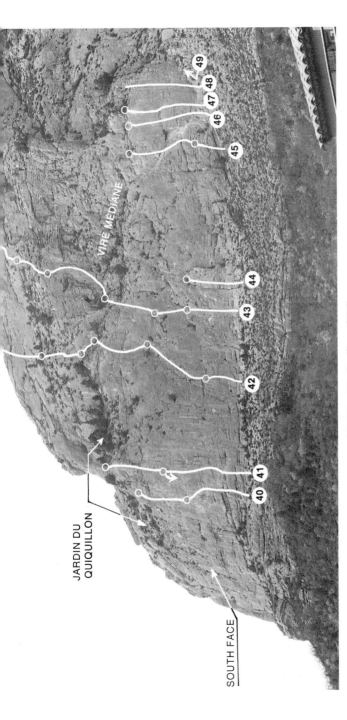

SOUTH FACE

JARDIN DU
QUIQUILLON

VIRE MÉDIANE

OP (40 - 49) Orpièrre, SE Face

QUIQUILLON, SOUTH EAST FACE

OP 40 Vivement la Bombe 50m, L1:6b, L2:6c

OP 41 Heureusement il y a la Mer 80m, L1:6b, L2:6c

OP 42 Le Ramier 160m, L1:4c, L2:5b, L3:4c, L4:3b, L5:5a

OP 43 La Grotte 170m, L1:5b, L2:5b, L3:6a, L4:4b, L5:5c, L6:5b, L7:5c

OP 44 La Jungle en Folie 30m, 4c

OP 45 Demain les Loups 45m, L1:6a, L2:7a

OP 46 On Achève Bien les Chevaux 45m, 6c

OP 47 Panique en Ouganda 45m, 7a-

OP 48 Suer aux Tripes 45m, 7a

OP 49 Terreur en Antartique 45m, 7a-

93

SISTERON

Map Ref: *Michelin Motoring Atlas, page 146, A3.*

Area Maps: IGN 3340e, L=(3217.5, 888.6). MICH 81.6.

Guidebook: *Topo Guide d'Escalade de Sisteron.*

Climate/Climbing Season: Precipitation (rain/snow) 600mm on 75 days of the year. Climbing can reasonably be expected between April and November.

Restrictions: Temporary restrictions (weekend climbing only) due to road tunnel construction are now lifted.

Rock and Protection: Bedded limestone folded vertically. When viewed end on from the town these beds form parallel ribs. The vertical faces of each bedding plane provide the climbing and although the rock is fissured and flaky it is hard and sound on the S face (Grande Dalle). Bolt protection is good and it is only necessary to carry quick draws (although small to medium size Rocks and Friends could be placed on the crack climbs). Double 50m ropes are recommended for the abseil descents.

Situation: Sisteron lies on the N85 48km S of Gap, 39km W of Digne, some 140km equidistant from Grenoble and Marseille. The cliff lies on the E bank of the River Durance, immediately opposite the town. Département Alpes de Haute-Provence (No.04).

Access: This could hardly be easier! Below the car park/viewpoint adjacent to the main road running through Sisteron a bridge (Pont de la Baume) crosses the river. Discover a road at the N end of the car park to cross the bridge and turn S (on the D4) to find lay-by parking opposite the cottages below the cliff. A path leads up to a large rift and the S face to the R (1 minute).

Camping etc: There are plenty of hotels in town and a large quiet car park (with water tap) down by the side of the river, S of the Pont de la Baume (very narrow access road) provides a pleasant site for camper vans. Camping 2km N of la Baume at Plan de la Baume is open between May and October.

Crag Facts: The crag, the W flank of the Montagne de la Baume, stands opposite and overlooks the medieval town of Sisteron. Viewed from the town the parallel ends of the limestone bedding planes thrust vertically upwards - part of a great fold in the earth's skin. The softer rocks between the beds have been eroded away to present the skeletal ribs of white limestone thrown into dramatic relief. The climbing lies on the faces of these bedding planes. A deep rift to the R, the Dalle du Pli, provides two faces, one slabby the other overhanging. R of this forming the S face, the Grande Dalle, forms the end of the crag. In all there are some 55 routes from 30m to 60m ranging from 5a to 7c. Wind can be a severe problem here, especially in the Dalle du Pli.

CRAG CHAT

At Sisteron the River Durance squeezes through a gap in the white mountain limestone of Provence. On one side lies the fortified town, built of rock and built into rock. Its jumble of buildings, narrow streets, arches, buttresses and twisting steps, tumble skywards to a majestic summit castle. Opposite lies the steeper high W face of la Baume, its aesthetic rock architecture floodlit at night to provide one of the most famous tourist features in Provence. Round the corner, hidden from the town, and sunlit during the day the S face looks serenely down the Durance. Fully bolted it now provides a wide range of interest for the sport climber.

Although cut and tunnelled by the busy N85 and popular with tourists Sisteron retains great character and charm. There are plenty of shops and cafés and prices remain reasonable. The crag itself is now also tunnelled by the new autoroute, running along the opposite bank of the Durance the construction of which put a temporary restriction on climbing, during weekdays. The now finished scheme lessens traffic through the town itself.

The deep, dark rift to the right of the crag is known as La Dalle du Pli. Once inside its bowels it will be found that the L wall is slabby and fossiliferous and the R wall (the back of Grande Dalle) is overhanging. A number of fierce cracks cut this R wall. Both walls offer a number of worthwhile bolted climbs. It may also be found that a fierce wind constantly screams through the rift. Its apparent offer of shelter being largely illusory.

Just round the corner, hardly detectable from the town, lies the large S face and here can be found some excellent climbing with over 30 routes offering a wide spread of difficulty from 5a to 7b (British grading Mild Very Severe 4b to E5 6c). The easier routes tend to follow cracks and fissures whilst the harder climbs take the challenge of the blank faces. Fine open climbing that often provides a safe haven from the wind whistling down the Durance Valley.

SELECTED CLIMBS AT SISTERON:
Deux et Demi (SI 6), Bambino (SI 8)

DEUX ET DEMI: 35m, 5a. (British grading - Mild Very Severe, 4a/b).

First Ascent: Not known but re-equipped in 1985.

Location: South Face (Grande Dalle).

Route Facts: Walking right from the deep rift, the point where the access path reaches the cliff, a slabby face seamed by cracks will be found in approximately 100m. Just above the ground a large diamond-shaped block within the face, outlined by the cracks, marks the bottom section of the climb.

L1, 35m, 5a. Take the right side of the diamond then follow the continuation crack

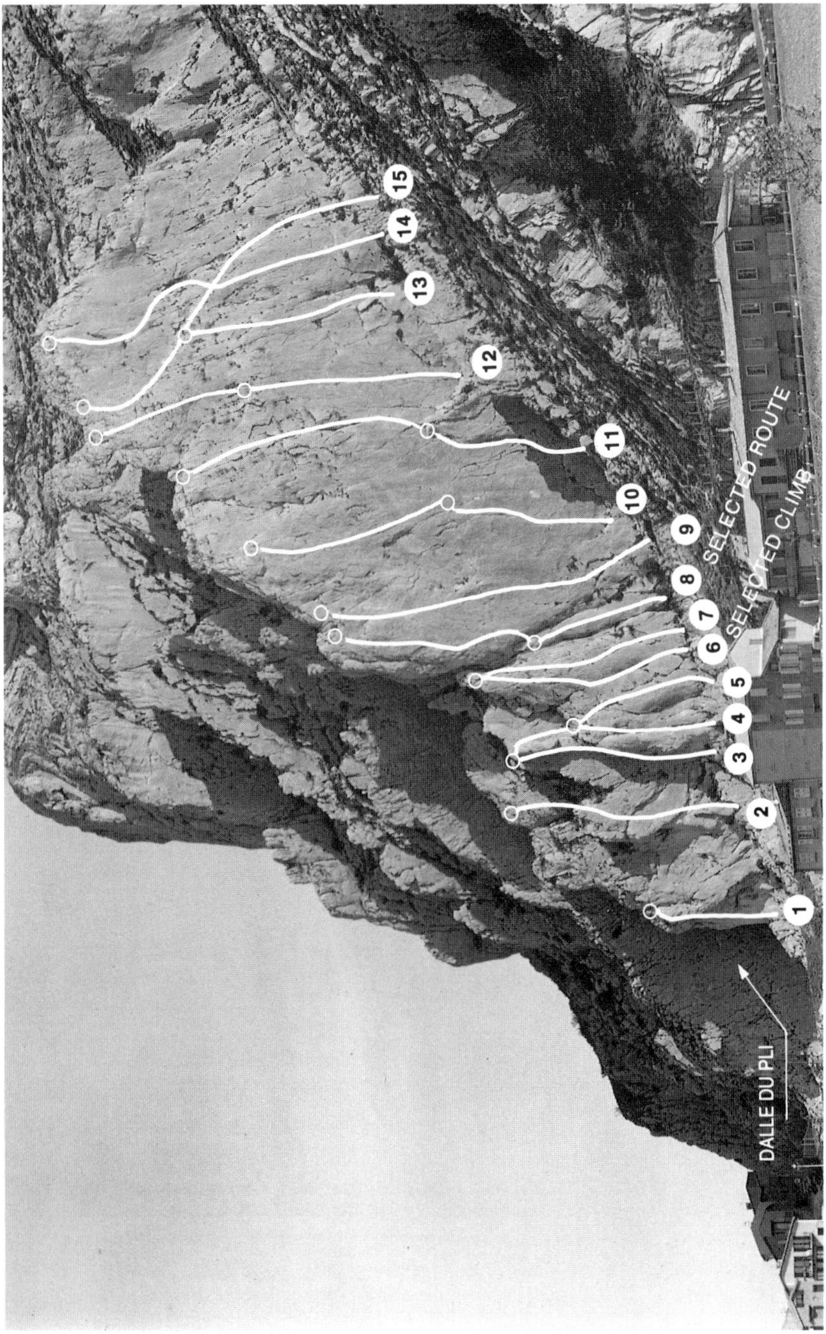

1
2
3
4
5
6
7
8
9
10
11
12
13
14
15
SELECTED ROUTE
SELECTED CLIMB
DALLE DU PLI

SI (1 - 15) Sisteron, Grande Dalle - S Face

Climber on Rose des Sables (7a/b), Mur du Nombril area, Buoux

Irmgard Braun on Pesanteur ou la Grâce (6c/7a), Secteur La Derive, Buoux

HIT LIST (From L to R)

DALLE DU PLI - LEFT WALL (Petite Dalle)
Géant Jaune 30m, 5c. The third route in.
Starky 30m, 5b. Climbs the wall immediately right of the notice boards.
Poussières D'Étoiles 60m, L1:6a, L2:6a

DALLE DU PLI - RIGHT WALL (Devers)
Shimoda 20m, 7c/8a. The left-hand, banana-shaped, crack.
2001, Les Doigts De L'Espace 20m, 7a. The straighter crack right of above.
Crack 5m, 6a.The left crack of the V.
Super Crack 7m, 7a. The right crack of the V.

SOUTH FACE - GRANDE DALLE

SI 1	**Fronton** 20m, 6b	
SI 2	**Excalibur** 30m, 6c	
SI 3	**Le Dièdre** 20m, 5b	
SI 4	**Clog** 20m, 5b	
SI 5	**Mégalomaniaque** 20m, 6c	
SI 6	**DEUX ET DEMI** 35m, 5a. SELECTED ROUTE (see p.95).	
SI 7	**Deux Trois Quart** 35m, 6a	
SI 8	**BAMBINO** 50m, 6c. SELECTED ROUTE (see below).	
SI 9	**Le Braqueur du Poubelle** 40m, 6b	
SI 10	**Les Cannelures** 60m, L1:6a+, L2:6b	
SI 11	**La Dülfer** 70m, L1:5b, L2:6a	
SI 12	**Ballade au Bout du Monde** 60m, L1:6c, L2:6a	
SI 13	**Transdalle Express** 45m, 6a+	
SI 14	**Libre Errance** 65m, 6a	
SI 15	**La Traversée** 65m, L1:5b, L2:5b	

above. This is steeper and more awkward than it looks from below but once a small ledge is gained a few metres above the diamond the difficulties ease. Continue up the crack until it breaks up on the shoulder of the buttress. Move diagonally right then ascend more directly to the tip of the pillar. Abseil point insitu.

BAMBINO: 50m, 6c. (British grading - E4, 6a).
First Ascent: 1985
Location: A line up the left edge of the main section of the S face.
Route Facts: The route starts up the front face of the little sandwiched pillar marking the ledge edge of the main section of Grande Dalle.

Sl (6) Sisteron, 'Deux et Demi' (5a)

L1, 50m, 6c. Climb the front face of the pillar approximately centrally. At the top of the pillar is a flat ledge and possible belay (insitu chain). Move right onto the front face of the upper buttress and climb steeply to a bulge. Pass this directly or take a slightly easier route to the right (both are finger strenuous). Continue directly to another bulge and climb the face of this using an undercut flake edge on the left. The angle eases slightly and soon an abseil chain marks the end of the route.

ROUTE CHAT

Two totally different propositions. Both enjoyable and satisfying, both difficult for their grade, but one in a much higher league of difficulty than the other. Don't worry if you don't climb at Bambino standard, Deux et Demi is a satisfying enough climb in its own right, taking a most obvious line up the S face.

The diamond block, cut by deep cracks, unmistakably marks the climb. This part of the face is crazed with cracks and predominantly, for the hands if not for the feet, this is a crack climb. The name is a play on words with the meaning that if care is not taken the sharp rock may reduce your middle finger to half its former glory. So take care.

I found the initial stages of the route surprisingly awkward and quite run out between bolts. It may be advisable to carry a few small to medium sized Rocks to supplement the bolt protection if you feel you are pushing the grade. A long pitch, which shouldn't really be split as the upper section is notably easier than the bottom. A double rope abseil is needed for descent. There is ample opportunity to place protection.

Dennis Gray recommended Bambino. Suffering from broken ribs he hadn't actually climbed the route himself but had been sufficiently impressed by its appearance to point Dave Birkett and myself in its direction. It proved a demanding climb. Tackled in one pitch it gave 50m of sustained effort with the upper edge of the buttress offering a real fly on the wall feeling.

Even the bottom pillar, looking insignificant from below, proves to be extremely tricky. Choice of footwear is important here (good edging boot required) for the rock is extremely smooth and compact offering only tiny matchstick edges. Once the top of the pillar is reached it may be tempting to belay but the real challenge is to keep on going up the even steeper ground above.

Fingery but not pockety the holds rarely seem to get better than small edged sharp flakes. Mysteriously, these are massively painful for the fingers but cruelly insignificant and rounded for the feet. There is little respite throughout and a small overlap appearing soon after leaving the pillar constitutes the technical crux. A direct ascent is the most difficult but it is possible to detour right (although blind moves must be made) at a slightly easier grade. Throughout, position, high on the vertical ledge edge of the great face of Grande Dalle is tremendous. Yet the leader may be forgiven for not noticing this as the effort required to ascend remains intense. Long after the crux is negotiated a further overlap provides food for thought before the abseil chain can be greeted. A fine view across to Sisteron and time now to relax, slowly regaining feeling in fingers strained by 50m of verticality. Even Dave was moved to say he found it quite hard for a classic route. But he was younger then.

BUOUX

Map Ref: *Michelin Motoring Atlas, page 159, D1.*

Area Maps: IGN 3142e, L=(3173.7, 843.0-845-5). MICH 81.14.

Guidebook: *Buoux* by Jean-Baptiste Tribout

Climate/Climbing Season: Precipitation (rain/snow) 700m to1,000m on 60 to 70 days of the year. Climbing from April to October inclusive. The best seasons are spring (April and May) and autumn (September and October).

Restrictions: Initially the massive influx of climbers on the tiny local community of Buoux caused some conflict. After negotiation by CAF on behalf of climbers, rules and agreements have been drawn up which allow climbers to continue. The area remains sensitive and the rules are to be rigorously adhered to. There is strictly no wild camping, no overnight parking or fires, no access or right to trespass (sunbathe or picnic) in the meadows below the crag (these are now fenced off). No climbing is now allowed on the cliffs directly above the road - Falaise des Confines - as parking here severely constricts the road (under no circumstances park here either). There are now three parking areas for climbers: (1) On the L below the road immediately after the base of the valley is reached; (2) In the wood to the right - marked by litter bins (use them) - in a further 250 metres; (3) After the end of the surfaced road, a track continues and in about a further 250 metres parking will be found on the R. Carefully note that the surfaced track does a U-turn and leads up to a parking area - this is for tourists visiting the Roman fort on the cliffs opposite the crag - climbers are NOT ALLOWED TO PARK HERE.

Rock and Protection: Rough textured limestone honeycombed with pockets, generally it is of excellent quality. It was once described as the gritstone, limestone, granite crag - an apt summation of the rock's qualities. All routes are bolted and only quick draws need be carried.

Situation: Some 65km SE of Avignon, 8km S of Apt, this extensive crag (the N rim of a sunken valley) runs above the narrow cul-de-sac road which passes through the tiny

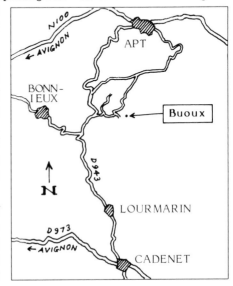

village of Buoux. Département Vaucluse (No.84).

Access: When travelling S it is usual to leave the Autoroute du Soleil (A7) at the Avignon S junction (the one before Cavaillon) following the D22 and then the D100 to Apt. The D113 leads directly from Apt to Buoux. In all cases take the worn paths that descend to cross the stream running through the valley. On the N bank of the stream a path/track traverses beneath the entire length of the crag and access to the various parts of the cliff is made (steeply) from this. From parking places (1) & (2) (described above) a path leads directly to the stream where a crossing can be made by balancing across strategically placed logs. From parking place (3) (the best for access to Pilier des Fourmis) it is necessary to walk back along the track to the junction with the surfaced road. From here a path drops through the trees towards the stream and then along to a small footbridge crossing (15 minutes to reach the foot of Pilier des Fourmis). Do not attempt to descend through the meadow and playingfield - attached to the school-type buildings - below the road. These are now fenced off and it is obvious that access is forbidden.

Camping etc: The two main bases are Apt and Bonnieux. Each has its merits. Apt is the largest centre with a pleasant family-run campsite. This also has static caravans which can be rented quite cheaply and a small café and shop (limited supplies). The attractions of Apt are reached in a few minutes walk and include supermarket, cafés, an incredible market on Saturday and Wednesday mornings, where the narrow streets become a continuous line of stalls, hustle and bustle; a wine cavern where the famous "petrol pumps" dispatch the wine of Lubéron into your own container all too cheaply!; banks *(change),* post office, cinema et al. Unfortunately the campsite can be rather crowded at peak periods and becomes muddy after rain.

Bonnieux is the classic Provence mountain village perched on a commanding rocky hill. Although facilities in the village are limited, possibly the best pizzas in France can be found here. The campsite is spacious and generally feels quiet, although it does seem exposed to the wind at times. A number of *gîtes* are available in the village. During peak periods a mobile van boot repairer and equipment seller - *Cordonnier des Falaises* - operates from car park 2.

Crag Facts: This is the premier sport climbing cliff of Europe and attracts a large international contingent. The cliffs stretch for almost 1km with some 300 routes from 20m to 100m ranging from 5c to 8c - although one should be able to climb a minimum of French 6b to enjoy the climbing here. The easier routes (still hard!) tend to be very popular and queuing is usual at peak periods. Basically the cliff stretches from W to E in four easily recognisable sections. Firstly comes (A) the West Face which overlooks the winding descent approach road from Buoux village and this turns a corner to face S before a tree-filled break separates it from the next long line of cliff. This is accessible from car parks 1 and 2. The next straight section of cliff (B) comprises a number of different *secteurs* but it heightens and impends impressively to end at the great tower-like corner of Pilier des Fourmis (the highest point). The L half of this is accessible from car parks 1 and 2 and the R end from car park 3. R of this (C) the cliff effectively forms a large square-cut recess to provide a number of key *secteurs*. Most obviously the massively pocketed back wall is the Mur du Styx. To the R of the Styx wall the permitted climbing area ends with (D) the Mur du Bout du Monde and the Chouca cave. This is situated at a point just before the cliffs overlook the Auberge des Sequins - the restaurant and café found at the end of the unsurfaced track, reached after passing car park 3. This area is most accessible from car park 3 - strictly no access or parking at the Auberge des Sequins.

In greater detail the areas described above comprise the following. Area (A) The Face Ouest (West Face) turns the corner to face S and become Secteur la Derive and Secteur Autoroute (the clean wall seen high above and slightly L of the car park 2). Area (B) begins after the break with Secteur Emoro and proceeds through Secteur Marabounta, Secteur GVB, Mur Zappa, Secteur Salinas above which lies Secteur Diamants to end with the pillar-like buttress of Secteur Pilier des Fourmis. Area (C) starts with the overhanging L wall of the square recess, Secteur Spectre followed by Secteur TCF. Mur du Nombril forms a small bay on the L side of the flat back wall to the R of which, and separated by the distinctive elephant trunk-like nose of Courage Fuyons, lies Mur du Styx which forms the distinctive flat back wall. Area (D), Mur du Bout du Monde, lies just R of this.

CRAG CHAT

Situated in Provence on the northern flanks of the wild upland chain of mountains known as the Montagne du Lubéron the cliff forms the northern rim of the deep cut wooded and secretive valley of l'Aigue-Brun. Opposite are further cliffs (climbing no longer permitted) and Fort Rnes perched on an island of rock. On the narrow descent road from the tiny Buoux village most, seeing the hay cart and farm implements resting in a cave cut from the rock, will think they have returned to another age. A feeling compounded by the impressive and extensive prehistoric (?) dwellings cut into the cliff and the deep tangle of tree and briar that carpet the valley. The oaks colour wonderfully in autumn, butterflies fill the warm air in summer - this is an intriguing area of considerable natural beauty. Yet it is the crag which climbers now know as Buoux, rising to startling proportions in its central - Pilier des Fourmis - area, that most commands the attention.

In the modern history of sport climbing Buoux has universally been recognised as the place where "it's all at". It offers a high concentration of accessible, highly demanding, perfectly protected, routes. Of these technically desperate climbs some have, at a particular period in time, been awarded "hardest route in the world" status. Understandably, Buoux has been described both as, "the greatest cliff in the world" and "an unadventurous pocket pulling gymnasium". Take your pick, but personally I would tend to sympathise with the former, for despite its shortcoming (and my own), I have always found Buoux a magical place to climb.

The earliest recorded climbing took place as early as 1958, most notably in the great overhanging cave above the path leading to the Fort. But this was largely aid climbing and development was sporadic. It wasn't until the 1980s with the advent of the modern expansion bolt protection that the really intense development and realisation of the crag's full potential took off. Today routes like *Chouca* 8a/b, *Les Main Sales* 8b, *La Rose et le Vampire* 8b, *La Rage de Vivre* 8b/c, *Le Minimum* 8b/c and *Agincourt* 9a represent the leading edge of free (bolt protected) climbing possibility.

A combination of rock qualities make the climbing at Buoux quite distinctive. The granular limestone offers pockets ranging from single slim finger to full body size. While a high friction factor does make it possible to smear the feet, generally arms - battered by the ferocious angle of climbing - demand more positive assistance. However, it quickly becomes apparent that a test of memory is required to place the toes in recessed pockets hidden by the steep angle of dangle. Once passed they can be quite impossible to see. It will also be found that fingers wear out and damage rapidly!

For the most part the rock is very steep, bulging and overhanging although some slabby areas (Secteur Derive, Secteur Zappa and the R side of Mur du Styx, for example) can be found. The climbing tends to be very finger strenuous involving merciless pocket pulling. Therefore it is worth reiterating that unless you climb at least 6b (English E2 5b/c) there isn't really much joy to be had at Buoux.

However, if you are climbing well then the total Buoux experience is really something. Even given the fact the climbing is seldom dangerous, biting the Buoux bullet to run it out at the maximum end of your performance range, prepared to fall off, is an adrenalin-surging trip. Quite addictive.

HIT LIST (From L to R)

WEST FACE
BU 1 Elixir de Violence 8a
BU 2 Les Mains Sales 8b

SECTEUR AUTOROUTE
BU 7 Songe Sucré 7a
BU 8 Be-Bop Tango 7a
BU 9 Le Dernier Problème des Alpes 6b
BU 10 Parties Carrées 7c
BU 11 Viol de Corbeau 7b/c
BU 12 Autoroute du Soleil 7c.
A famous test piece with a highly
polished crux that maintains the grade.

SECTEUR LA DERIVE
BU 3 Pesanteur ou la Grâce 6c/7a
BU 4 La Calfouette 5c
BU 5 Ring Art 6b
BU 6 L'Afrique Physique 6b

BU 13   **Valse aux Adieu** 7a/b
BU 14   **Belle de Cadix** 7a/b
BU 15   **L'Amour à la Plage** 6a/b

SECTEUR EMORO (This, the first slabby wall above the access route, is now so highly polished that any grades given are only nominal.)
BU 16   **L'Emoro** 6a
BU 17   **Sexpistol** 6b
BU 18   **La No** 5a

SECTEUR MARABOUNTA
BU 19   **Archi-Hyper-Ultra-Active** 7a
BU 20   **Commes des Bêtes** 7b
BU 21   **Franco-Belge** 5c
BU 22   **Marabounta** 6a
BU 23   **Pas de Pet** 7b

SECTEUR GB
BU 24   **Rien Ne Va Plus** 7b/c
BU 25   **L'Escoube** 7a
BU 26   **Souche à Mex** L1:6c, L2:6b/c
BU 27   **Pepsicomane** L1:6a/b, L1:5c. The first pitch can also be done direct at a similar grade. It is usual to lower off after the first pitch.
BU 28   **Congé Chimique** 6b/c
BU 29   **GVB** L1:6a, L2:6a. Starting from the higher ledge to the R, reached by scrambling.

MUR ZAPPA
BU 30   **PGF** L1:6b/c, L2:7a. Note that the second pitch is found by walking L across the ledge and climbs the upper wall in the Secteur les Diamants area.
BU 31   **Zappamaniac** 6b/c. Very polished
BU 32   **Bal des Lazes** 5c. The enjoyable crack/groove.
BU 33   **Shabada Swing** 6b/c

SECTEUR SALINAS
BU 34   **Cap'tain Crochet** 7a/b
BU 35   **Antinéa** 6b/c
BU 36   **Salinas** L1:6b/c, L2:7a, L3:6c. The upper two pitches are found on Secteur les Diamants above.

SECTEUR LES DIAMANTS
BU 30   **PGF** L2:7a
BU 36   **Salinas** L2:7a, L3:6c
BU 37   **Les Diamants Sont Éternels** 7a. One of the great routes, bolts notoriously spaced.

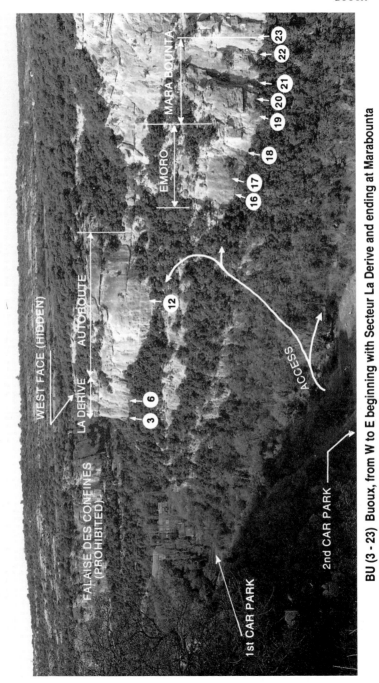

BU (3 - 23) Buoux, from W to E beginning with Secteur La Derive and ending at Marabounta

105

BU (24 - 37) Buoux from W to E GVB to Pilier des Fourmis

BU (38 - 45) Buoux, Secteur Pilier des Fourmis

BU (41 - 73) Buoux from W to E, Pilier des Fourmis to Chouca Cave

SECTEUR PILIER DES FOURMIS

BU 38 **Gougousse** L1:5c, L2:6b, L3:7a/b

BU 39 **Sourire Hawaii** 6b/c

BU 40 **Black Stage** 6b/c

BU 41 **PILIER DES FOURMIS** 100m, L1:5c, L2:6b, L3:7a. SELECTED ROUTE (see p. 110).

SECTEUR SPECTRE

BU 42 **Vaugneray's Sisters** 6c/7a

BU 43 **Comme un Loup Blessé** 6c/7a

BU 44 **Bonne Nouvelle des Étoiles** 6b

BU 45 **Les Barouilles** 5b

SECTEUR TCF

BU 46 **Requiem** 7c

BU 47 **La Cage aux Orchidées** 7b. An extra bolt in the middle section has (marginally) recently reduced the fear factor.

BU 48 **TCF** 7a

BU 49 **Camembert Fergusson** 7a

BU 50 **Alambic Sortie Sud** 6b

MUR DU NOMBRIL

BU 52 **Rêve d'un Papillon** 8a

BU 53 **Nombril de Venus** 6c. It should be carefully noted that a 50m rope is not long enough to lower back to the ground. Numerous accidents have occurred here with the end of the rope running through the belay plate.

BU 54 **Rose des Sables** 7a/b. Follows the nose from its base to move R into the o/h crack of the next route to finish.

BU 55 **Courage Fuyons** 7a. Moves out L to the edge then back R to the hanging flake crack.

BU 56 **Os Court** 7b/c. The overhanging wall R of the above route utilises a technical and strenuous sequence of chipped holds.

MUR DU STYX

BU 57 **Mélodie Gaël** 6b

BU 58 **La Rape** 6b

BU 59 **Endéavor** 6a/b

BU 60 **Récréactivité** 6a/b

BU 61 **Buffet Froid** 6b/c

BU 62 **Ultime Violence** 7a

BU 63 **Rhinoféroce** 6c/7a

BU 64 **Le Hasard Fait Bien Les Choses** 7b

BU 65 **Plus de Trois Fois c'est Jouer Avec** 6c/7a

BU 66 **Scaravageur** 7a

BU 67 **Kilo de Frite Physique** 6c/7a

BU 68 **Proxima Nox** 6c

BU 69 **Le Voyage de l'Incrédule** 6a/b. A fine slab with a wonderfully polished start.

MUR DU BOUT DU MONDE

BU 70 No Man's Land 7a/b. A traverse R is followed by strenuous and sustained climbing up the arête - a tremendous route.

BU 71 **Harlem Desir** 7c

BU 72 **La Rose et le Vampire** 8b

BU 73 **Chouca** 8a. Possibly the most famous climb of its grade in Europe.

SELECTED CLIMB AT BUOUX: Pilier des Fourmis (BU 41)

PILIER DES FOURMIS: 100m, L1:5c, L2:6b, L3:7a free/6b with aid. (British grading - E4, 5a, 5c, 6b- free/or using a couple of points of aid on pitch 3 then overall grade becomes E2, 5c).

First Ascent: Pierre Coquillon, Raymond Coulon, Jean Gay, Pierre Gras, 27 January 1968 with aid. First free ascent unknown.

Location: The central and highest point of Buoux. A high profile line which takes the diagonal right edge of the pillar rising from the square-cut cave at mid height.

Route Facts: From the tiny footbridge crossing the stream (accessed from car park No.3) a steep path leads directly to the edge of the buttress and then passes the foot of the route. Some 30m R of the front of the buttress a recessed corner rises vertically from the trees to mark the start.

L1, 50m, 5c. Climb the corner directly to a small cave recess. (Possible belay here, and it is probably best to do so.) Step L and climb directly to easier ground. Bear L to enter the cave. Bolt belay on the far L wall of this. (A long 50m if done in one pitch!)

L2, 30m, 6b. Move up the wall immediately L of the cave, climbing first diagonally R then diagonally L to surmount the small overlaps. The angle now eases slightly and a long diagonal ramp leads R to a small cave recess and belay.

L3, 20m, 7a (6b with aid). Step right and climb to a ledge on the very edge of the buttress. Move up left to a large flat hold from which can be clipped a bolt runner. Rock steeply up to the thread above and pass this (crux section) to become established in the shallow scoop above. Bear right up the steep shallow groove until easier climbing leads directly to the top. A tremendous pitch.

Descent: Probably the easiest method is to walk R to abseil from a chain or tree above the Styx Wall (the back wall of the recess). Double 50m ropes are essential to reach the ground and the anchor must be near the edge to achieve this. As this

BU (8 - 14) Buoux, Secteur Autoroute, with climbers on (from L to R) -
'Autoroute du Soleil' (7c), 'Valse aux Adieux' (7b), 'Belle de Cadix' (7b)

BU (24 - 28) Buoux Secteur GVB , with climbers on (from L to R) - 'Souche à Mex' (6c), 'Pepsicomane' (6b), and the arête of 'Congé Chimique' (6b/c)

Climber on Miroir du Fou (6b), Verdon

Above: Tête de Chien, South Face, climber on Corto Maltese (7a+)
Below: Bill Birkett on the superb Chez Herazade (6b), Secteur de la Grotte, Fontvieille

**BU (41) Buoux, just above the crux on pitch three of
'Pilier des Fourmis' (7a free)**

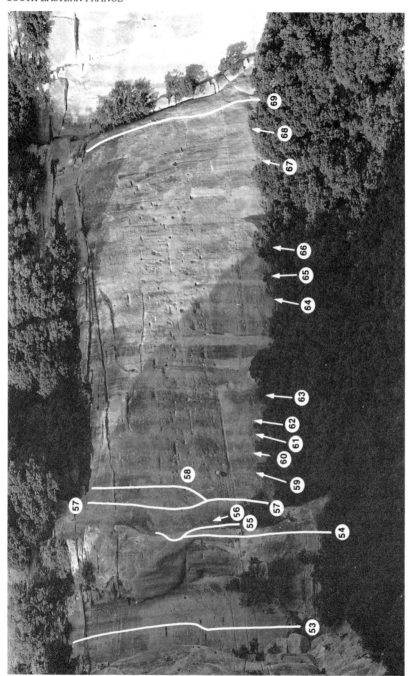

BU (52 - 69) Buoux, from L to R - Mur du Nombril and Mur du Styx

is a very busy area, great care must be exercised to ensure no one is climbing directly below when lowering the ropes or abseiling. No stones or debris must be dropped and this should be carefully watched.

ROUTE CHAT

Of all the excellent and famous routes on this magnificent crag Pilier des Fourmis is the undisputed classic. It really does have everything. Length: three quite different pitches increasing in difficulty. Line: the easiest traceable route up some very impressive ground. Position: fantastic exposure on the very edge of the buttress with overhangs below and above. Quality: sustained and varied climbing on perfect rock, with a masterful crux section taking a knife edge line of possibility between the bulging S and the overhanging E faces.

It also plays a dual role. Those looking for full value technical difficulty will be well pleased with a free lead of the demanding crux section. Whilst those who do not quite feel up to 7a on the day can still climb this superb route by simply using a couple of points of aid (long slings insitu) limited to a 5m section of this 100m route. Most choose the latter course but make no mistake, whatever option, this is still a very demanding climb.

The long vertical corner start lifts rapidly from the trees and gloom into the bright sunshine. Although it is possible to continue right up into the large cave above it may be better to belay, so avoiding communication difficulties and rope drag. Retrospectively, having already blundered and suffered, I recommend starting after the intense excess heat of the afternoon sun has abated somewhat.

The intriguing nature of the caves also adds another dimension to the route. Cut square and regular, with flat bottom and a sump to catch the rainwater, they were obviously sculpted by man. Who were these first climbers at Buoux who cut rectangular holes for seating wooden posts, carved lines of steps that rise through the vertical in an ingenious three-dimensional solution, and built stone walls converting this sheer face into a vertical city?

Moving out from the cave marks a noticeable increase in the technical difficulty. The aim is to keep as near to the R edge of the buttress as possible and the mistake of trending L (a bolt line does lead this way) should be avoided. By the time the small cave recess is reached, this time a natural creation, exposure is intense and the rock below completely undercut.

Next comes the crux. A narrow passage of hope amidst a sea of overhangs. It's as though a giant hand has taken the front of the buttress and squeezed its face, indenting it so only a thin nose of rock separates one side from the other, to provide continuity between the bulges. A gripping position whether you opt to grab the aid slings or not. Completing it free demands a gymnastic rockover with the right heel hooked around the flat flake handhold. Higher handholds are affected by undercutting the pockets in the bulge above, until a high, small fingerhold can just be reached. A power move follows to pass the steepest section into the sanctuary of a shallow scoop. Despite its formidable appearance when precariously balanced in the bottom of it, a reasonable quantity of hidden pockets keep you adequately supplied until the pitch relents and the top can be gained.

An intense and fulfilling experience, climbing Pilier des Fourmis offers more than many of the much harder but shorter routes at Buoux. This opinion grew naturally with the ascent. One which heightened, like the colour of the crag, from the flat grey of a clouded morning, through the deepening definition of white and black at midday, to the vivid orange fire that creeps over the buttress at evening time, finally to live emblazoned in memory, long after the actual rock has vanished from view.

VERDON

Map Ref: *Michelin Motoring Atlas, page 162, C2.*

Area Maps: IGN 3442e, L=(3171, 926,2). MICH 81.18.

Guidebook: *Topo Guide des Voies d'Escalade du Verdon.*

Climate/Climbing Season: Precipitation (rain/snow) 950mm on 85 days of the year. Climbing is best between April to June and September to November (inclusive) with the closed winter season stretching from December to March. Occasionally it can be still too cold and snowy in April and generally July and August are unpleasantly hot.

Restrictions: No wild camping is allowed. Car thieves frequently operate from the parking areas and nothing of value should be left.

Rock and Protection: Hard limestone, very compact but seamed by sharp-edged cracks and pocketed with the famous *gouttes d'eau* (water pockets). Whilst some of the oldest classics have now been fully bolted up, along with all the modern harder routes, there are still routes (rapidly diminishing) where it is necessary to carry a rack of gear. It is therefore important to check the current status of an individual route before climbing.

Situation: La Palud forms the centre and base, placed equidistantly between Castellane and Moustiers on the D952. Some 100km NE of Aix-En-Provence and 50km S of Digne. Département Alpes de Haute-Provence (No.4).

Access: There are two main approaches when heading S. (1) This way is blessed with marvellous mountain scenery and reduces the autoroute tolls. From Lyon continue on the N6 to Grenoble, take the N75 through Sisteron to branch off on the N85 to Castellane. From Castellane take the D952 to La Palud. (2) This is probably the quickest route; follow the Autoroute du Soleil A7 S from Lyon to turn off at Avignon Sud and the N100 to Manosque via Apt. Take the D6 through Valensole to Riez and continue on the D952 first to Moustiers then to La Palud.

From La Palud a circular road (a 23km loop) - the Route des Crêtes - leads to and along the rim of the gorge before returning to La Palud. Access to the top of most of the climbs lies from the *belvédère* car parks along this route. Abseil descent to the start of the individual route is usual. Whilst some climbs can be reached on foot, the bottom of the gorge can only be gained by car at one point. This car park is known as the Couloir Samson and is situated at the upstream (NW) end of all the climbing. Lying directly below the popular viewpoint of the Point Sublime, it is reached from the La Palud to Castellane D952 road. Some 8km E of La Palud a café and tourist shops mark the viewpoint Point Sublime, a little way after this on the R (just before the D952 leads through a short tunnel) a road leads down to the car park. A track/path descends from this to follow the base of the gorge.

La Palud - Camping etc: Even though it remains a small unspoilt village La Palud is now geared to being the climbing centre for the "le Grand Canyon du Verdon". The main climbers' campsite is Jean Paul's (Jean Paul Audibert) Camping de Bourbon which lies just R of the D952 when descending into the village from Moustiers. Accommodation is plentiful and comes in the form of a youth hostel (Auberge de Jeunesse) with no age barrier, a *gîte,* two cafés and a few hotels. There is a general store/small supermarket next to the petrol station and a small climbing shop Le Perroquet Vert run by Cherry Harrop. The post office will exchange Eurocheques but the nearest banks are at Moustiers or Castellane. Those wishing to find quieter family-type camping with better facilities may wish to make the 50km round trip each day and camp in Castellane where there are two

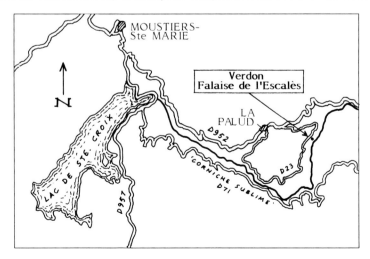

campsites. The two telephones in the centre of La Palud are frequently busy or out of order.

Crag Facts: A rock climbing mecca providing Europe's principal adventure/sport climbing arena. Commencing at the Couloir Samson, the Verdon River progressing first S then W to Lake Saint Croix for some 20 miles/32km, has carved a magnificent limestone gorge of awe-inspiring proportions. At its highest point the rim reaches an altitude of 2,800ft/930m to plunge some 2,000ft/610m to the river below. The walls of the gorge are predominantly vertical and clean cut to provide continuous climbing interest to an unbroken height of 1,000ft/300m. Practically all the climbing is spread beneath the road known as the Route des Crêtes for a discontinuous length of something like 9 miles/15km. The variety is mind boggling and ranges from short 20m routes to 14 pitch monsters of almost Alpine character and seriousness. Some routes can be reached from walking along the bottom of the gorge, others can be reached on foot from the rim, others rise above the road but the majority are reached by multi-abseil. The famous Verdon fear factor - abseiling, often in space, into the unknown to climb a long and demanding route sometimes from a hanging stance: many climbs have no safe escape by abseil - commitment par excellence. There are over 1,600 routes ranging in difficulty from 5a to 8b but with the average range of difficulty being from 6b to 7a. Routes vary in length and seriousness from 20m to 300m.

Starting with the upstream NE end of the gorge the basic topography is as follows; facing Couloir Samson on the opposite side of the river (true L bank) lies the overhanging and formidable Falaise du Duc (300m high). The gorge then narrows (foot access through a series of tunnels) to form the major climbing cliff of the gorge, the massive Falaise de l'Escalès. A few routes here start from the bottom of the gorge, these are best reached on foot through the tunnels - notably Ula and La Demande. However, the vast majority are started by abseil from the rim and are reached from the combined car pull-off points and fenced look-out stations (known as *belvédères*) on the Route des Crêtes. In clockwise direction the first of these is the Belvédère du Trescaïre (note that two hairpin bends, one above the other, each provide a parking space), next comes Belvédère de la Carelle and finally Belvédère de la Dent d'Aire gives a fine view up the gorge and along the Falaise de l'Escalès. Some of these latter routes start from hanging stances but most begin from a series of very large tree-filled ledges situated approximately half way up the cliff.

Driving clockwise around the Route des Crêtes (proceeding downstream) the main areas occur in the following order. The Falaise de l'Escalès the major cliff of the area which consists of the following sections - Secteur Éperon Sublime (routes accessed from Belvédère du Trescaïre) with most routes starting from the large ledge named Terrasse Mediane, Secteur la Demande, Secteur Pichenibule (routes accessed from Belvédère de la Carelle) with routes starting from Jardin des

Écureuils, Secteur Fenrir, Secteur Chrysalis with routes starting from Jardin des Bananes, and nearing the end of the Falaise Secteur Frimes et Châtiments opposite the Belvédère de la Dent d'Aire.

The road then passes over a col to wind its way down to a road tunnel. The wall immediately above the road pierced by the tunnel (facing SE) is Secteur Miroir du Fou. Above the road to the R are the minor cliffs of Secteurs Mur de Sale Temp and Septième Saut. Below the road, reached from the other side of the tunnel are Secteur Taies de Porcelaine. Despite their brevity and being somewhat remote from the gorge walls proper there are many worthwhile climbs in this area, which, combined with ease of accessibility, make it an attractive alternative.

Continuing along the road and after passing through a second road tunnel the flanks of the gorge again offer two notable cliffs. A number of buildings on the left are known as Malines and include a CAF hut Le Chalet de la Malines. Below this can be found the Falaise des Malines and reached from the same point, but sited upstream, the Falaise de l'Eycharme. Nearing the end of the road loop comes the Belvédère Maugue (a marked car park) and below this can be found the Falaise de l'Imbut. The road continues to reach La Palud in a further 2.5 miles/4km.

Obviously many of the climbs here are serious propositions. In addition to technical difficulty, the state of the protection (not all routes are bolted throughout) should be ascertained as well as the length and sustained nature of the climbing. Beware not to be caught in a thunderstorm or in rain; escape by abseil is not always possible. Lightning is a serious hazard. Take note of both the prevailing and predicted weather conditions. It can be furnace-hot in the midday sun and care should be taken to avoid sunburn and dehydration. Conversely if the sun disappears it can become unpleasantly cold. Double full 50m ropes are essential. Check the protection status of the individual route you intend to climb, it may be necessary to carry a rack of gear in addition to quick draws. Take care if wading the river (to visit Falaise du Duc, for example) as the flow is controlled by a dam further upstream. It can vary from a lazy trickle to a sweeping torrent.

CRAG CHAT

The bone-hard white limestone flanks of the Verdon gorge provide the finest free climbing experience in Europe. It is a vertical world of massive proportions with bulging walls, soaring cracks and elegant pillars stretching limitlessly up. Wild Haute-Provence beauty, Mediterranean sunshine, magnificent climbing.

Whilst the climbing is invariably sustained in nature its character and difficulty does vary enormously. Amongst the verticality there are some notable roof problems and a few easier-angled slabs. Mammoth walls and bold pillars, separated by long cracks, proliferate. The cracks take nut and Friend protection but the walls and pillars generally do not. Fortunately the rock is pocketed by *gouttes d'eau* and seamed by sharp cracks. This phenomenon and the bolt

119

protection has made Verdon a free climbers paradise.

My first visit to Verdon was the result of being forced reluctantly away from an Alpine holiday. A series of hard times due to bad weather - winter conditions arriving prematurely in September - culminated in my partner refusing to climb any longer in the mountains. Heading for La Palud I imagined it to be very much a poor man's alternative to real mountaineering.

The reality, the pure unadulterated physical challenge of climbing up those massive walls and cracks, freedom of movement carrying only a minimum of equipment and wearing only shorts, rock boots and chalk bag, captivated me to such an extent that it completely changed my attitude. This free climbing I found was the most natural and profound type of climbing I had every experienced.

In addition to its raw climbing appeal and physical grandeur I also found Haute-Provence proved to be a naturally beautiful and unspoilt region. A quiet open space virtually devoid of artificial barriers. A captivating blend of white limestone hills, rough stony pastures, aromatic wild herbs, fields of purple lavender and small pleasant villages. Thankfully, despite the influx of climbers, this charm endures.

Despite its pure enjoyment the climbing here has its serious side. Many routes are reached only by multi-abseils, often in space, and it is necessary to pendule in to the next abseil point. Always abseil on double 50m ropes with the ends knotted if it is not possible to see the position of the rope in relation to the next abseil point.

Also adding a certain character to the area, both a blessing and a curse, are the numerous bushes of gnarled and twisted maritime pines that cling to the face. From a distance the sheer scale of the cliff makes their presence look like tiny clumps of vegetation. In actuality they generally take on the size of a large Christmas tree. Despite their often flimsy appearance, their tenacious grip in the tiniest fissure in the rock, combined with their high strength, can provide a welcome hold, sling runner or stance. Unfortunately they can also completely snag a carelessly thrown rope. A jammed rope in the middle of a Verdon wall is a nightmare. Beware also the potency of the dagger-like branches to puncture bare skin.

Despite the Mediterranean influence and generally good weather La Palud and the rim of the gorge are sited at the relatively high altitude of 900 metres. Many climbers have arrived at Easter time to find it snowing. Warm sunny spring and autumn days can be accompanied by night frosts. It is also worth noting that La Palud is sited in a kind of hollow which holds the autumnal mists when the gorge itself is bathed in sunshine.

Although it is very hot during July and August it is possible to climb even on the highest sections of the cliff. Beware though, of dehydration and sunburn. I have never carried water, even on the longest routes here during August, but that is a personal decision to climb as light and as fast as possible. Many do carry a lightweight water bottle. Although tempting to climb in the bare minimum, a sleeved T-shirt and track suit bottoms can be rolled down to offer some protection should you start to burn or if the weather takes a turn for the worse.

Getting a preview of the cliffs is not easy without a major hike. However, there are a few accessible point which offer excellent views and these are worth detailing. At the upstream end the Point Sublime gives a dramatic look downstream into the narrows, but only really provides views of Falaise du Duc (L) and the striking arête of Éperon Sublime (R) which marks the upstream end of the major area - Falaise de l'Escalès.

Following the Route des Crêtes clockwise above the cliffs provides one outstanding viewpoint of the Falaise de l'Escalès just a little way before the summit of the col is reached. Even so, only half of this major cliff can be seen. This extends from the Frimes et Châtiment wall to the Pichenibule section.

Probably the best way to view the gorge and put things in perspective is to take the short hike along the bottom of the gorge itself. This starts at Couloir Samson and emerges at the CAF hut, Le Chalet de la Malines, some 15km downstream (car pick-up advised). The gorge itself terminates in the blue water of Lake St Croix. After a few hot days climbing I strongly recommend you do likewise.

HIT LIST

FALAISE DE L'ESCALÈS (From R to L)
SECTEUR ÉPERON SUBLIME

AA Abseil Point - Dièdre des Rappels L1:40m, L2:40m, L3:15m abseils
        descend the route of the same name to Balcon de l'Ascension.

VR 1   **Dièdre des Rappels** L1:5c, L2:6b+, L3:6a+

VR 2   **Tuyau d'Orgue** L1:6c, L2:6b, L3:5c

AB Abseil Point - Douce Sublimation 5 abseils to reach Jardin Mediane.

AC Abseil Point - Luna Bong L1:40m, L2:45m, L3:30m, L4:30m, L3:25m
        abseils reach Jardin Mediane. On the first descent this famous out-in-space abseil requires a swing to reach the next belay station/chains. Remember to kick off the lip of the overhang, to get swinging, before you pass it.

VR 3   **Éperon Sublime** L1:5b, L2:5b, L3:5c, L4:5c, L5:6a, L6:6c or 5c & AO, L7:5c.This great classic receives many ascents - few of which are entirely free!

VR 4   **Douce Sublimination** L1:7a, L2:6b+, L3:6b+, L4:6b, L5:6b+, L6:5a, L7:5b

VR 5   **Caca Boudin** L1:6c, L2:6a+, L3:7a, L4:7a, L5:6c+, L6:5c

VR 6   **Troglobule** L1:3b, L2:6b+, L3:7a, L4:6b, L5:5b, L6, 5c

VR 7   **Luna Bong** L1:5b, L2:5b, L3:6a, L4:5c, L5:5c, L6:6c or 5c & AO. A tremendous crack/chimney climb with plenty of hand jamming.

VR 8   **Nécronomicon** L1:6b+, L2:5c

VR 9   **Triomphe d'Éros** L1:6a, L2:6c+, L3:6c, L4:6a, L5:6c

SECTEUR DEMANDE

AD Abseil Point - Massacre L1:20m, L2:50m to reach start ledge of route VR 11 only. Routes starting from bottom of gorge are best accessed by walking from Couloir Samson (abseil descent not recommended).

VR 10   **Solanut** L1:3b, L2:4c, L3:6b+,L4:6c, L5:5c, L6:6a, L7:4c

VR 11   **Baiser Sanglant** L1:6c, L2:6b+, L3:5c

VR 12   **LA DEMANDE** 400m, L1:5c, L2:5c, L3:6a, L4:5c, L5:5c, L6:5b, L7:5c, L8:5c, L9:6a, L10:5c, L11:5b. SELECTED ROUTE (see p. 128).

VR 13   **ULA** L1:5c, L2:5b, L3:6a, L4:5b, L5:5c, L6:5c, L7:6a, L8:5c, L9:6a, L10:5c, L11:5c. One of the best wide cracks and an absolute must.

SECTEUR PICHENIBULE

AE Abseil Point - Dalles Grises L1:35m, L2:20m, L3:45m, L4:45m abseils to reach Jardin des Écureuils. Note short 2nd abseil maintains correct abseil stations/trees. For routes starting beneath Jardin des Écureuils, 2/3 abseils are made down route to be climbed.

VR 14   **Les Barjots (by Footcroûte variation)** L1:6b, L2:6a, L3:6a+, L4:5c, L5:3b. A celebrated off-width first pitch.

VR 15   **Mangoustine Scatophage** L1:6c, L2:6a+, L3:6c, L4:5b, L5:4c. Some use a sky-hook on pocketed first pitch (tut-tut).

VR 16   **Pilier des Écureuils** L1:5c, L2:6a+, L3:5c, L4:4c (these four pitches lie below Jardin des Écureuils and are well worth doing).

VR 17   **Dingomaniaque** L1:5c, L2:6a, L3:6a+, L4:6c, L5:6c. Now well bolted (numerous variations) - brilliant climbing.

VR 18   **A l'Est des Bens** 6a. Top pitch only often top roped.

VR 19   **L'Arabe en Décomposition** 6b

VR 20   **L'Arabe Dément** L1:6a, L2:6a

VR 21   **Dalles Grises** L1:4c, L2:4c, L3:4c, L4:4c. the popular route of Verdon which despite its rather scruffy (many small bushes) appearance provides excellent climbing at a reasonable grade.

VR 22   **Afin Que Nul Ne Meure** L1:5c, L2:5c, L3:6a, L4:5c, L5:6a. Slabby climbing of some quality.

VR 23   **Pichenibule** L1:5c, L2:5c, L3:6a, L4:5c (these four pitches lie below Jardin des Écureuils - not often ascended), L5:5c, L6:5c, L7:6a+, L8:6b, L9:6c, L10:6b, L11:7b or 6c & AO, L12:5b.

VR 24   **Rideaux de Gwendal** L1:6b+, L2:6b+, L3:5c, L4:5a. although the full route starts from the ground it is described here as an alternative finish to VR 23 starting from the top of L8 of that route. Excellent climbing, somewhat easier than VR 23 (often accessed by abseil).

VR 25   **Papy On Sight** 7c+. A test piece - mostly top roped.

SECTEUR FENRIR

In this section abseil is by access down each individual route apart from the point below;

AF Abseil Point - Golem L1:35m, L2:35m, L3:50m (last abseil from the garden).

VR 26   **Troisième Ciel** L1:7a, L2:5c (Direct 7a+).

VR 27   **Fenrir** L1:7a, L2:7c+, L3:5c, L4:5c, L5:6b, L6:6c, L7:6a

VR 28   **L'Ange en Décomposition** L1:6c, L2:7a, L3:6a

VR 29   **Rêve de Fer** L1:6b, L2:6b, L3:6b

VR 30   **Golem** L1:6c+, L2:6c, L3:6c, L4:6b, L5:6a

SECTEUR CHRYSALIS

AG Abseil Point - Durandalle

VR 31   **Chrysalis** L1:7a, L2:6b+, L3:7b+, L4:6c, L5:6c+

VR 32   **Éperon des Bananes** L1:5b, L2:5c, L3:4c, L4:6b, L5:5b, L6:5c, L7:4c, L8:6a, L9:4b

SECTEUR FRIMES ET CHÂTIMENTS

AH Abseil Point - Frimes et Châtiments

VR 33   **Mission Impossible** 7b

VR 34   **Les Frères Caramels Mous** L1:7a+, L2:7a

VR 35   **Surveiller et Punir** L1:6b, L2:6a, L3:7b, L4:6c+. Once claimed to be the finest route in France - indeed the top two pitches provide superlative wall climbing.

VR 36   **Frimes et Châtiments** L1:5c, L2:6c+, L3:6b, L4:6b

VR 37   **Mort à Venise** L1:6a+, L2:6c

SECTEUR MIROIR DU FOU (From L to R)

VR 38   **LE MIROIR DU FOU** 60m,L1:6c, L2:6b. SELECTED ROUTE (see p. 132).

VR 39   **La Dulfer du Fou** 6a+

VR 40   **La Pirouette Enchantée** 6c+

VR 41   **Le Graîn de Folie** L1:7a, L2:6b+

FALAISE DE L'EYCHARME (No phototopo)
L'Estemporanée 8 pitches, hardest 6c or A2.

FALAISE DES MALINES (No phototopo)
Éperon BB 7 pitches, hardest 5c.

FALAISE DE L'IMPUT (No phototopo)
Le Roumagou 8 pitches, hardest 6b.

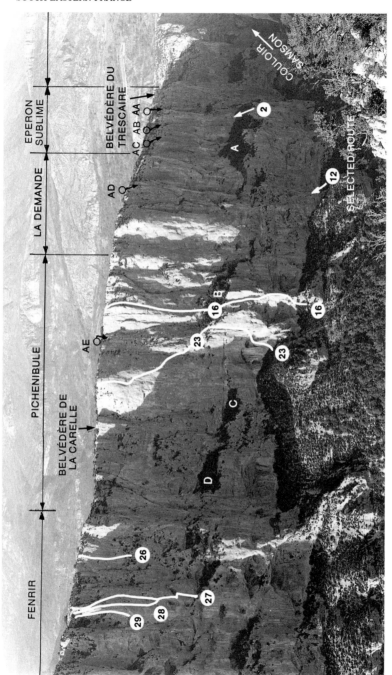

VR (1 - 29 Verdon, Falaise de l'Escalès, from R to L - Secteur Eperon Sublime to Secteur Frimes et Châtiments.
A = Terrasse Mediane, B = Jardin des Écureuils, C = Jardin de la Marcelin, D = Jardin de la Gravatation, E = Jardin des Bananes,
F = Jardin des Suisses. Abseil Access Points are (for this and the other Verdon photo-topos) denoted as follows: AA, AB etc. -
refer to text HIT LIST for full details

VR (26 - 37) See caption page 124

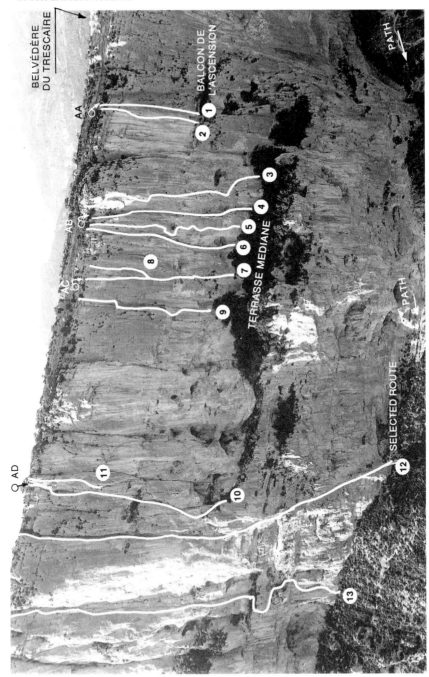

VR (1 - 13) Verdon, Falaise de l'Escalès, from R to L - Secteur Eperon Sublime to Secteur Demande

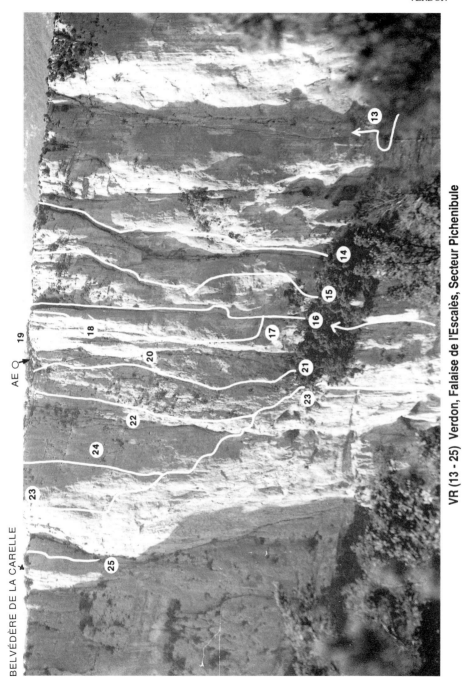

VR (13 - 25) Verdon, Falaise de l'Escalès, Secteur Pichenibule

VR (33 - 37) Verdon, Falaise de l'Escalès looking N from Secteur Frimes et Châtiments to Secteur Pichenibule

SELECTED LONG ROUTE AT VERDON:
LA DEMANDE (VR 12)

LA DEMANDE: 400m, L1:5c, L2:5c, L3:6a, L4:5c, L5:5c, L6:5b, L7:5c, L8:5c, L9:6a, L10:5c, L11:5b. (British grading E1, 4c/5a, 5a, 5a/b, 5a, 5a, 4c, 5a, 5a, 5b, 5a, 4c.)

First Ascent: Joel Coqueugniot and François Guillot, 29 October 1968.

Protection: Predominantly crack climbing, this route has recently been re-equipped throughout. The insitu gear (bolts) is now very good but often quite spaced, therefore a small rack of gear - nuts from Rock 4 size upwards and a couple of Friends (1 & 2.5) - is recommended

Route Considerations: For a roped party of two the ascent can reasonably be expected to take between 5 and 7 hours. Teams in front can slow this down. A water bottle must be a personal decision, balancing the dehydration factor with extra weight (in addition to walk-in footwear) and can be particularly troublesome on the restrictive top chimney section. Be prepared, clothing wise, for both hot and cold conditions.

Location and Access: This striking crack/chimney line lies within the first quarter of Falaise de l'Escalès (working downstream or right to left looking at the

128

VR (12) Verdon, Falaise de l'Escalès, in the crux final chimney of 'La Demande'

crag). The best approach is via the foot tunnels that lead down the gorge from the Couloir Samson. This approach necessitates a car drop at the Couloir Samson and pick up on the appropriate belvédère car park on the Route des Crêtes loop road above the climb. There is no direct walkable connection along the top of the gorge between the top of the climb and Couloir Samson. On leaving the car park at the base of Couloir Samson follow the path along the gorge then rise up some steps to enter the tunnels and continue through these (long dark sections, a small torch may be helpful). Finally emerge into the daylight to follow the path traversing the scree above the river. Soon the path nears the foot of the cliff, moves along its foot and after passing a sizeable cave leaves it again. This cave marks the start of a large bay whose L end is defined by a rib of rock. An unmistakable diagonal crack line rises leftwards from the rib. Gain the base of the rib by scrambling through scree and vegetation above the path (25 minutes). It is usual to gear up at the car park and approach carrying trainers which are then carried up the climb (don't forget your rock boots when leaving the car). At the top go R to descend slightly to Belvédère Trescaïre, or L to ascend slightly to Belvédère de la Carelle, both on the Route des Crêtes loop road. The climb takes full sunshine from early morning until mid afternoon.

Route Facts: A very striking natural line which follows a R to L diagonal crack leading to a deep chimney system. On reaching the foot of the rib/pillar scramble up for 10m to reach a belay ledge.

L1, 30m, 5c. Follow the crack keeping to the R side of the pillar to gain a belay ledge.

L2, 45m, 5c. Move left (don't attempt to go straight above) to gain the crack and follow it to a tree belay.

L3, 40m, 6a. Continue up the steepening crack on good hand jams.

L4, 40m, 5c. Follow the crack and then a groove which forms a ramp.

L5, 30m, 5c. The crack.

L6, 18m, 5b. Move left and pull into the crack following it to a belay at a point beneath where it begins to overhang. This pitch marks the start of the upper chimney section.

L7, 33m, 5c. Don't climb the overhanging corner crack above (despite the presence of insitu gear), but move R to gain a shallow corner groove on the opposite side of the chimney. Continue up this groove over a bulge until it is possible to traverse back L to regain the main crack system.

L8, 24m, 5c. Climb the corner crack to a scoop belay.

L9, 45m, 6a. The crux pitch. Move up to and over the overhang following the corner crack. Above the crack widens to a chimney. Bridge up this with increasing interest (passing a jammed block which forms a possible but restricted belay ledge - not recommended) to reach a stance. Even after re-equipping, this and the next pitch are notoriously run-out.

L10, 45m, 5c. Continue up the chimney/corner. Again some wide bridging is necessary.

L11, 45m, 5b. Easier more broken climbing, but still with some interesting sections, passes a few trees and intermittent walls to reach the top of the gorge.

ROUTE CHAT

La Demande was the first route to be climbed in the whole of the Verdon gorge. From a prominent toe of rock just above the river at the bottom of the gorge a long crack system curves to meet a vertical chimney rift. In all it sweeps unbroken for virtually 400 metres, the most elegant natural line of weakness up the Falaise de l'Escalès.

Falling within the lower category of difficulty for Verdon (British E1), it is perhaps the most popular and famous climb here. But don't underestimate or undervalue it; a fine-tuned route description, excellent insitu gear, et al., do nothing to shorten its sheer length. There are no easy sections; pitch follows pitch relentlessly with mounting exposure. The sustained crux chimney section, technically high in its grade, lies near the top. For this section there is no possibility of placing protection between the fixed point and it feels distinctly serious. All in all a route offering tremendous value.

The climbing is surprisingly varied with sections of pure hand jamming and

VR (38 - 41) Verdon, Secteur Miroir du Fou, the climber is approaching the crux of
'Miroir du Fou' (6c)

bridging proving relatively short. This is because the rock, in places resembling Swiss cheese, is liberally scalloped by *gouttes d'eau*. These sharp-edged, sometimes painful, water-worn pockets are of great significance in making the impossible possible. They vary from single slim finger *mono doigts* to those that comfortably take a full hand or toe.

Standing at the bottom looking up to the distant top is a daunting experience. The commitment required at this point feels Alpine in scale. An impression further compounded when after a couple of hours' climbing you are still seemingly a long way from the top, having made little apparent progress.

Nevertheless, a steady determined approach should be adopted rather than a mad dash. This is particularly important at the beginning - take a good look at the line before starting to climb. Early on its is quite easy to stray and in doing so much vital time will be lost dealing with the ensuing unnecessarily difficult and unprotected climbing.

The crack on pitch 3 proves to be a steep exercise in jamming and it may be some compensation to know that technically this pitch is equal in difficulty to anything else on the route. Even on its completion however, there is still a fair distance to go to gain the start of the upper chimney section.

Finally on pitch 6 you enter the chimney section and at last feel as if you are making some headway. At the end of the pitch the corner crack overhangs alarmingly. Sundry insitu gear looks tempting. However, the way lies to the right. When Ron Fawcett made his famous solo attempt in the early 1980s he climbed straight up it and (by his own admission) nearly fell off in doing so.

The long crux chimney section (pitch 9) now lies only a little way ahead. Although technically pitch 3 is comparable the chimney will most definitely be found to be the crux. Sustained bridging, on now-tired legs, and considerable air space between fixed protection see to that. Another fine pitch follows before a rather bitter-sweet pitch weaves through tree and rock to reach the top.

Elated on completion of this, Verdon's premier route, François Guillot made La Demande - proposing to his girlfriend. Simultaneously he gained a wife, named a magnificent rock climb and with Joel Coqueugniot, opened Europe's finest rock climbing arena. That's style.

SELECTED SHORT ROUTE AT VERDON:
Le Miroir du Fou (VR 38)

LE MIROIR DU FOU: 60m, L1:6c, L2:6b. (British grading - E3+, 6a, 5b.)

First Ascent: Jacques Perrier, 1979.

Protection: All insitu bolts.

Location and Access: The most easily accessible wall in Verdon. Travelling clockwise on the Route des Crêtes takes you first along the rim of Falaise de l'Escalès and then over the summit of the pass to wind steeply down to pass through a road tunnel. The clean white wall L of the tunnel marks the start of the route. Ample parking space just before the entrance of the tunnel. Stroll across to the foot of the route (1 minute or less). The wall faces south-east and takes the sun until mid afternoon.

Route Facts: The route starts in a little bay just left of and higher than a pointed flake.

L1, 30m, 6c. Climb the scoopy wall directly until bolts lead diagonally right. Follow these, finally traversing horizontally to make difficult moves across to gain a narrow ledge and chain belay.

L2, 30m, 6b. Step right and move straight up the wall until it is easier to trend diagonally leftwards to gain a hanging flake/corner crack. Climb it and continue directly to the top.

Descent: If no one is climbing below then a 50m abseil leads to the road - watch out for cars! Alternatively walk L (looking at crag) and scramble down.

ROUTE CHAT

In an area famed for its hairy abseils and long committing climbs the novel accessibility and position of this engaging route have established it as a Verdon favourite. Climbing a beautiful grey/white wall of limestone, it is in full view of all passing tourists. Starting just above the roadside it first climbs directly and then breaks diagonally right eventually to make a precarious traverse above the mouth of the road tunnel. Finally it soars aesthetically up the headwall. A perfect choreograph for maximum public acclaim - if you get it right.

It is the best to leave your ascent until the heat of the sun has moved on. For whilst foot friction is a premium requirement, small finger-end pockets have to be used, and are so much the more pleasant to handle when the temperature has cooled slightly. Always interesting, the climbing increases in intensity the higher you get.

Nearing the end of the first pitch, you begin to feel the strain and begin to wish it was all over, then the crux suddenly materialises. At this point all you want to do is reach out and grab the belay chain to relieve those throbbing fingers and toes. Unfortunately both footholds and handholds diminish to painful proportions.

Careful pre-inspection from the ground will pay dividends as a crucial footpocket does exist and is essential to reach the belay ledge. This section seems ridiculously polished. Its hard gloss surface and the predicament in which it places you perhaps inspired the route name. In contrast, assuming you make it with any strength left, the top pitch is pure pleasure. A steady supply of pockets, some of them bigger than one finger size, keep you the right side of stable.

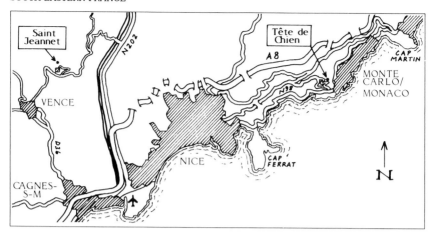

BAOU DE SAINT JEANNET

Map Ref: *Michelin Motoring Atlas, page 165, D3.*

Area Maps: IGN 3642e, L=(3172.6, 986,8). MICH 84.9.

Guidebook: *Sun Rock* by Nicholas Mailänder.

Climate/Climbing Season: Precipitation (rain/snow) 1,000mm on 75 days of the year. Statistically the wettest months are October, November, March and May. However, in summer it is generally too hot to climb here and the best periods are spring and autumn. It is also a noted winter venue.

Restrictions: Climbers should not attempt to drive through the narrow main street of Saint Jeannet.

Rock and Protection: Hard compact grey/white limestone predominates. Protection is insitu but comprises of old pegs on some routes, therefore a small rack of nuts from small to medium size Rocks may be thought beneficial.

Situation: This large rock bastion rises directly from the village of Saint Jeannet which in turn is some 3.5km NE of Vence and 12km NW of Nice. Département Alpes Maritimes (No.6).

Access: Leave autoroute A8 at Cagnes. Follow the D36 N to Vence then follow the D2210 NE branching up to Saint Jeannet. If travelling up or down the coast from another area don't be tempted to drive along the coastal road nearby or drive through Nice - stick to the autoroute. Access to all areas is on foot from a car park just below the road on the L immediately before the village is entered. Walk through the village a little way until, passing the Hotel Le St Barbe on the L, a street leads up R. Wind your way rising through the narrow connecting streets to reach the road leaving the town at its highest point. This becomes a track which zigzags up the hillside through the trees to pass some circular water tanks. Direction now depends on which part of the cliff you intend to visit. The SW face is reached by contouring round to the L, the SE by continuing directly up. A path leads roughly up the middle of the SE face passing through its four tiers to the summit (allow 1 hour to reach the SW face and the middle section of the SE face). Descent from the SW face is made by this path. For access specifically to the 2nd Ressaut of the SE face pass the water storage tanks to find the path steepening and ascending diagonally L up the hillside to a point just L of centre of the 1st Ressaut (the first tier of cliffs). Above lies a tree-filled break (inaccessible) and to the R a buttress of rock. Scramble up and R to climb the recess separating the buttress from the main crag. Gain the top of the buttress then traverse horizontally R along the ledge until a short ascent up a tree-filled break gives access to the ledge below the 2nd Ressaut. Immediately above lies the central section of this cliff and the fine open corner (starting from a cave) of La Super-Tavan. Walk L to find Mur Noir and R to find L'Ange.

Camping etc: Les Cent Chênes in Saint Jeannet bas below the main village towards Gattières. Although officially closed during the winter months climbers staying here do not usually experience any problems. Nearest all-year camping is at nearby Tourrette situated a little E of Vence. Small shops etc. in Saint Jeannet and water available at the car park.

Crag Facts: A visually striking feature; the craggy mountain above Saint Jeannet has a relatively long history, with climbing beginning here in 1940. The crag really comprises two main sections. The high SW face is the traditional area and has some 42 routes from 150m to 200m ranging in difficulty from 3c-7b. Many of these long routes include vegetated ledges and cracks and much of the gear consists of old pegs. The SE face is tiered to offer short but clean faces of excellent limestone, these are generally modern bolt-equipped one-pitch routes. There are four tiers *(ressauts)* of cliffs and these are classified, from bottom to top, Ressaut 1 to Ressaut 4. There are some 200 routes from 20m to 40m ranging in difficulty from 3c to 7b. Additionally if the main street is followed through the village a track continues, passing the church of Notre Dame des Champs, to reach a modern developed area in the woods just above the track to the R. This is La Source with some 90 routes from 15m to 25m ranging from 4c to 7c. The 2nd Ressaut, from which the routes detailed have been selected, comprise of three main sections; L, Central, and R.

CRAG CHAT

The elevated scenic village of Saint Jeannet, with its narrow streets, red clay tiled roofs and church tower, clings to a shoulder on the hillside beneath the great rock

SJ Baou de Saint Jeannet, the Ressauts of the SE Face

SJ (1 - 5) Baou de Saint Jeannet, 2nd Ressaut L side

HIT LIST (From L to R)
2nd RESSAUT - LEFT SIDE

SJ 1   **La Dalle a Dudu** 6c
SJ 2   **Les Travailleurs** L1:6c, L2:7a
SJ 3   **MUR NOIR** 35m, L1:6a, L2:6c+. SELECTED ROUTE (see p. 140).
SJ 4   **La Voie Lactée** 6b
SJ 5   **Le Mur de Sa Vie** 4c

SJ (6 - 16) Baou de Saint Jeanette, 2nd Ressaut Central Section

2nd RESSAUT   **SJ (17 - 22) Baou de Saint Jeannet, 2nd Ressaut R Side**

SJ 6	**Solexine** 7a
SJ 7	**La Super-Tavan** 7a
SJ 8	**La Tavan** 6c
SJ 9	**Mephisto** 6c
SJ 10	**La Plantation** 7a
SJ 11	**L'I** 6b
SJ 12	**L'Ibis** 6b
SJ 13	**Le Chameau** 7a
SJ 14	**La Dame** 5c
SJ 15	**La Spinach** 5b
SJ 16	**Le Grand Chariot** 5c

2nd RESSAUT - RIGHT SIDE

SJ 17	**La Bouffique** 6b
SJ 18	**La Veuve** 6a
SJ 19	**L'ANGE** 25m, 6c. SELECTED ROUTE (see p. 140).
SJ 20	**La Femelle** 7a
SJ 21	**L'Os du Grimpeur** 4b
SJ 22	**L'Os Dudu Grimpeur** 6b

cliff of Baou de Saint Jeannet. In many respects it epitomises a high Alpine village. The immediately detectable differences being its warm climate and unspoilt nature.

The commanding summit of the rock is at an altitude of around 800 metres with rapid ascent made from the lowly coastal plain below. Trees surround the village and shrubs spread across the higher steeper ground. In autumn, possibly the best time to climb here, it becomes a collage of colour.

The crag is well sited geographically to offer climbing when other key areas suffer from adverse weather conditions. If wet and cold at Verdon, Saint Jeannet can be hot and dry. In winter, because of its greater altitude, it can be pleasantly warm here whilst still too hot to climb at nearby Tête de Chien. Unfortunately in summer it can become a furnace. However, the generally favourable climate combined with a choice of three separate areas, each of quite different character, make this an enjoyable climbing ground of some importance.

SELECTED CLIMBS AT BAOU DE SAINT JEANNET (2ND RESSAUT): Mur Noir (SJ 3), L'Ange (SJ 19)

MUR NOIR: 35m, L1:6a, L2:6c+. (British grading - E3+, 5b, 6a+.)

First Ascent: Unknown

Location: Left side of the 2nd Ressaut.

Route Facts: This route starts under a slight scoop on the R side of the black stained wall, just L of a gully.
L1, 15m, 6a. Climb the scoop, name painted on rock, to a flake. Move up to a larger scoop. Traverse out diagonally left until the wall can be climbed directly to a small ledge stance. Insitu gear is spaced but can be backed up with small to medium size Rocks.
L2, 20m, 6c (3 old pegs and a new bolt protect this pitch). Step R and climb the steep wall to belay on a bush at the top.

Descent: There is a break in the cliffs 200m to the right but it is probably best to abseil (double 50m ropes).

L'ANGE: 25m, 6c. (British grading - E3, 6a.)
First Ascent: Not known

Location: Right side of the 2nd Ressaut.

Route Facts: Before the crag breaks into two final little nose buttresses and ends, a slabby wall stands out from a corner. The route starts beneath the centre of this wall.
L1, 25m, 6c. The bottom steep section provides the crux. Move up the little groove.

At its top step up and right to a white finger flake jug (bolt with long sling) and pull up onto the wall above. Continue up the centre of the wall trending left slightly to gain an undercut flake. Move up diagonally left from this until possible to climb directly to the top. Belay ledge.

Descent: Abseil or walk off over to the R.

ROUTE CHAT

Although it may seem surprising to choose two routes from the 2nd Ressaut rather than one of the longer (up to 180m) more traditional routes from the SW face there is good reason. Even the best routes on the longer face have sections of loose rock and vegetation and much of the insitu equipment is now well past its prime.

The two routes selected however, both on immaculate limestone, offer superb and very different climbing. They have a distinctive character and will be long remembered. The standard of difficulty is quite high, with the 2nd pitch of Mur Noir being top end 6c (British 6a), but both receive many ascents.

The initial pitch of Mur Noir feels quite serious and you may wish to back up insitu peg protection with nut runners. The main interest arrives when moving diagonally left onto the face of the wall, it becomes very steep with long reaches to the horizontal breaks. These are adequate but it is a strenuous business, and strangely reminiscent of the upper wall of Shrike on Clogwyn Du'r Arddu, Snowdonia.

The next section from the belay provides delectable climbing up the steep wall. The type I love the most, technical rather than strenuous, utilising small but positive finger holds and flakes. Precise footwork essential.

L'Ange may only be one pitch, but it is perfect. Right from the start it tries to outface you, with the easy-looking groove pushing you out as you attempt to use best the awkwardly placed holds. Pulling out onto the wall above proves to be the crux, forcing you to make a long reach to the white finger flake whilst holding a poor layaway. A tremendous move but with a long sling hanging from the bolt if you want to cheat. Suddenly the angle eases and excellent pocket holds lead right up the centre of the wall. Nearing the top you move slightly left to centralise your position on the headwall and then it's straight up for the belay ledge. "Go-ee", pure and memorably fine.

TÊTE DE CHIEN

Map Ref: *Michelin Motoring Atlas, page 165, E3.*

Area Maps: IGN 3642e. MICH 84.10.

Guidebook: *Sun Rock* by Nicholas Mailänder.

Climate/Climbing Season: Precipitation (rain/snow) 900mm on 65 days of the year. Noted as a winter, spring and autumn venue. In summer it is too hot during the day.

Restrictions: No wild camping.

Rock and Protection: Very hard, glaring white limestone. There are sharp flake holds and plentiful small pockets but the rock is polished in places. All gear is modern and insitu and it is only really necessary to carry quick draws. However, it is possible to place small to medium size Rocks on some of the routes.

Situation: Tête de Chien is a great head of limestone standing above Cap-d'Ail, Monte Carlo, Monaco. Don't worry, you don't need to show your passport. The head is reached by driving S from the little town of La Turbie. In the centre of Turbie descend to pass the Central Square car park and continue on a minor road to reach the small car park at the summit of the head in 2km. Département Alpes Maritimes (No.6).

Access: Descend from the R side (looking out) of the car park to find a track leading through a short tunnel. On the other side cross a flat square area and leave it by a constructed/walled path and steps. Follow zigzagging down these until the constructed path traverses across open hillside with limestone scree slopes below. (The path continues under a small steep overhanging band of crag known as La Barre Supérieure and continues to pass further bands of crags known collectively as La Loubière. Eventually this path descends to the hairpin bends of the D37 which rises from Cap-d'Ail to La Turbie.) Break L off the constructed path to follow a steep worn path down the scree. After descending through a rock bluff via a gully the path turns L to find the amphitheatre of the S face.

Camping etc: A number of old fortification tunnels on the descent track/path below the car park could provide useful bivouac sites. Overnight dossing on the car park seems to be tolerated if a low profile is kept and there are only a small number of cars. Tents must not be erected. There is no water. Water and supplies, plentiful small supermarkets, and cheap hotel accommodation in La Turbie. Nearest campsites are some 10km distant at Peillon and Menton.

Crag Facts: Basically the head of Tête de Chien comprises three main sections; the SW Face which turns to form a great white wall - the real front face of the head - the S Face. This extends R to form the higher but more broken SE-facing Grand

TT (12) Tête de Chien, S Face, climber on the white wall of 'Corto Maltese' (7a+) with Monaco Palace below

Face which does not hold many worthwhile climbs. Above this to the right (looking in) and actually situated directly below the car park (accessed by a steep scramble down a gully from the flat square area beyond the tunnel) forming a shoulder to the main head is the Paroi du Fort. Only the SW and S faces are dealt with here. Taking the area as a whole (including La Loubière not detailed here) there are some 240 routes from 25m to 70m ranging in difficulty from 4b to 8b. Even in early spring and late autumn it can be hot, hot, hot. Climbing is just bearable but don't forget the sunglasses. It is best to forget the crag during the summer months and remember it again in winter. The local French grading here (I have graded to match the nationally accepted norm) seems to equate directly with the British technical grading, this can be quite a shock if you are not prepared.

CRAG CHAT

Much magazine attention has been turned to this crag in recent years, probably because of the stunningly photogenic nature of the S Face. Looking across at a climber on the brilliant white wall of the S Face with the glamorous backdrop of the Monaco Royal Harbour and Palace below does hold a certain charisma.

Purely from these impressions and from the raw statistics it would be easy to get a false impression of the breadth of climbing available here. Many of the climbs are quite short. Most visiting climbers on an Easter holiday, subjecting themselves to the midday heat to maximise climbing time, will have had their fill after a couple of days. Most of the worthwhile climbs fall within the hard category and there isn't a great deal to be had below 6a.

Just before the parking space an electronically controlled gate and fortified castle building may cause some speculation. In actual fact it is the Monaco National Communication and Broadcasting Centre which is why the Radio Monaco (the only station worth listening to?) reception which you have struggled with throughout southern France has never been better! The head of Tête de Chien does occupy a wonderfully commanding position and even if you do not spend the night here it is worth taking some time to admire the view. If you do stay to watch the stars emerge and the lights begin to twinkle down in Monaco, keep an eye on your supplies. Ironically the Dog's Head is infested by hungry and fearless stray cats.

HIT LIST (From L to R)

SOUTH WEST FACE

TT 1 **Jonathon** L1:6a, L2:6b, L3:6c

TT 2 **Bail à la Salamandre** L1:7a, L2:6a+

TT 3 **Périferique Ouest** L1:8a+, L2:6c

TT 4 **Les Années Lumières** 6c

TT 5 **LA DALLE À JULES** 20m, 6b. SELECTED ROUTE (see p. 147).

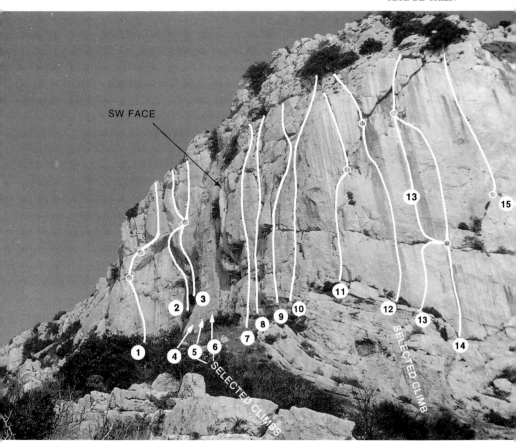

TT (1 - 15) Tête de Chien, SW & S Faces

TT 6	**DOCTEUR FATALIS** 20m, 5c. SELECTED ROUTE (see p. 147).
TT 7	**Mur des Lamentations** 6a
TT 8	**Le Pilier Puffo** 5c
TT 9	**Petrouchka** 5c
TT 10	**Impeccable** 6a

SOUTH FACE

TT 11 **Bleue** L1:5c, L2:7a
TT 12 **CORTO MALTESE** 30m, L:7a+, L2:6b.
SELECTED ROUTE (see p. 147).
TT 13 **Les Passagers du Vent** L1:6b, L2:6c, L3:6b
TT 14 **Qui s'y Jette s'y Coupe** L1:7a+, L2:7a+
TT 15 **Athos** 7a

TT (4 - 6) Tête de Chien, the pillar of the SW Face

SELECTED ROUTES AT TÊTE DE CHIEN:
La Dalle à Jules (TT 5), Docteur Fatalis (TT 6), Corto Maltese (TT 12) see page 143

LA DALLE À JULES: 20m, 6b. (British grading - E2, 5c.)

Location: R side of amphitheatre SW Face.

First Ascent: Unknown

Route Facts: To the R of the recessed amphitheatre of the SW Face stands a pillar, just R of a small cave. This route starts on the L side of the pillar.

L1, 20m, 6b. Starting from the shoulder on the left climb a scoop in the wall then move up R to gain a triangular niche. Step left move up a flake crack then aim for and climb the centre of the wall. Make a difficult move up the wall to gain the base of a large distinct triangular niche. Bridge up this pull out awkwardly left and continue to the belay chain. Lower off from this point.

DOCTEUR FATALIS: 20m, 5c. (British grading - HVS, 5a.)

Location: R side of amphitheatre SW Face.

Route Facts: This starts just to the R of La Dalle à Jules at the lowest point of the front face of the pillar.

L1, 20m, 5c. A most obvious flake crack fault line. Climb the elongated flake hole and continue ascending diagonally R to reach a pinnacle flake. A diagonal crack leads up from this to a small roof on the R edge of the pillar. Pull over this then move L to the obvious large niche (junction with La Dalle à Jules). Bridge up the groove move out awkwardly L and continue to the belay chain. Lower off from here.

CORTO MALTESE: 30m, L1:7a+, L2:6b. (British grading - E5, 6b+.)

Location and Access: This route climbs the white wall on the S Face. Continue traversing round R from the SE face to find a sloping ledge beneath the wall in approximately 100 metres.

First Ascent: Not known

Route Facts: Directly beneath the wall there is a sloping narrow ledge. From the highest point rises a curving corner/crack line. Start some 20m R of this at a faint broad black streak. Name painted on rock.

L1, 20m, 7a+. Climb directly to the break, immediately finger strenuous. Continue through the bulge to pull onto the wall and follow the bolts more or less directly until moves across lead L to easier ground. (Possible lower-off at this point.) Continue directly to belay beneath the overlap.

L2, 10m, 6b. Climb the curving crack/groove to finish.

ROUTE CHAT

La Dalle à Jules and Docteur Fatalis can be considered to be sister routes, climbing a tapering pillar to join just before the top belay anchor is reached. Despite their close proximity they are quite different in standard and nature. Docteur Fatalis is the better, more natural route, giving consistently interesting climbing on quite positive holds. There is no particular crux - it is interesting all the way. La Dalle à Jules is quite a different proposition. All goes well at about 5c standard until the top wall is reached below the large triangular niche. Much harder than the rest of the route, a really long reach is required to pass the crux. The fingerholds feel very slippery indeed and the strategically placed bolt runner gets frequent use. A point of aid bypasses the difficulty and keeps the standard at around 5c.

On the S Face things are very different. This may be the area of high glamour but for most of the day the heat is intense. Like a giant mirror the rock reflects a blinding white light. Fingers feel burnt and blistered even before you begin to cram them into those sharp tiny pockets. An ascent here, akin to lying on a bed of nails I imagine, is as much a test of raising your pain barrier as being able to make the high technical grade.

Some route names and grades are painted on the rock. The grades seem well out of order; here equate French 6a directly with British 6a. Corto Maltese seems to be one of the most aesthetic lines. Three bolt runners and finger pockets, for me immediately painful beyond the call of duty, take you to the break. Continue above in the same desperate vein, at about 6c/7a, until one move separates you from the lower off point. This is the most finger-painful section of all and must equate free to 7a+/7b.

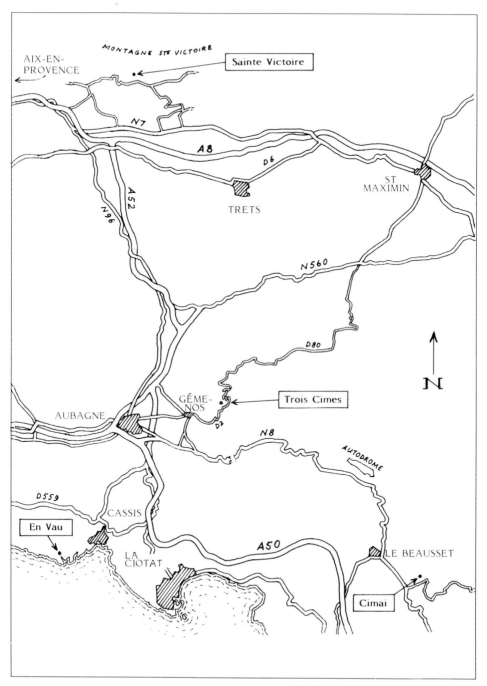

AIX-EN-PROVENCE

MONTAGNE STE VICTOIRE

Sainte Victoire

N7

A8

D6

A52

N96

ST MAXIMIN

TRETS

N560

D80

N

GÉMENOS

Trois Cimes

D2

AUBAGNE

N8

AUTODROME

D559

CASSIS

En Vau

LA CIOTAT

A50

LE BEAUSSET

Cimai

SAINTE VICTOIRE

Map Ref: *Michelin Motoring Atlas, page 159, E3.*

Area Maps: IGN 3244. MICH 84.3/4.

Guidebook: *Escalade dans le massif de la Sainte-Victoire. Les Deux Aiguilles, Le Signal,* an Edisud Guide. *Sun Rock* by Nicholas Mailänder.

Climate/Climbing Season: Precipitation (rain/snow) 700mm on 65 days of the year. Maximum in October. Because the cliffs are south-facing there is climbing on the lower cliffs to be had here for 12 months of the year. It can be too hot in summer, conversely the mistral can make it unpleasantly cold and windy.

Restrictions: No fires, no wild camping. The car park is notorious for thieves - leave absolutely nothing of value in your vehicle.

Rock and Protection: This varies from area to area. Much insitu gear was destroyed or seriously weakened in the great summer fire of 1989 therefore it is advisable to take a full range of Rocks and small selection of Friends, making the final selection beneath the particular route. However, most routes have now been re-bolted.

Situation: 15km E of Aix en Provence. With the main climbing area located near the tiny village of St Antonin. Département Bouches du Rhône (No.13).

Access: Leave Aix en Provence by the D17 in the direction of Le Tholonet, St Antonin and Puyloubier (the road is signed Route des Cézanne). Pass through St Antonin (blink and you will miss it) to find in a further 600 metres parking spaces on both sides of the road. From the car park nearest the crag a path leads through the trees (regrown?) and up the hillside to reach the Paroi des Deux Aiguilles, a series of buttresses which run along the base of the mountain (30 minutes).

Camping etc: There are campsites at Beaurecueil and Puyloubier. Nearest huge supermarkets in Aix. Limited supplies can be had in Puyloubier and there is a climbing shop here run by Daniel Gorgeon. There is a water fountain at St Antonin.

Crag Facts: This beautiful mountain, Montagne Sainte Victoire, forms a great plateau ridge stretching for some 7km at an altitude of around 1,000m. Its precipitous milky white S face consists of three distinct limestone bands rising a full 400m from the wooded slopes below. The bottom band is the cleanest and most continuous presenting a series of steep slabby faces. The middle area is made up of more broken stratified rock and scree. Crowning both, the upper band of limestone soars majestically to the summit rim in a series of ribs, buttresses and pillars. The visual effect is quite stunning. Overall there are some 500 routes from 40m to 400m in length. Perhaps the most popular and accessible area occupying the bottom band is the Paroi des Deux Aiguilles and here alone can be found 200 routes from 40m to 100m ranging in difficulty from 4b to 8a. Some of these routes have to be protected with nut runners but many are now fully bolted and offer some excellent sport climbing.

CRAG CHAT

In the dry hot summer of 1989 a terrible fire, fuelled by strong winds, swept the area, burning the woods below and sweeping the full height of the crag. Many communities had to fight to save their homes. Today, thankfully, new growth is bursting through but it will be some time before the woods are replenished to their former glory. The local community remains, understandably, extremely sensitive on the issue of fire. In addition to the obvious rule of no fires, anyone climbing here should really refrain from smoking, discarding matches or leaving any rubbish (glass bottles etc.) that may amplify the sun's rays and start another blaze.

The famous great white mountain rising from the Mediterranean plains just E of Aix is perhaps the most revered natural feature in the whole of Provence. The artist Cézanne, painting it repeatedly, brought it to the attention of a wider world. It is easy to see his fascination. The ivory white rock captures and intensifies every light and mood. If the sky is angry then Sainte Victoire is black, if the sky is clear blue, the mountain lives, if the sun sets red then the hillside becomes a wall of flame.

Climbing began here in the 1940s and moved to the steep slabby walls of Paroi des Deux Aiguilles in the 1970s. At that time the area developed a reputation for some of the hardest and boldest free climbs in France. Pegs were well spaced and often skyhooks were used to protect crux moves. Today many modern routes have joined the older classics and these sport good bolt protection.

Since the fire all old insitu gear should not be trusted. The heat was intense even high on the crag, and in a number of places flakes of rock exfoliated. Even some time later this was particularly obvious on the lower sections, brilliant white patches where the flakes had departed, stood out against the flame-blackened whole. Fire apart the limestone is of high quality and gives excellent flake and pocket holds. Despite its shiny appearance the rock is generally quite rough in texture and gives a surprisingly high degree of friction.

The climate can be extremely variable on this mountain. Although it faces due S, therefore fully exposed to the sun all day, and strongly influenced by the Mediterranean - it can be very windy here. Invisible from below the constant fight against the cold buffeting of the infamous mistral can make climbing a tedious affair.

CROIX DE PROVENCE

LE TUNNEL DU GARAGAÏ

TRACE NOIR

SV (1 - 9) Sainte Victoire, from L to R, The Paroi Deux Aiguilles stretch along the foot of this impressive mountain. The Croix de Provence can be seen at the top L of the photograph

SV (9 - 24) Sainte Victoire, The Paroi Deux Aiguilles

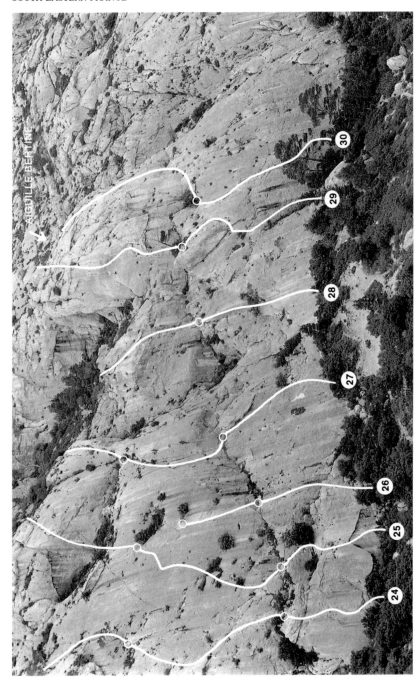

AIGUILLE BERTINE

30

29

28

27

26

25

24

SV (24 - 30) Sainte Victoire, The Paroi Deux Aiguilles with the Aiguille Bertine on the R

SV (30 - 35) Sainte Victoire, the Paroi Deux Aiguilles

HIT LIST

PAROI DES DEUX AIGUILLES (From L to R)

SV 1	**La Yanneck** L1:4b, L2:5c, L3:5b
SV 2	**Dérélita** 7a
SV 3	**Flagrant Délire** 6c+
SV 4	**Choflagom** 7b
SV 5	**Gnai** 6c
SV 6	**Supervers** 6b
SV 7	**Miss Maple** 7a
SV 8	**La Lequer** 6b
SV 9	**La Dédouille** 7a
SV 10	**La Présence** 7a
SV 11	**Escarpolettissime** L1:3b, L2:7b+
SV 12	**La Mégotine** 4c
SV 13	**La Croucouniaque** 5b
SV 14	**Les Rognures d'Ongles d'Allah** 4b
SV 15	**Arrosoir et Persil** L1:7b+, L2:5c
SV 16	**La Barnett** L1:7a+, L2:5c
SV 17	**La Martine** L1:6b, L2:6c, L3:5b
SV 18	**La Reposante** L1:5b, L2:6a, L3:4c
SV 19	**La DJ** L1:5c, L2:5b, L3:6a
SV 20	**Diédre des Tordus** L1:5c, L2:5b, L3:3b
SV 21	**Planquez les Femmes** 7a
SV 22	**Erotissimo** 7c
SV 23	**Cuni Lingus** 6c
SV 24	**Les Deux Ecailles** L1:4c, L2:5a, L3:3b
SV 25	**Le Boulon du Millieu** L1:4c, L2:5a, L3:3b
SV 26	**Clitomax** L1:6a, L2:6b
SV 27	**Le Quatre Quart** L1:5b, L2:5c, L3:4b
SV 28	**Les Plattes Dalles** L1:4b, L2:4a
SV 29	**La ULK** L1:4c, L2:5c
SV 30	**LE GRAND PARCOURS** 450m, 5b. SELECTED ROUTE (see p. 157).
SV 31	**La Lévitation** L1:7a
SV 32	**Messaline** 6b
SV 33	**La Tamanrasset** 6c. A classic system of steep cracks, nuts advised.
SV 34	**Les Crêpes Centrifuges** 6b+
SV 35	**La Boule** 8a+

SELECTED CLIMB ON SAINTE VICTOIRE: Le Grand Parcours (SV 30)

LE GRAND PARCOURS: 450m, 5b. (British grading - Very Severe, 4c.)
First Ascent: Not known.

Location and Access: This route starts up the Aiguille Bertine of the Paroi des Deux Aiguilles but continues to reach the summit of the mountain climbing the outstanding pillar known as Le Signal. Continue along the approach path ascending to meet a well-defined horizontal path traversing beneath the barrier cliffs of the Paroi des Deux Aiguilles. The triangular and most obviously pointed of them, Aiguille Bertine, lies some 100m to the L.

Route Considerations: Allow 3 hours for a party of three prepared to climb Alpine style or solo the easier sections. Immense care should be taken not to dislodge any loose stones (many have been loosened by the fire) - this would have potentially disastrous consequences for parties climbing below. Trainers should be carried for the descent is long and arduous.

Route Facts: The climb starts some 12m L of the very foot of the crag and roughly equidistant from some large boulders on the L of the crag.

450m. Climb the wall (5b) and trend L to pass a ledge (burnt out tree) until the wall eases. Belay. Move up then cross the slab to ledges and trees. Belay. Move out R around the rib to ledges. Continue R then follow up the buttress. Belay. Continue easily now to the top of the Aiguille and begin to climb in Alpine style. Move up R and scramble up towards the next buttress. Much loose scree and rock abounds since the fire. Easy slabs on the right of this lead up to the path - *trace noir*. Move L along this then climb up to and along the crest of the next buttress (this appears as a long rib of rock when viewed from the ground). This leads to the foot of the final impressive nose of rock the bottom part consisting of a fine pillar defined by the 'Y' crack. Climb to the fork in the 'Y' (5b). Belay. Take the L arm of the crack which is quite steep and awkward but well protected (perhaps one move of 5c but made easier by a point of aid) to emerge onto the shoulder. Belay. The angle now eases. Climb up the ramp a little way until it is preferable to climb the wall directly. Trend R to the arête and follow more broken ground to the summit plateau.

Descent: Follow the vague path along the edge of the summit plateau leading L (west) towards the large cross (Croix de Provence). A little way before this is reached a large cave opens on the L (le Tunnel du Garagäi). Scramble steeply (easy) down into this and through the arch. On exiting immediately bear L (looking out) to make a descending traverse of a scree slope to gain a horizontal path occasionally marked by small cairns and black paint marks. This is the *trace noir* path that leads across the tops of the Paroi des Deux Aiguilles to descend safely

157

to the base of the cliffs at their R end. Continue directly down the hill to find the approach path leading from the car park (presuming no gear has been left at the foot of the climb). Note: on leaving the cave do not descend too far before moving

SV (30) Sainte Victoire, looking up the full height of the mountain from the Aiguille Bertine on the Paroi des Aiguilles to the final pillar of Le Signal - the line of 'Le Grand Parcours'

L. Allow 2 hours from the top of the climb to return to the car park.

ROUTE CHAT

An aesthetic and appealing line that rightfully explores this great mountain from bottom to top. Rising from the conical tip of Aiguille Bertine it moves up to gain the sharply defined rib of rock issuing from the foot of a most impressive final nose - Le Signal. The bottom half of the nose consists of a pillar defined by a Y-shaped crack. An unmistakably challenging feature even when seen from the car park.

This long route will suit those who quest for adventure. Not only does it take you up into the very special mountain environment of Sainte Victoire, it also provides some high quality climbing. The crux is, where it should be, right at the top.

The initial wall, despite fire damage, provides some very entertaining and technical climbing. The holds are good and the standard is actually lower than you would at first imagine. Some climbers treat the ascent of Aiguille Bertine as an entity in itself and descend from there, which is a pity because the real attraction of the route lies in the fact that it takes you all the way to the summit of the mountain.

When you cross the *trace noir* it is worth fixing its position on the flanks of the mountain in your mind's eye (possibly marking it with a recognisable cairn). It isn't always straightforward to follow on the way down. Particularly on the initial stages from the cave it is very easy to descend too far down the scree slope and miss the path.

The next section climbs what now looks like a buttress but is in fact the long rib. It is rather broken but still enjoyable. Those confident on British 4a may wish to move together Alpine style or solo it to save time.

Whatever your chosen mode of ascent you should arrive at the foot of the nose. It looked impressive from the ground and close proximity does nothing to dispel the image. The chimney is climbed with some interest to reach a belay at the split in the Y. The left crack bulges for a short way and one or two single moves may reach a technical standard of 5c/6a, depending on your height and reach. Insitu gear will help those who are struggling though there is nothing in the climbing above British Very Severe. An alternative climbs the actual nose to the L of the cracks but this is considerably harder - grade 6b - and not really in keeping with the rest of the route.

The crack soon eases and a belay is taken on the shoulder ramp. Proceed a little way up this before cracks and weaknesses take you easily up again to the arête. This leads to the top with no further problems. The view across Provence and out across the flat plains to the Mediterranean is superb. Over to the south-south-east you will notice another range of mountains topped by a white golf-ball - this is the Massif de la Sainte Baume.

SAINTE-BAUME, TROIS CIMES

Map Ref: *Michelin Motoring Atlas, page 160, B3.*

Area Maps: IGN 3245 3345w. MICH 84.14.

Guidebook: *Escalade dans le massif de la Sainte Baume,* an Edisud guide.

Climate/Climbing Season: Precipitation (rain/snow) 600mm on 50 days of the year, heaviest in October but averaging 6 wet days per month between October and March (inclusive). Its SE-facing aspect, proximity to the Mediterranean, and 700-metre altitude means that climbing is possible all year round. However, it can be too hot in summer and too cold in winter depending on the individual season.

Restrictions: It appears that wild camping is permissible but thieving is a problem in the area.

Rock and Protection: Limestone generally good but a little blocky and care should be taken in places. Gear insitu but a small rack of small to medium size Rocks may be useful.

Situation: Near the Mediterranean, some 20km E of Marseille, within the upland chain of Massif de la Sainte Baume. Département Bouches du Rhône (No.13).

Access: Following the A52 autoroute SE from Aix a turn off-off for Gémenos will be reached in 29km. Take this and follow the D396 into Gémenos. Exit on the D2 heading E to find the three pillars, Trois Cimes, rising above (to the west of) the road D2 in 5km. At the hairpin there is plenty of parking space before a low metal gate which prevents vehicular access up the steep winding track. Follow the track until directly below the end pillar then scramble directly up to the buttress (20 minutes). Note planting operations may mean that the area beneath the crag will one day be afforested.

Camping etc: Gémenos has a campsite, a water fountain and several small supermarkets.

Crag Facts: Trois Cimes is a convenient crag for an evening or short day. The Massif de la Sainte Baume is a parallel, more southerly, mountain chain to Sainte Victoire and holds numerous crags and climbing areas. Within La Massif de la Galére, which includes Trois Cimes, may be found some 120 routes from 30m to 80m, ranging in difficulty from 3c to 7a

CRAG CHAT

A pleasant mountainous area of considerable character. Effectively the Massif de la Sainte Baume forms the last mountain chain rising from the plains of Provence before reaching the Mediterranean. For some reason the crags around here do not seem as popular and therefore not as well equipped as the nearby ones of Sainte

Victoire and Luberon. This is a little hard to understand as the climbing here is of a high quality even if some areas are a little loose in places. The unmistakable and striking pillars of Trois Cimes are in fact part of a group of crags collectively known as La Massif de la Galére. Plainly visible from here, looking NE beyond the hairpins and pass of Col de l'Espigoulier, is the fine cliff of Bau de Bartagne - recognised by the huge golf-ball radar station crowning its summit (note the fine pillar known as La Walker de la Provence in the centre of the face).

Many of the routes were pioneered in the same era as the classic aid routes of the Vercors and therefore old aid pegs abound. If the insitu gear looks suspect it is better to place nuts; fortunately the rock here does run to 'natural' protection placements. The more popular routes do have good insitu gear, a combination of peg and bolts, and there are quite a few easier routes in the British Severe category to be found.

Although wild camping does seem permissible here thieving is apparently a problem and the scores of burnt out car wrecks below the hairpin bends of the pass (they can't all be accidents despite the severity of the mountain road) seems to suggest that this is a prime dumping ground for stolen cars. Better to stick to the campsite, keeping the car clear of valuables.

SB (2) Sainte-Baume, the outstanding final headwall of 'Arête Est de la Cime Sud' (6a)

CIME NORD

CIME CENTRALE

CIME SUD

SB (1 - 7) Sainte-Baume, Trois Cimes

HIT LIST

CIME SUD

SB 1   **Quasimodo** 120m, L1:5c, L2:4c, L3:5c, L4:6a

SB 2   **ARÊTE EST** 80m, L1:5c, L2:5a, L3:6a. SELECTED ROUTE (see below).

CIME CENTRALE

SB 3   **Arête du Toit** 90m, L1:5c, L2:3b, L3:3b

SB 4   **Éperon Central** 120m, L1:5c, L2:4b, L3:7a or AO.

SB 5   **Le Slicteux** 120m, L1:4b, L2:6a, L3:5b

CIME NORD

SB 6   **Le Spigolo** 100m, L1:7a, L2:5b, L3:7a

SB 7   **Pilier d'Angle** 110m, L1:5b, L2:5b, L3:5c

SELECTED CLIMB AT TROIS CIME:
Arête Est de la Cime Sud (SB 2)

ARÊTE EST DE LA CIME SUD: 80m, L1:5c, L2:5a, L3:6a. (British grading E1, 5a, 4b, 5c.)

Location: Front face of the most southerly pillar - La Cime Sud.

First Ascent: André Coudray, Georges Livanos, 2 January 1943.

Route Facts: Start up the front face just L of the R edge of the pillar.

L1, 30m, 5c. Climb up to the bush and continue to the overhang above. Move delicately right to a crack. Move into this (pitch crux) and follow it and the rib above to gain a good ledge and bolt belay.

L2, 20m, 5a. Climb up to gain some blocky ledges on the R then step L to gain a groove. Follow this and the weakness above to trend slightly L and up to the large terrace.

Walk across to the foot of the headwall.

L3, 30m, 6a. Climb the cracks just L of the front face of the pillar. At half height move R across a blank section (insitu aid, if used, considerably reduces the difficulty of this short hard section) to make a high reach to gain the continuation of the cracks. Follow these to an overlap. Step R and then up to gain the top.

Descent: Walk S and descend quite easily to make a circuitous journey back to the R edge of the pillar.

ROUTE CHAT

Our arrival was at night amidst a heavy and prolonged thunderstorm. Despite the intense flashes of the lightning, we missed the crag completely. As the journey progressed up the tortuous pass of the Col de l'Espigoulier it rapidly took on a nightmarish intensity. The road in front was hit by lightning, whilst rivers of mud, rocks and debris flowed across it freely suggesting imminent landslide. With nowhere safe to stop or turn, it seemed progress upwards was the best choice. With visibility through the deluge mainly zero, hairpins were overshot, tyres and passengers screeched until arrival at the tiny village of Plan d'Aups some 10km beyond our intended stopping point.

The following day of sunshine and cloudless sky revealed just how daunting the pass really is. It also revealed an attractive crag of three while pillars which under ordinary circumstances would be quite impossible to miss.

The route, taking the front face of the pillar consists of three pitches, each with its own particular interest. Located in wonderfully wild mountain surroundings, the tiny hairpin road far below emphasizes the scale of the limestone scarps and soaring walls. Fine views across the hills and out to the hazy blue Mediterranean abound and that certain freshness of the air that comes with mountain terrain speeds you to the foot of the climb.

First appearances suggest that the lower section of the pillar, despite the brilliant white colour of the rock, may be rather broken in nature. In execution this is not the case, sharp juggy holds provide a surprisingly fine pitch. The crux section of this pitch, moving right beneath the initial overhang to gain and climb the crack on the edge of the pillar, provides delectable climbing.

The final headwall is, as it looks, quite outstanding. Although short, the crux of the route is both technical and precarious. On checking with the other two members of our party, Dave Birkett and Trevor Jones, they also followed with some precise sequence of moves: the right hand utilises a small pocket and the left foot is smeared until a high layaway flake can be taken with the left hand. Right foot placed in the pocket and the right hand raised to grasp a crack high to the right. Insitu protection is good and if used as a point of aid (the party in front of us did just that) it would reduce the overall standard of difficulty of this excellent route to HVS.

LES CALANQUES, EN VAU

Map Ref: *Michelin Motoring Atlas, page 160, A3.*

Area Maps: IGN 3145e and 3245e, L=(3105.0-3106.0, 856.7-857.2). MICH 84.13.

Guidebook: *Escalade dans le massif des Calanques En Vau*, an Edisud guide. *Sun Rock* by Nicholas Mailänder.

Climate/Climbing Season: Precipitation (rain/snow) 600mm on 50 days of the year. Climbing possible all year round.

Restrictions: Wild camping is strictly prohibited in the area as a whole - there is a high fire risk. However, it has long been the tradition for climbers to bivouac in the valley of En Vau itself (romantic perhaps, but there is no water and no sanitary arrangements). Thieving in this area is a serious business, only the car parks in Cassis can be considered safe to leave a vehicle. Leave no valuables in the car. Individuals or couples should remain on their guard.

Rock and Protection: Limestone of good quality, polished in places. Generally all gear is insitu, mainly this takes the form of peg protection although some of it is now of dubious worth. The popular routes have mainly been re-equipped but a small rack of gear may be considered worthwhile.

Situation: On the Mediterranean coast immediately W of Cassis, some 15km E of Marseille. Département Bouches du Rhône (No.13).

Access: Cassis can be reached by driving along the D559 from Marseilles or by quitting the autoroute A50 at the signed junction. There are two park and walk approaches in both of which your car/contents are at considerable risk from theft.

(1) From the centre of Cassis follow signs and small roads above the sea to Port Miou and then Les Calanques. The road ends at a car park at the head of the Calanque de Port Miou. Walk along the waterfront passing the old quarry workings and continue along the well-defined path (the correct path is marked by black paint) which leads through the woods first to the head of Calanque de Port-Pin and then up the wooded hillside beyond to gain a level plateau. The marked path now makes a very steep descent down a gully to the head of Calanque En Vau (30 minutes).

(2) Some 5km W of Cassis on the N559 a small road leads to a barrier at the Col de la Gardiole. Park here. Follow the track which continues through the wood of la Fontasse passing the Maison Forestière to descend into the dry valley of Calanques En Vau. Walk along this to its head (30 minutes).

Probably the best approach however is to take a boat from the harbour front at Cassis. Safe parking (fee charged and early arrival to get a place essential). There are numerous small boats making regular tourist trips to the sea inlets of Les Calanques and they are used to taking climbers specifically to En Vau. Make it clear before sailing (a) that you only wish to go to En Vau, (b) that you require return at a definite time and day. A return trip costs around £5.00 and is well worth it.

Camping etc: There is a campsite at Cassis open from April to October. If intending to stay in the area for more than one day I would recommend it. Camping by the side of the D559 on an unguarded site is very risky. Thieving is rampant and people have been attacked even in locked cars. Cassis is an upmarket tourist resort and everything is available - at a price.

Crag Facts: En Vau is the prime climbing locality in this long famous Calanques region. The Calanques themselves are deeply cut limestone valleys running like fingers from the Mediterranean into the wild upland afforested plateau of the surrounding coastal area. Some are sea-filled, others only partly so - En Vau for perhaps half of its length. The sides of these valleys form excellent limestone cliffs up to a height of some 140m. It can be extremely hot here and it is essential to take a good quantity of water in even if only staying for the day. The cliffs at En Vau are simply classified in two groups, those on the NE side of the valley (the left side looking down the valley out to sea) are known as the Falaise de Gauche de la Calanque d'En Vau and include the two distinct detached pinnacles rising from the floor of the valley, the Petite Aiguille (seen by the beach) and the Grande Aiguille. Those on the opposite side (on the right looking out to sea) are the Falaise de Droite de la Calanque d'En Vau. There are some 175 routes from 80m to 140m in height ranging in difficulty from 3c to 7a. Even in midsummer, midday temperatures can resemble those of a furnace, but climbs in the shade can be found.

CRAG CHAT

At its best En Vau can provide outstanding climbing in a wild and beautiful setting. A wide range of difficulty is available on the superb sun-kissed white limestone sometimes rising directly from the blue Mediterranean. Outside the Alps this is perhaps one of France's most traditional climbing regions and climbing began here in the early 1930s. The atmosphere is easy and relaxed, the summer heat making a bathe in the Mediterranean or a naked laze on the beach, along with the boat-landed tourists, an attractive and easy alternative.

Despite its popularity in the evening or later in the season, a rather special secluded atmosphere does persist and some do stay overnight in the valley taking in enough supplies for a few days. However, since a series of damaging fires the police have tightened up and it is possible that you may be fined and moved on. Also, staying overnight means leaving a vehicle unattended for a long period. Quite frankly I don't recommend this.

If you decide to park and walk, then the approach from the head of Calanque de Port Miou is probably the safest option. The area is busy during the daylight hours and a lot of small boats moor here. Leave nothing at all of value in your car.

HIT LIST

FALAISE DE GAUCHE (Proceeding up the valley from the beach)

EV 1   **PETITE AIGUILLE** 30m, 5a. SELECTED ROUTE (see P. 169).
EV 2   **La Saphir** 100m, 4b. Basically follows the ridge.
EV 3   **La Sans Nom** 90m, L1:4b, L2:3b, L3:4a
EV 4   **Pilier de la Sirène** 100m, L1:5c, L2:4c, L3:3c
EV 5   **Couloir de la Sirène** 100m, L1:5c, L2:4a, L3:3b

EV (1 - 2) Les Calanques, En Vau, Petite Aiguille

EV (3 - 7 Les Calanques, En Vau, Falaise de Gauche - 'Super Sirenè' area

EV 6   **SUPER SIRÈNE** 100m, L1:6b, L2:6c, L3:4c. SELECTED ROUTE (see below).

EV 7   **Sirène Liautard** 100m, 4c

GRANDE AIGUILLE
La Paillon 35m, 4a. Takes the L edge of the SE (seaward) face, a crack then moves through a cave of the final finger to climb in its inside edge.
Voie Abeille 20m, 3b. Climbs SE face from botom R to top L. The normal line of ascent.

FALAISE DE DROITE
Opposite the Petite Aiguille and for a little distance up the valley steep short walls rise abruptly from the path. There are now numerous modern bolted one-pitch sport climbs here - names and sometimes grades painted on the rock.

SELECTED ROUTES AT EN VAU: Petite Aiguille (EV 1), Super Sirène (EV 6)

PETITE AIGUILLE: 30m, 5a. (British grading - Mild Very Severe, 4b.)
Location: Seaward face (SE face) of the Petite Aiguille, the unmistakable rock pinnacle approximately 100 metres beyond the beach, Falaise de Gauche de la Calanque d'En Vau.
First Ascent: Henri Barrin, 1932
Route Facts: Start at the centre of the face.

L1, 30m, 5a. Climb straight up for a few metres then move L to the flake. Up this and L onto the arête. Step up and follow the flake crack which leads diagonally back R to a good corner ledge. Climb directly up the steep corner (crux) and follow the crack to the top of the pinnacle.

Descent: Abseil from the insitu ring taking care not to snag the rope in the crack below.

SUPER SIRÈNE: 100m, L1:6b, L2:6c, L3:4c. (British grading - E3, 5c, 6a, 4a.)
Location: On the Falaise de Gauche a few hundred metres along the path leading up the valley of En Vau (a couple of minutes beyond the Petite Aiguille and some way before the Grande Aiguille) a very striking pillar of rock rises from behind the bushes. The route takes the centre of this and is reached by scrambling up through the bushes for perhaps 30m.
First Ascent: Paul Guérin and Gaston Rebuffat, 30 March 1941.

Route Facts: This takes the front face of the central, tallest and most elegant pillar. Start at the foot of the pillar.

L1, 40m, 6b. Climb the face of the pillar by the line of least resistance to a belay ledge on the R.

L2, 40m, 6c. Move up and left under the protruding nose to make some difficult technical moves to gain the arête above. Follow this to a stance.

L3, 30m, 4c. Continue easily up the exposed arête to the top.

Descent: This may be made down the gully to the L (looking in) but involves some tricky rock walls at the top or more straightforwardly down the gully over to the R.

ROUTE CHAT

Rising from the floor of the valley just beyond the beach the distinct pinnacle of Petite Aiguille is the most immediately identifiable feature in En Vau. An obvious challenge it was perhaps the first rock climb of the area - its back face (La Face à la Mer) being first ascended in 1913. With its top notch finger of rock it has an uncanny resemblance to Napes Needle in the English Lake District. It provides a number of worthwhile climbs which go well with a lazy day spent mainly on the beach.

The actual route described is fully titled Directe de Gauche de la Diagonale - variation "a", and is probably the most satisfying way to reach the top. Of course it is highly polished in places and shouldn't be underestimated. Those new to climbing here may find the corner crux particularly steep and difficult. Pegs mark numerous other ways up the pinnacle should alternatives be sought.

The pillar of Super Sirène provides a spectacularly beautiful and challenging climb. Famous Alpine guide, photographer and author, the late Gaston Rebuffat, cut his teeth on Les Calanques and made the first ascent of this route, with his companion Paul Guérin, in 1941.

Today the rock may be highly polished but the insitu pegs are sensibly spaced and apparently quite solid. The long first pitch gives sustained wall climbing but it is the second pitch which proves to be both the hardest and the best. The crux, moving up and left to reach the arête, is short but difficult. Above it the exposed, finely balanced knife edge arête provides a stimulating lead. The top section is technically a lot easier but the heightening sense of exposure up the tip of the pillar makes for an exciting finish.

If the pegs are used for aid, which is still most often the case, the grade diminishes to around HVS. If that is your top grade, or the high polish and intense heat force it upon you, do it. For as you would expect of a climb with this pedigree it remains an elegant and remarkable climb which shouldn't be missed.

CIMAI

Map Ref: *Michelin Motoring Atlas, page 160, C3.*

Area Maps: IGN 3346, L=(3103.4, 885.0). MICH 84.15.

Guidebook: *Sun Rock* by Nicholas Mailänder.

Climate/Climbing Season: Precipitation (rain) 700mm on 60 days of the year. Climbing possible all year round.

Restrictions: None

Rock and Protection: Limestone. Protection all insitu bolts, only quick draws need be carried.

Situation: Overlooking the D462, 2km NE of the small village of Sainte Anne d'Evenos, 8km NW of Toulon. Département Var (No.83).

Access: Sainte Anne d'Evenos is reached along the N8. Following the A52 autoroute SE from Aix a turn off for Gémenos will be found in 29km. Take this and follow the D396 through Gémenos to join the N8 (6km W of Aubagne). Turn L to reach the village of Sainte Anne d'Evenos in 32km. Halfway through the village turn L onto the D462 and rise up a hill to pass beneath the crag in 2km. A flat area on the L (care crossing drainage ditch) and the verge on the R provide parking. The L section of the cliff is reached by first following the track then a steeper path leading directly to its base (5 minutes).

Camping etc: Wild camping is possible but not recommended. There is an *auberge* a further 2km up the road and a couple of cafés and a water fountain in Sainte Anne d'Evenos but little else. Nearest camping is in Toulon at La Seyne sur Mer.

Crag Facts: Imagine a standing wave first frozen, then sliced along its length to leave a long clean face; this is Cimai. It is divided into two main sections, L and R, divided by a deep gully (used for descent, with one abseil). Although much of the fence is vertical or overhanging, providing a feast of hard climbing, there are numerous diagonal cracks and breaks which provide easier ways. There are some 150 routes from 40m to 80m and ranging in difficulty from 5a to 8b. The crag faces SE and it can be very hot here; conversely it does seem to catch the wind.

CRAG CHAT

Cimai has risen to the status of an alternative hard climbing locality to Buoux. Although the rock here is very different, being much harder and sharper, there are many bolted routes in the upper spectrum of difficulty. This does not mean to say there are no easier routes to be found. There are and these offer multi pitch length and follow striking lines which will appeal to many.

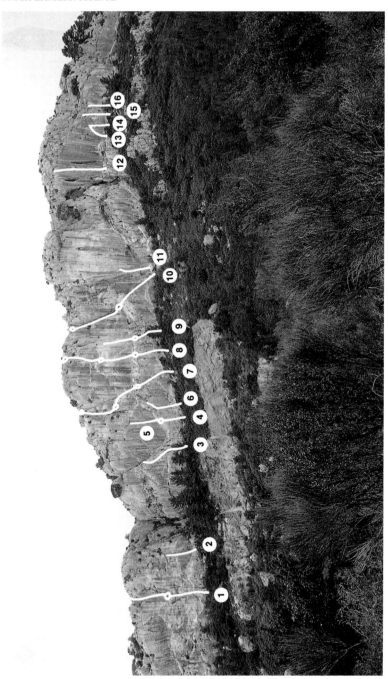

CM (1 - 16) Cimai

Although the crag is divided into L and R sections, by the descent gully, it will be observed that the R portion is somewhat the longest. The crest of the sectioned wall of limestone rises and falls in waves and troughs, to offer a number of buttresses. Between the waves will be found diagonal weaknesses offering crack climbing and in-between these face climbing of varying steepness (although seldom less than vertical).

Very much a roadside crag, climbing here is particularly popular on a summer's evening when the sun leaves the face. The package is an attractive one with the steep hillside below falling into a tree-filled gorge. The wind apart, the crag can also form an effective sun trap and provides a reliable winter venue.

Extensive quarrying operations have been carried out here in the past but all now seems quiet. A number of ruined buildings can be found and a few level areas where it would be possible to pitch a tent. However, one team who pitched here awoke to a lightning storm so severe they retreated back to their car. It was fortunate they did so, for on return in the morning they found the tent completely flattened by a huge boulder which, dislodged by the storm, had rolled down from the cliff above!

HIT LIST (From L to R)

LEFT SIDE

CM 1   **Anal Plus** L1:6b, L2:6a
CM 2   **RODÉO** 25m, 7a+. SELECTED ROUTE (see p. 174).

RIGHT SIDE

CM 3   **Le Crapaud** 6c
CM 4   **Alice au Pays des Merveilles** 5b
CM 5   **En un Combat Douteux** 8a
CM 6   **Sous l'Oeil de Bouddha** 6a+
CM 7   **LE CHAT HUANT** 80m, L1:5a, L2:5b, L3:5c. SELECTED ROUTE (see p. 174).
CM 8   **El Condor Pasa** L1:5c, L2:7a, L3:7a
CM 9   **Le Surplomb des Bois** L1:5a, L2:7a
CM 10   **La Jean Bert** L1:4b, L2:4c, L3:4b
CM 11   **Le Pillier des Clodus** 7b
CM 12   **Orange Mécanique** 8a
CM 13   **Energie Douce** 7b+
CM 14   **Vive la Vie** 7a
CM 15   **Tropique du Cancer** 6b
CM 16   **Café Crème** 6b

SELECTED ROUTES AT CIMAI: Rodéo (CM 2), Le Chat Huant (CM 7)

RODÉO: 25m, 7a+. (British Grading - E5, 6b.)

Location: Where the path meets the L section of the crag there is a small roofless ruin and an obvious tufa pillar on the wall above.

First Ascent: Unknown

Route Facts: Start by scrambling to a rock ledge above the ruined building. A tufa pillar soars up the leaning wall - this is the line.

L1, 25m, 7a+. Step left and move up to gain and follow the pillar. At its top pull over onto the slabby wall and continue a little way to a lower-off point.

Descent: Lower off.

LE CHAT HUANT: 80m, L1:5a, L2:5b, L3:5c. (British grading - Hard Very Severe, 4a, 4c, 5a.)

Location: Traverse R along the foot of the cliff some 200m beyond the large gully.

First Ascent: Unknown

Route Facts: A line of diagonal corners lead up from R to L, start beneath these.

L1, 25m, 5a. A surprisingly awkward start leads to the ledge beneath the first large corner. This is climbed more easily to a ledge belay.

L2, 25m, 5b. Make an awkward start to gain and follow the ramp and crack. Pass a difficult constriction and continue in the same line to a junction with the overhanging headwall above. Traverse delicately left to a small pedestal and two-bolt belay.

L3, 30m, 5c. The next section constitutes the crux. Step L round the corner to gain a chimney. Bridge steeply up this, then continue more easily directly to the top.

Descent: The descent gully will be found over to the L. A large bolt provides the abseil anchor. Make one abseil then scramble easily down to the path which traverses the foot of the cliff.

ROUTE CHAT

The hanging tufa pillar of Rodéo provides a sustained and strenuous challenge. Starting some way above the ground, making the first tentative pinch of the flange-like rib seems precarious. A slap with the hand and the flange responds with a hollow metallic sound. Will it stay attached to the face? Should you or shouldn't you commit yourself?

Grip the tufa and clip the bolt - you're on your way. A fingerhold here and a pinch there, sometimes laying-off the edge, sometimes bridging onto the face, sometimes using tiny toeholds on the flange. The higher you get the higher

CM(2) Dave Birkett on the tufa pillar of 'Rodéo', a modern classic

pitched is the noise from the pillar. Inevitably when all else begins to fail and gravity takes it toll the inspiration for the name becomes obvious. You grasp the pillar between the knees, pinch its mane and will those arms to recover and carry you on over the top of this unique ride.

Le Chat Huant is a three-pitch route of consistently high quality and increasing difficulty. Whilst there is ample opportunity to pause en route to admire the surroundings, wonder at the overhanging walls, when the harder sections of climbing do arise they demand full concentration.

Don't be put off by the difficulty of the insignificant looking initial corner which leads in a few metres to a ledge and the corner proper. Don't be misled either; it really is quite awkward. The remainder of the first pitch is absorbing without being difficult, but on the second pitch the difficulty is resumed. The diagonal corner proves most demanding at a constricting overhang but continues with interest until it arrives at the overhanging headwall.

With no way directly up the wall at the grade allotted, a traverse left is forced. This proves quite delectable, providing positive holds on rock that is needle-sharp. A belay with a view is taken and a pleasant opportunity granted to savour the position.

Immediately on leaving the stance the climb steps up a gear. Round the corner is an overhanging chimney, getting established in this is the objective. First step up, then reach high to the left to find a finger slot. This is just adequate enough to enable a balancey move around the bulging rib and up into the exposed bottomless chimney groove. Once established weight can then be shifted from the arms into a bridging position. A series of steep moves are now necessary to gain the continuation chimney. Once reached it marks the end of a very exciting crux section and you can again allow your mind to relax knowing the climb is in the bag.

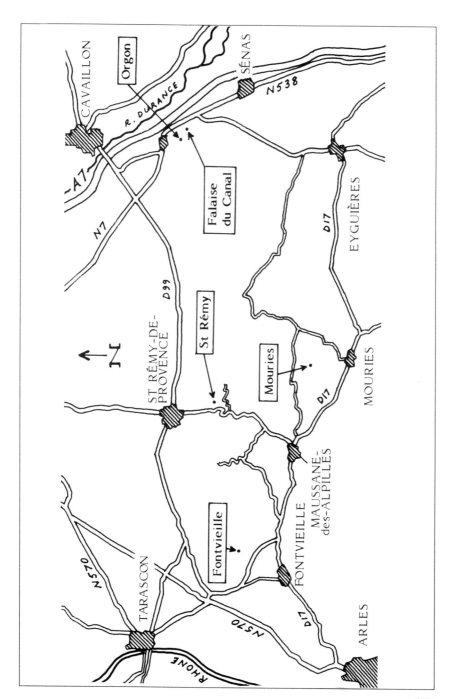

CAVAILLON

Orgon

SÉNAS

N538

R. DURANCE

Falaise
du Canal

EYGUIÈRES

A7

D17

N7

D99

N

ST RÉMY-DE-
PROVENCE

St Rémy

Mouries

MOURIES

D17

MAUSSANE-
des-ALPILLES

Fontvieille

FONTVIEILLE

ARLES

N570

TARASCON

N570

D17

RHONE

ORGON, FALAISE DU CANAL

Map Ref: *Michelin Motoring Atlas, page 158, C2.*

Area Maps: IGN 3142w. MICH 81.12.

Guidebook: *Les Alpilles* by Serge Jaulin.

Climate/Climbing Season: Precipitation (rain/snow) 600mm on 50 days of the year. The wettest month is October and on average it rains 6 days a month between October and March (inclusive). Depending on prevailing conditions climbing can be had all year round. Generally the crag faces E and loses the sun in the afternoon (a considerable bonus in the hot summer months).

Restrictions: None - although this is a semi-urban environment and wild camping is not recommended.

Rock and Protection: Limestone, sometimes friable. All bolt-protection, only quick draws need be carried.

Situation: Orgon and this cliff mark the E end of a beautiful upland chain of hills known as Les Alpilles. Located 6km S of Cavaillon and 2km S of Orgon. Département Bouches-du-Rhône (No.13).

Access: Exiting Orgon S on the N7 a minor road leads off to the R, just after passing the last few (rather derelict) buildings of the town. The road follows down the R (W) bank of a small canal and soon deteriorates to become a rough dirt/mud track. Continue along it until the cliff appears on the R, parking spaces about half-way along the cliff. (Allow a few seconds to reach the crag.)

Camping etc: Although there is a campsite at Orgon - Camping de la Vallée Heureuse, reached by taking a (signed) road leading up R from the canal road - they apparently do not welcome climbers. The nearest recommended campsite is just up the road at Cavaillon although for Les Alpilles generally campsites at Saint Gabriel, Fontvieille, Maussane and Saint-Rémy are all popular.

Crag Facts: This relatively recently developed cliff stretches above the canal. Without exception it is a sport climbing crag and all routes are bolt-protected with descent by lower-off or abseil. Many of the names of the routes are written on the rock and this makes identification on the ground a simple affair. At the time of writing there are some 34 routes from 15m to 35m in length ranging in difficulty from 4c to 8b.

CRAG CHAT

This cliff literally forms the last drop of Les Alpilles onto the plains of the Durance River. The crag environment, rising from the almost swamp-like, semi-industrialised plains of the Durance is best described as interesting. For those who do try wild camping it will be discovered that this apparently derelict environment actually comes to life at night. Bats swarm from the caves and a ceaseless cacophony of noise, led by the rampant bullfrog who massively inhabits the surrounding swamps, will be experienced from dusk to daybreak.

Despite any aesthetic shortcoming the quality of climbing here, particularly in the harder bracket, is first class. The physical composition is quite interesting and changes from its slabby R end through a series of ribs and corners to an undercut and largely overhanging middle section. Finally, on the far L end, a square-cut pillar of brilliantly white limestone offers two long sustained wall climbs (4th Dimension 7a and Univers en Expansion 7a+) of impeccable quality. The former requires every millimetre of stretch on a 65m-rope to lower off and reach the ground, but for the latter (furthest L-hand route) a belay is usually taken on the top of the short pillar.

Some of the rock is rather friable and it will be noticed by those tackling Couer de Loup 7c+ that vital holds have been glued/epoxied back in place. Generally however the rock is reliable, worst in the overhanging cave sections but quite sound on the slabby right end where most of the easier routes are to be found.

HIT LIST (From R to L)

FC 1	**Lettre Majuscle** 4c		FC 18	**Bébé Chanteur** 7c
FC 2	**L'Espagnol** 5a		FC 19	**Lisa** 7b+
FC 3	**Mort aux Cons** 6a		FC 20	**Chantez Tout** 7a
FC 4	**Tchao** 6a		FC 21	**Antonin Paysan du**
FC 5	**Histoire d'un Jour** 6b			**Causse** 6c
FC 6	**Voyage en Mappenmonde**		FC 22	**Morgane** 7a+
	7a+		FC 23	**Mélusine** 7a
FC 7	**Calinette** 7a+		FC 24	**Squeletor nous Gonfle** 6c
FC 8	**La Sieste à l'Ombre** 6c+/7a		FC 25	**Vent d'Est** 8b (Not deter-
FC 9	**Pousse au Rête** 6a			mined at time of writing.)
FC 10	**Gris Souris** 7a		FC 26	**Cacou** 7c+/8a
FC 11	**La Jument de Fernand** 6b		FC 27	**Couer de Loup** 7c+/8a
FC 12	**Binjamin Bigoudi** 6b+		FC 28	**4th Dimension** 7a
FC 13	**Les Methes Sauvages** 6c+		FC 29	**Univers en Expansion**
FC 15	**En Catimini** 7a+			7a+ (hard)
FC 16	**La Black Music** 7b			

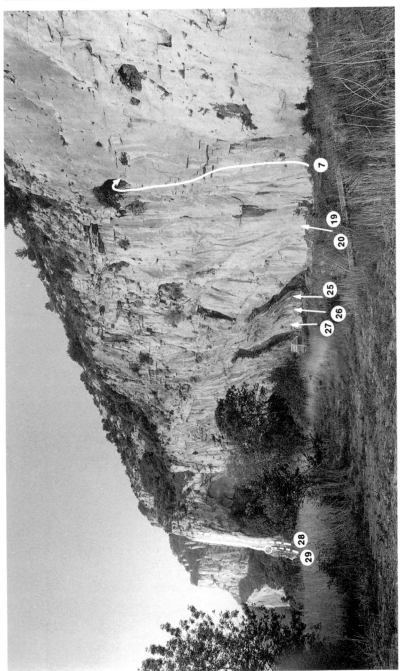

FC (7 - 29) Falaise du Canal, Orgon, looking along the length of the crag from its slabby R end to the pillar at the far L

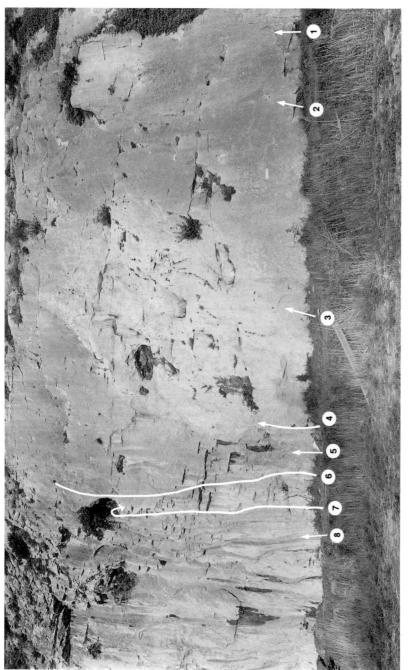

FC (1 - 8) Falaise du Canal, Orgon, the slabby R end

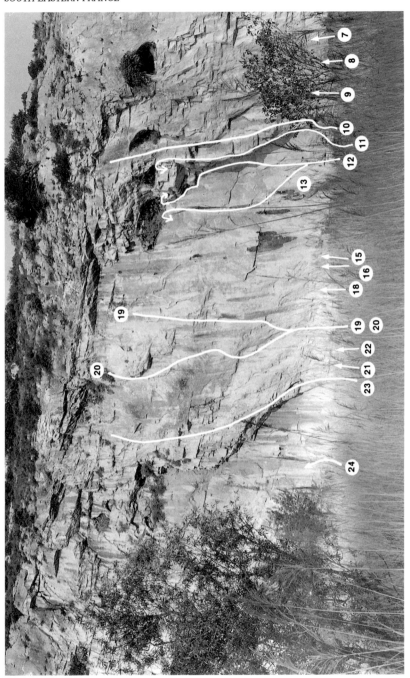

FC (7 - 24) Falaise du Canal, Orgon

ORGON

Map Ref: *Michelin Motoring Atlas, page 158, C2.*

Area Maps: IGN 3142w. MICH 81.12.

Guidebook: *Orgon* by P.Duret.

Climate/Climbing Season: Precipitation (rain/snow) 600mm on 50 days of the year. The wettest month is October and on average it rains 6 days a month between October and March (inclusive). Depending on prevailing conditions climbing can be had all year round. Generally the main crag faces E and loses the sun in the afternoon (a considerable bonus in the hot summer months).

Restrictions: No wild camping, fires etc.

Rock and Protection: Limestone, sometimes friable. All bolt-protection, only quick draws need be carried.

Situation: Some 50km NW of Aix-en-Provence Orgon marks the E end of a beautiful upland chain of hills known as Les Alpilles. Located 6km S of Cavaillon and 1.5km S of Orgon. The cliffs of Orgon and the area described here are situated directly above the campsite and lake of Vallée Heureuse. Département Bouches-du-Rhône (No.13).

Access: There are two approaches, the first leading over the top of the rim into the valley and the second directly through the campsite. (1) In Orgon find the minor road leading from the village up the hillside towards the prominent church on the hill - la route de la Notre-Dame-de-Beauregard. Before the col is reached a parking space in the pines on the right will be found (note, this cannot be seen from the crag and if the car is left here leave nothing else of value). Follow the road to the col then bear right to find the main section of crag detailed here (10 minutes). (2) Leaving Orgon S on the N7 a minor road leads off to the R, just as the last few (rather derelict) buildings of the town are passed. The road follows down the R (W) bank of a small canal and soon deteriorates to become a rough dirt/mud track. Immediately prior to the road losing its surface a steep track winds up to the R (signed Camping de la Vallée Heureuse). Follow this to a parking place outside the campsite. Walk through the campsite and up to the cliffs forming the NE flanks of this horseshoe valley (15 minutes).

Camping etc: Although there is a campsite perfectly situated beneath these cliffs - Camping de la Vallée Heureuse - at the time of writing they apparently do not welcome climbers. This may change in the future, but until then the nearest recommended campsite is just up the road at Cavaillon. For Les Alpilles generally campsites at Saint Gabriel, Fontvieille, Maussane and Saint Rémy are all popular.

Crag Facts: A traditional climbing ground now extensively bolted, all the routes fall into the sport climbing category. Within this circular bowl of cliffs there are some 135 routes from 25m to 70m in length and ranging from 3c to 7b+. The section of cliff selected, the NW wall of the bowl, constitutes the most popular area.

CRAG CHAT

This slice of the crag constitutes a slabby to vertical limestone wall of around 20m to 35m in height. The R side of the wall is smaller but steeper and to its L, beyond the notch in the skyline, a deep cave makes for a formidable roof problem. Generally the crag provides warm, dry climbing until the sun leaves it sometime around mid-afternoon. Sheltered from wind, notably Le Mistral, it is a popular all year round venue.

There are a few steep harder routes, notably Sur le Fleuve Amour crossing the roof of the great cave, but more typically it offers slabby wall climbing that suits the climber of average ability. The easiest standard of difficulty is around Very Severe but the plentiful bolt placements will encourage most to push their standard some way beyond this.

HIT LIST (From L to R)

OR 1   **Jeux Sans Frontière** 6b+
OR 2   **La Minute de M. Cyclopède** 6c
OR 3   **Sur le Fleuve Amour** 7b+
OR 4   **La Porte Tragique** 5c
OR 5   **Wall Street** 6a
OR 6   **Mistoufi** 5c
OR 7   **Séance Nocturne** 6a+
OR 8   **Zégavolta** 6b
OR 9   **Les Déménageurs** 6a
OR 10   **Radio Active** 5b
OR 11   **RFM** 6a
OR 12   **Coproduction** 6c
OR 13   **La Frite Mystérieuse** 6c+
OR 14   **Rolling Stone** 7b
OR 15   **Genesis** 6b+

OR (1 - 15) Orgon

MOURIÈS

Map Ref: *Michelin Motoring Atlas, page 158, B2.*

Area Maps: IGN 3042w, L=(3159.8, 803.5-805.2). MICH 83.10.

Guidebook: *Les Alpilles* by Serge Jaulin.

Climate/Climbing Season: Precipitation (rain/snow) 600mm on 50 days of the year. Wettest month is October. Facing due N and due S this crag generally offers all year round climbing possibility.

Restrictions: No wild camping or vehicular access is permitted. This is a Red Alert fire risk area and smoking or any type of fire is strictly forbidden. Towards the E end of the reef archaeological sites are being excavated and these should be left strictly undisturbed. An extremely sensitive area, regularly patrolled, contravention of these rules may lead to an absolute ban on climbing - tolerated at the moment.

Rock and Protection: A very compact brilliant white limestone of excellent quality. Purely a sport climbing crag and only quick draws need be carried.

Situation: This crag lies on the southernmost flanks of the upland chain of hills known as Les Alpilles. Some 50km NW of Aix-en-Provence, 45km S of Avignon, 20km E of Arles and 2km N of Mouries. Département Bouches-du-Rhône (No.13).

Access: In the centre of the small town of Mouries turn off the D17 and head N following signs for the Auberge de Servanne and the golf course. Keep on this minor surfaced road (no road number) passing both the forks R to the *auberge* and the golf course until at the sharp L-hand bend a parking space can be identified on the R (CARS MUST BE LEFT HERE). A track (and small bridge crossing the irrigation canal) bears off R just beyond the car park and a dirt track leads along soon to pass under the first section of cliff (its W end) and continues more or less parallel to it (3 minutes to the W end and 15 minutes to its E end).

Camping etc: Supplies can be obtained in Mouries and despite its size there are a number of banks offering *change* (finding them open is another problem). There is a campsite on the D5 some 2km W of the town itself.

Crag Facts: This is possibly the most important crag in Les Alpilles and consists of a single knife edge reef of limestone running due E to W. This means that it faces N, virtually always in the shade apart from evening time during the summer months, and S, virtually always in the sunshine. The N face contains the most important sections and tends to be either vertical or gently impending. The S face, more broken with less climbing, tends to be slabbier and the routes easier. This is the place for steep technical wall climbing and without exception all routes are single pitch to a lower-off. Detailing the N face from R to L (W to E) and lastly the

S face the first section to be encountered (the W end of the reef) is known as the Falaise du Parking. This rapidly disappears into pine trees and shielding scrub to become Face Nord Secteurs Oliviers. For these two areas leave the track and walk along underneath the crag. As the track passes through pine trees and begins to ascend a hill an overgrown track forks R and fades into the scrub. The path leading from this gains access to the first area of real importance, Nord Mur du Bout du Monde followed by Du Singe. The face then breaks up slightly. The next area is best reached by staying with the main track until it crests the hill and begins to descend into an open grassed area known as La Prairie. First on the R comes a small buttress known as Face Mur du Couer and just past this an obvious notch in the reef, profiled by a distinctive nose of rock which cannot be missed. This notch provides easy scrambling access through to the S face. Past the notch lies another important area, firstly Face Nord Falaise de la Prairie followed by Face Nord Prairie Centrale which effectively ends the climbing on the N face. The last buttress, isolated by another gap in the reef, stands above an archaeological dig and is not climbed on (at the time of writing). Entrance to the S face is gained via the notch described above (this is the easiest and shortest route to the climbs) and immediately L (W) of this (now facing the S face) is the Face Sud Secteur Tamalou (the only section of the S face to be detailed here). There are some 200 routes from 25m to 35m in length and ranging from 3c to 8b+ in difficulty.

CRAG CHAT

This up-ended reef of limestone not only offers a considerable volume of climbing but is also sited in a most agreeable environment. To the N are rolling pine-clad hills and olive groves and to the S gentle cultivated plains (and almost directly below a new golf course) stretching across to the mouth of the Rhône issuing into the Mediterranean.

If ever there was a "designer crag" this is it. Two opposite faces enabling one to optimise the prevailing conditions: in the baking heat of summer the cool of the N face, in winter the sun on the S. Two faces quite contrary in nature. The N, the most important, being generally vertical or slightly steeper and famed for its routes of 7a. The S, easier angled and generally offering routes of a more amenable standard.

The compact hard nature of the rock, with surprisingly few pockets, offers positive if small holds. The flat, flaky breaks make for very fingery and technical climbing. Specifically in terms of physical movement, although the comparison may at first appear ridiculous, the climbing feels very similar to that experienced on the British rhyolite walls of Dinas Cromlech or Pavey Ark. A splendid contrast to the pockets of Buoux. If one were to criticise, then it could be said that much of the climbing feels quite similar in character - only more, or less, difficult. But, considering the overall ambiance of the area, that would seem a mere trifle.

MO (1 - 13) Mouriès, Face Nord du Bout du Monde (R) & Face de Singe (L)

HIT LIST (From R to L)

FACE NORD MUR DU BOUT DU MONDE AND DU SINGE

MO	1	**Sans Importante** 6a+
MO	2	**Les Yeux Verts de l'Été** 6b
MO	3	**À Coups de Pied dans le Cul** 6c
MO	4	**Bisous dans le Cou** 6c
MO	5	**Chronique Martienne** 7a
MO	6	**Super Fruite** 7a
MO	7	**Ceux Qui Vont Mourir te Saluent** 7b+
MO	8	**Au Bout du Monde** 7c. The route of the wall - for those with the ability to climb it.
MO	9	**Big Mac** 7b
MO	10	**Les Petites Douceurs de la Vie** 7c+
MO	11	**Métro** 7a

MO 12   **Mourir au Hasard** 7c
MO 13   **Félicitad** 7c

FACE NORD FALAISE DE LA PRAIRIE
MO 14   **Bivouac sur la Lune** 6b+
MO 15   **Ballade d'Arlequin** 6a
MO 16   **Grosse Brute Technique** 6c
MO 17   **En Voiture Simone** 7b
MO 18   **Les Ours** 5c
MO 19   **Gloubi Boulga** 6b
MO 20   **Sucettes à l'Anis** 6c+
MO 21   **Nuits Calines** 7c
MO 22   **BCBG** 7b

MO (14 - 22) Mouriès, Face Nord, Falaise de Prairie

MO (22 - 29) Mouriès, Face Nord Prairie Centrale

MO 23   **Chemins du Paradis** 6a
MO 24   **Quatre pas dans l'Étrange** 5c
MO 25   **Divergences** 7a
MO 26   **À Voile et à Vapeur** 6c

FACE NORD PRAIRIE CENTRALE
MO 27   **Canyon Street** 5c
MO 28   **Corbeau Solitaire** 3c
MO 29   **Via Velpa** 4b

**MO (9) Mouriès, Face Nord du Bout du Monde,
climber in action on 'Big Mac' (7b)**

MO (30 - 42) Mouriès,Face Nord Prairie Centrale

MO 30	**Bonjour le Soleil** 6a
MO 31	**Un Doux Calin** 7b
MO 32	**Du Glucose pour Noémie** 7b
MO 33	**Du Bruit pour les Brutes** 6c. A powerful and popular route.
MO 34	**La Saison des Amours** 7b
MO 35	**Vol de Jour** 7a
MO 36	**Le Mandarin Orgueilleux** 6a+
MO 37	**Brouillard de Violence** 6a+
MO 38	**Le Pion** 7a
MO 39	**L'Oreille en Coin** 7a
MO 40	**Vol de Nuit** 6c
MO 41	**Du Rififi sur les Alpilles** 6c
MO 42	**Souffle Douceur** 6c

MO (43 - 52) Mouriès, Face Sud, Secteur Tamalou

FACE SUD SECTEUR TAMALOU ET JEUNES LOUPS (From R to L)

MO 43	**Croquemitouffle** 6a	
MO 44	**Recalcitrouille** 6a+	
MO 45	**Rubrique à Bras** 5c	
MO 46	**Vaisseaux de Pierre** 6a	
MO 47	**L'Inconnue** 6a	
MO 48	**Gueule d'Enfer** 6c	
MO 49	**Tamalou** 5c	
MO 50	**Goupil Main Rouge** 6b	
MO 51	**La Belle Histoire** 6b	
MO 52	**Le Yeti la Haut** 5c.	

SAINT-RÉMY

Map Ref: *Michelin Motoring Atlas, page 158, B2.*

Area Maps: IGN 3042w, L=(3159.3, 801.1). MICH 80.20 and 81.12.

Guidebook: *Les Alpilles* by Serge Jaulin.

Climate/Climbing Season: Precipitation (rain/snow) 600mm on 50 days of the year. The wettest month is October and on average it rains 6 days a month between October and March (inclusive). Rather exposed to wind making it rather a cold winter venue.

Restrictions: No wild camping etc.

Rock and Protection: Hard limestone with small finger-painful pockets. All sport climbing, only quick draws need be carried.

Situation: Placed roughly centrally in the chain of hills known as Les Alpilles, some 25km S of Avignon and 55km NW of Aix-en-Provence. Located high on the hillside just above the D5 from Saint-Rémy to Maussane. Département Bouches-du-Rhône (No.13).

Access: The D5 leaves Saint-Rémy in a southerly direction passing the famous Roman remains of Ruines de Glanum to rise up a steep pass. Some way before the col of the pass, the sheer white wall and prow of the crag will be seen on the E side of the road. Numerous parking places by the side of the road from where a steep path leads directly up to the crag (10 minutes).

Camping etc: Saint-Rémy is the nearest and probably the best for shopping. Saint Gabriel, Fontvieille and Maussane are equally popular.

Crag Facts: Most of the climbing lies on the W-facing vertical white walls of limestone as seen from the road - Falaise du Mont Gausier. For those interested in routes of 7b to 8a status the Mur de Chocoline just to its left (obscured from below) is a must. There are some 30 routes from 30m to 50m in length and ranging from 6a to 8a in difficulty. Only a few route names are written on the rock and identification can be difficult.

CRAG CHAT

Les Alpilles consists of an elevated chain of limestone reefs running parallel to and contrasting savagely with the flat plains on either side. Razor-like and often knife-edged, the vertical walls of brilliant white limestone rise from a fragrant mixture of upland scrub and pine. The contrasting colours of vegetation and rock, and the exotic sweet smells of the herbs, make this wild untamed region one of the most breathtaking in Provence.

SR (1 - 14) Saint-Rémy, Falaise du Mont Gausier

HIT LIST (From R to L)

SR	1	**Éperon des Alpilles** 6a
SR	2	**L'Amie Dalle** 6a
SR	3	**Les Gladiateurs** 7a
SR	4	**Ils Sont Fous ces Romains** 6c
SR	5	**Leve Toi et Marche** 6a
SR	6	**L'Ancien** 6b
SR	7	**Couer de Pigeon** 6b
SR	8	**Aux Quatre Vents** 6b
SR	9	**Impasse des Intimes** 7a
SR	10	**Ca Petille** 6c
SR	11	**Byen Manze Kreol** 6c
SR	12	**Les Tisseurs d'Orb** 6b. Very sharp pockets.
SR	13	**Tablac Belin Tout Va Bien** 6c
SR	14	**La Grande Muraille** 6a+

Occupying a commanding position high on the hillside Falaise du Mont Gausier offers magnificent views across Les Alpilles and out to the flat plains beyond. A sheer white wall providing immediate exposure. Nearby the elevated fortified village of Les Baux-de-Provence provides one of France's favourite tourist attractions - well worth a visit at the end of a day's climbing.

The routes are all steep and demanding, there is effectively little below British E2 5b in standard. Most utilise the sharp-edged pockets, often painfully small, and are often sustained in difficulty from beginning to end. Those with an eye for a line may tackle the prow of the buttress via Éperon des Alpilles 6a, one of the more traditional routes here. Care should be taken with the insitu gear, which at the time of writing was partly old pegs.

A mecca for those who like steep wall climbing, there are however a number of potential drawbacks worthy of consideration. Situated immediately next to the road this is a prime site for car break-ins. Its exposed position, facing west, means it is often wind buffeted. On the other hand, when the sun does reach it in the afternoon, the heat can be intense. All things considered, it is still a highly worthwhile venue.

FONTVIEILLE

Map Ref: *Michelin Motoring Atlas, page 158, B2.*

Area Maps: IGN 3042w, L=(3163.8, 792.4). MICH 83.10.

Guidebook: *Les Alpilles* by Serge Jaulin.

Climate/Climbing Season: Precipitation (rain/snow) 600mm on 50 days of the year. The wettest month is October and on average it rains 6 days a month between October and March (inclusive). Dependent on prevailing conditions climbing is possible all year round.

Restrictions: No wild camping, no fires and no vehicular access beyond the road.

Rock and Protection: The pocketed limestone, generally excellent, varies quite considerably in the type of climbing it offers. This is purely a sport climbing crag and only quick draws need be carried.

Situation: Some 60km NW of Aix-en-Provence the valley of Vallon de la Lècque cuts into the W end of a beautiful group of hills known as Les Alpilles. The cliffs forming the rim of the Vallon de la Lècque are located due N of the small town of Fontvieille. Collectively known by the name of the town, these lie some 8km SE of Tarascon and 5km W of Baux. Département Bouches-du-Rhône (No.13).

Access: The D33a cuts from the D17 to continue as the D33 to enter Saint Gabriel effectively forming the base of a triangular system of roads whose apex lies at Fontvieille. Half-way along the D33a, some 2.5km beyond the junction with the D17, there are some buildings and a minor road on the S of the road. At this point a track/dirt road runs off to the N. It is now necessary to park by the road or just along the track as vehicular access by climbers into this private valley is prohibited. Walk along the track, bear R at the first junction, then bear L by a row of cottages to enter Vallon de la Lècque. The main cliffs are found on the L side of the valley and a track branches up L until a further track (blocked by an iron barrier gate) leads up left in a short way to their lowest point, the unmistakable Secteur de la Grotte (25 minutes).

Camping etc: There are campsites at either Fontvieille, with small shops in the village, and at Saint Gabriel.

Crag Facts: This is an important cliff of some length and variety situated above the Vallon de la Lècque - a pine-filled valley of some beauty. Within its folds there once existed a small community. Most of these delightful houses have now been taken over as second and prestige homes for the influential. It is they who have objected to vehicular access by climbers and anyone found parking here will be asked to move on by the police. However, climbing is permitted and there are no problems with pedestrian access - in any case the short walk is very pleasant. Cars left by the road are of course extremely vulnerable to theft and nothing of value should be left inside.

Effectively the cliffs form the rim of the valley. The most important are those on the L, which facing SE get the sun until mid-afternoon. These cliffs are divided into a number of *secteurs*, L of Secteur de la Grotte (the unmistakable large cave at the point of arrival). Mur Mozart is a slabby wall containing a number of worthwhile routes (although it appears small and scrappy when viewed from below). The next *secteur*, R and above the cave is Mur du Ninou, marked by the large pillar/buttress on its R end known as Dune de la Lècque. Then comes Secteur Dace Nord Orme de la Lècque followed by Mur du Boubou Doux and Secteur le Bloc Penche - another distinct feature where a tall, slender pillar leans against the main cliff. Finally comes Secteur des Grands Yeux Noirs, the area R of two distinct chimney rifts jammed with large blocks, Secteur de l'Ecaille and ending with the tiny buttress of Secteur Plume d'Ange.

Of the cliffs so far developed on the R, NW-facing, side of the valley Secteur Ocean Mur Brésilien et Pagnol can be found by scrambling through the trees above the track before it branches off up to the L. There are some excellent climbs here - altogether some 135 routes from 20m to 50m in length ranging from 3c to 7c in difficulty. Most of the route names are clearly written on the rock.

CRAG CHAT

The cliffs of Fontvieille provide some of the best climbing in Les Alpilles. Everything from slabs to overhangs, and the different *secteurs* vary in character enormously. Although the routes seldom pass 30m in length enough will be found to sustain climbing interest for a number of days whether you climb in the grade 7s or at a more modest standard of difficulty.

Although I have made some attempt to rationalise the grades I'm sure there are still some wide discrepancies of difficulty particularly in the 5 to 6 (French) categories. It is not uncommon to fail on some of the 5s and then find relatively little difficulty on some of the 6as! This in part may be explained by the widely different types of climbing to be found - in any case it adds a certain spice.

Mur Mozart will attract the climber of average ability and one should not be put off by its appearance from below. There are plenty of good value routes to be found. The much-photographed Chez Herazade climbing the wall and roof immediately left of the cave Secteur de la Grotte is a tremendous route, one with an impact far outweighing its meagre length. For those with strong fingers the steep wall, in the gully, on the R side of Mur du Ninou offers a number of brilliant routes around the 7a (hard) category. Another keynote route (with its arête start) is Mine de Rien 6c+, on the right of the cave-scallop at the start of the Mur du Boubou Doux section.

A route with a particularly distinct character, Ecorne Lune 5c (British VS/HVS), climbs first under and then out over the arch formed by the leaning pillar of Le Bloc Penche. It shouldn't be missed. Fantastic climbing will be found to the R of the block-filled chimneys on Secteur des Grands Yeux Noirs, Je Ne Pense Qu'a Elles 6b, and both its direct and R variations, respectively L'Arrache-Couer 7b and Liquer Bleue 6b.

The sun usually lingers on the W rim of the valley until midday. To remain in the sun, especially when it has lost its midday intensity, the long, low wall of Secteur Océan Mur Bresilien et Pagnol just above the track on the opposite side of the valley, should be considered. Despite its brevity there are some excellent climbs here varying from the strenuous Captain Nemo 6c and Moby Dick 6b on the R side, to the slabbier and more relaxing Manon 6a and Marius 5c/6a on the far R. A perfect location to end the day.

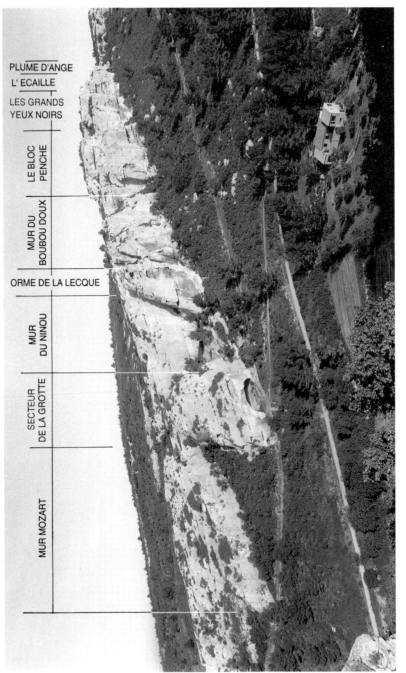

PLUME D'ANGE
L' ECAILLE
LES GRANDS YEUX NOIRS
LE BLOC PENCHE
MUR DU BOUBOU DOUX
ORME DE LA LECQUE
MUR DU NINOU
SECTEUR DE LA GROTTE
MUR MOZART

FO Fontvieille, looking the length of the main crag

HIT LIST (From L to R)

MUR MOZART

FO   1   Les Pieds dans les Nuages 6a
FO   2   Dialogue des Carmélites 6b
FO   3   La Flute Enchantée 6a
FO   4   Don Giovanni 6b
FO   5   Requiem 6b
FO   6   Les Damnes du Bitume 7a
FO   7   Toro Magic 4c
FO   8   Sourire 5b
FO   9   Plaisir 5c
FO 10   La Bistouquette 5b

SECTEUR DE LA GROTTE

FO 11   Chez Herazade 6b. A mini classic.
FO 12   Coup de Tête 7a
FO 13   Les Valseuses 6a+

MUR DU NINOU

FO 14   Gandalf 6c+
FO 15   Lune de Miel 6c
FO 16   P'Tits Calins 6b
FO 17   Youpala Turbo 6c
FO 18   Le Fou de Ninou 7a
FO 19   La Rousse au Chocolat 7a. Excellent

ORME DE LA LÈCQUE

FO 20   La Normale 4b
FO 21   Leviathan 6b
FO 22   Melisa 6b
FO 23   Flagada 6a+
FO 24   Bombix 5c

SECTEUR BOUBOU DOUX

FO 25   Mine de Rien 6c
FO 26   Boubou Doux 7c

LE BLOC PENCHE

FO 27   Plein Sud 5b
FO 28   L'Envers du Décor 6a

FO 29   **Écorne Lune** 6a. Tremendous but beware of nesting bees!
FO 30   **Cornelius** 6a
FO 31   **Derborance** 6b
FO 32   **BCBG** L1:6a, L2:5a

LES GRANDS YEUX NOIRS
FO 33   **C'est Beau Comme à Buoux** 6a
FO 34   **L'Arrache-Couer** 7b
FO 35   **Je Ne Pense Qu'a Elles** 6b. Superb.
FO 36   **Liquer Bleue** 6b
FO 37   **Au Pays des Grands Yeux Noirs** 6c
FO 38   **Je N'Aime Qu'Elles** 6c

L'ÉCAILLE
FO 39   **Go On** 5c
FO 40   **L'Écaille** 5c
FO 41   **Bruno Déboutonne** 6a
FO 42   **Quad** 6a
FO 43   **No Name** 6a

SECTEUR PLUME D'ANGE
   Plume D'Ange

SECTEUR OCÉAN MUR BRÉSILIEN ET PAGNOL (From R to L)
This long, low wall, hidden in the trees lies on the opposite side of the valley just above the road, it catches the evening sunshine.

   Nautilus 6c
   Captain Nemo 6c
   Moby Dick 6b
   Amazonie 6b
   Pais Tropical 7b
   Manon 6a. Pleasant slabby climbing on the far R end.
   Marius 6a. Ditto.

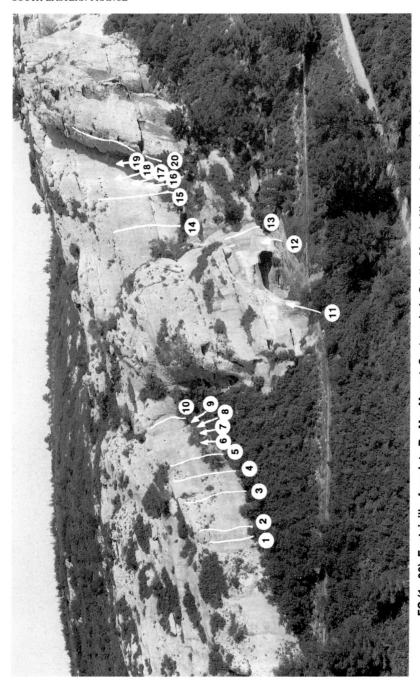

FO (1 - 20) Fontvieille, from L to R - Mur Mozart, Secteur de la Grotte, Mur du Ninou & Orme de la Lecque

FO (21 - 26) Fontvieille, N Face of Orme de la Lecque & Mur du Boubou Doux

FO (27 - 32) Fontvieille, Secteur Le Bloc Penche

FO (33 - 43) Fontvielle, Secteur Les Grands Yeux Noire & L'Ecaille

AREA 3 SOUTH WESTERN FRANCE

Moving W from the Rhône Valley and Lyon to the Atlantic, skirting along France's southern Pyrenean border covers a huge chunk of the country. It includes many fine crags and climbs yet is an area relatively unknown to the average British rock climber. Addressing this anomaly, I have detailed nine crags and nine selected climbs of outstanding quality in a circuit rotating from the Ardèche, through Languedoc down to and along the Pyrenees and back up through the Dordogne to end at La Rancune in the Massif du Sancy. A circuit well worth travelling with many excellent crags and a huge variety of climbing.

L'ARDÈCHE, MAZET PLAGE

Map Ref: *Michelin Motoring Atlas, page 143, D2.*

Area Maps: IGN 2839e, L=(3234.7, 748). MICH 80.8.

Guidebook: *Sites d'Escalade de L'Ardèche.*

Climate/Climbing Season: Precipitation (rain) 900mm on 68 days of the year. Climbing possible all year round.

Restrictions: No wild camping or bivouacking.

Rock and Protection: Limestone. All routes bolt-protected, only quick draws need be carried.

Situation: Although classified within L'Ardèche region this crag is located above the River Chassezac (which feeds into L'Ardèche) in a subsidiary valley, some 26km SW of Aubenas and 15km W of Vallon-Pont-d'Arc. Département Ardèche (No.7).

Access: Leave the D104 1km S of Maison Neuve and proceed W skirting the hamlet of Casteljau to reach Mazet Plage. Pass the campsite by the side of the road then bear R to cross the bridge above the river. Perhaps a 100m past this bridge, rising up a hill, parking will be found on the L verge. A little way up the road a track/path (no vehicular access - cars must not be taken down to the beach) leads down L (S) to reach the beach then bears R along this to reach the crag in a few hundred metres (5 minutes).

Isabelle Patissier, (world champion) on Chantez Tout (7a), Falaise du Canal, Orgon

Climber on Super Sirène (6c),
En Vau, Les Calanques

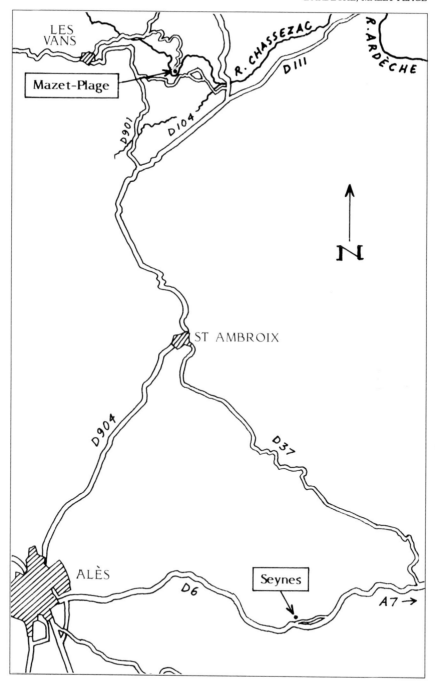

MP (1 - 10) Mazet Plage, L'Ardèche

HIT LIST (From L to R)

MP **1** **JUNIOR** 25m, 4b. SELECTED ROUTE (see p212).
MP **2** **Pilier Gris** 6b
MP **3** **Imagie Noire** 6c
MP **4** **Rando** 4b
MR **5** **MAUVAISE LIMONADE** 35m, 6a. SELECTED ROUTE (see p212).
MP **6** **Le Gellie** 4b
MP **7** **Semoule en Transmutation** 7a   MP **9**   **La Ro-Ro** 6c
MP **8** **Les Strates** 6a   MP **10**   **Le Bis-Bis** 6b

Camping etc: Campsites abound in this popular tourist resort. Mazet Plage is open between April and September. Up the road from the bridge is a VVF hut. Supermarkets and a climbing shop can be found in Aubenas.

Crag Facts: A popular sport climbing crag situated above the "beach" of the Chassezac River. The crag faces SW and becomes extremely hot in the afternoon. At this time it is usual to take to the river. There is one central wall and the LH end of this provides the main interest. In addition to this the crag extends in either direction to offer a few lesser climbs on the minor buttresses. Some 55 routes from 20m to 45m in length range in difficulty from 4b to 7a. Names of the routes are written on the rock at the foot of the climb.

CRAG CHAT

Although the region is named after the impressive limestone Gorge de l'Ardèche, where the river flows for some 30km through massive and seemingly endless cliffs, the main climbing is currently centred on cliffs some way outside the gorge. This is especially difficult to understand if you take one of the popular canoe trips downstream from Vallon-Pont-d'Arc and see the gorge's potential. Possibly the best cliffs currently within this group of small crags are Chauzon, Salavas, Chalet Plage and Mazet Plage. Chauzon takes the form of a horseshoe of cliffs mainly facing S actually above the Ardèche - temperatures here can be furnace-like even in midwinter. Salavas, just across the river from Vallon-Pont-d'Arc, faces NW and thankfully remains in the shade for most of the day. The Chalet Plage is located just downstream of Mazet Plage - they can be considered sister crags in nature and climbing content.

The S-facing crags can be considered a reliable winter venue and in summer provide a relaxed, fun place to climb. By turning W off Autoroute Soleil at Montélimar the area provides a worthwhile alternative to Provence and Côte d'Azur for a short break holiday. At weekends Mazet Plage can become extremely busy and is used extensively by climbing groups but it doesn't really seem to matter - bathing in the river is always an attractive alternative.

SELECTED CLIMBS AT MAZET PLAGE:
Junior (MP 1), Mauvaise Limonade (MP 5)

JUNIOR: 25m, 4b. (British grading - Very Severe, 4c.)

Location: The far L end of the central wall, Mazet Plage.

First Ascent: Unknown

Route Facts: Start at far L side before the rocks disappear into the bushes (there are a few isolated buttresses L of here).
L1, 25m, 4b. Climb the edge of the wall to an obvious flake groove at mid-height. Continue up this and then the wall above to a large ledge. There are many variations possible.

Descent: Abseil

MAUVAISE LIMONADE: 35m, 6a. (British grading - E1, 5b.)

Location: Centre of the central wall, Mazet Plage.

First Ascent: Unknown

Route Facts: Start about 25m R of a tree-filled break directly beneath the mid-point of a large roof marking the top of the crag.

L1, 35m, 6a. Climb the wall to the roof. Pull directly through this to a ledge and belay.

Descent: Abseil

ROUTE CHAT

Junior provides an excellent little route at its grade and by taking alternative lines to the R many variations on the theme exist. There are routes of similar nature to be found L again on a separate buttress rising from the bushes. The routes further to the R, with a few exceptions tend to be harder. Mauvaise Limonade takes in some interesting wall climbing, the chief characteristic of most of the routes here, but also throws in a considerable roof to add that something extra.

The roof is very well protected, bolts are strategically placed, but this does not alleviate the difficulties. First you have to commit yourself positively to gain the unseeable hold on the lip. Faith and a long reach are required here. Having got it, swing loose and make a strenuous pull up again to reach better holds above.

SEYNES

Map Ref: *Michelin Motoring Atlas, page 143, E4.*

Guidebook: *Escalades Falaise de Seynes* by Serge Imbert.

Climate/Climbing Season: Precipitation (rain/snow) 800mm on 75 days of the year. Wettest in October, driest in July.

Restrictions: The far L of the cliff, L section of Nouveau Monde, is out of bounds, due to nesting birds of prey, between 15 February and 15 June.

Rock and Protection: Hard, flaky limestone of good quality. Purely a sport climbing crag, only quick draws need be carried. Those climbing on a single rope and lowering-off (standard practice), should note that on many routes the minimum rope length requirement is 55m and on a number of routes a 60m is necessary to reach the ground.

Situation: Some 13km E of Alès, the crags lie just 2km W of the village of Seynes directly above the old (now bypassed) D6. Département Gard (No.30).

Access: Leave the D6 to enter Seynes then follow the now abandoned D6 W until in 2km the crags can be seen on the hillside above. Park below the individual buttress of your choice and walk directly to it (5 minutes).

Camping etc: Facilities in Seynes are limited but there is an excellent restaurant - La Farigoullette. Main supplies can be found at Alès. Nearest camping is some 8km distant (N along D7) at Les Fumades and 10km distant (S along D7) at Saint Jean de Ceyrargues.

Crag Facts: Strung along the hillside of Le Mont Bouquet above the old D7 these attractive S-facing crags presently comprise of five developed sections: to the R is Secteur Top Secret, immediately L of this isn't climbed on but L again is Secteur Diable par la Queue separated from Secteur Concerto by a scrub-filled gully. The L side of Concerto lowers in height to become a long, thin band of slabs known as Secteur Initiation. L again the largest, steepest and most impressive cliff is known as Nouveau Monde. At the time of writing only the R end of this cliff has been developed. It looks most attractive and its tufa pillars and blank impending walls will surely provide a high standard climbing ground par-excellence in the near future. Presently there are some 90 routes, 25m to 50m in length ranging in difficulty from 3b to 8b. The hardest are found on Nouveau Monde and the easiest on Initiation with a good spread of difficulty between. There is enough of interest here, whatever your standard of ability, to provide a good few days climbing.

CRAG CHAT

Strategically placed above the D6 to Alès, Seynes is a convenient stopping-off point for those heading either to the crags of the Ardèche (N) or to those of Languedoc (S). Despite the busy presence of the new D6 not far below the crag this is a wild region of rolling hills clad in dense scrub and pine. Peregrines and eagles are a regular sight and the L side of the crag is an important nesting site. Just beyond Alès, to the W, lies the Parc National des Cévennes - one of the most beautiful upland regions of France. Beyond this are the famous Gorges du Tarn and its tributary the Gorges de la Jonte (a remarkable climbing area - currently being developed).

When turning off into Seynes do not make the mistake of thinking that the crags visible on the hillside are those described here. In actual fact the developed cliffs are much more attractive but only visible after driving along the old road W for 2km. Top Secret is the most E of the band and the nearest to the road. It provides immaculate wall climbing, where good footwork is essential, on hard, flaky limestone. Those climbing at 6b will have little problem in completing all of the eight routes of the section in an afternoon.

It isn't unknown for it to rain heavily here but the S-facing aspect and clean nature of the rock means it dries very quickly. One March, some half an hour after one such deluge, we found the slabs of Initiation to be bone dry. We watched a tumbling group of young peregrines taking food from their mum on the wing before we moved on to sample the impending delights of the R end of Nouveau Monde. By this time the clouds had cleared and shorts only became the order of the day.

TOP SECRET

DIABLE PAR
LA QUEUE

CONCERTO

INITIATION

NOUVEAU
MONDE

SE Seynes, looking W along the crags

HIT LIST (From R to L)

SECTEUR TOP SECRET

SE	1	**Aphrodisiaque** 6a+
SE	2	**Pharmacie du Bon Dieu** 6a+
SE	3	**Top Secret** 6b+
SE	4	**Top Rove** 6a+
SE	5	**Fragment d'Univers** 6b
SE	6	**Soupçon** 6b+
SE	7	**Allégresse** 5c+

SECTEUR DU DIABLE PAR LA QUEUE

SE	8	**Tychodrome** 4c
SE	9	**Crécerelle** 5a
SE	10	**Verdon** 6a+
SE	11	**Le Rouge et le Noir** 6a+
SE	12	**Crème Renversée aux Abricots** 7a
SE	13	**Apocalypse Rock** 7a
SE	14	**Le Diable par la Queue** 6b+
SE	15	**Colouer Pourpre** 7a
SE	16	**Étroite Surveillance** 7a
SE	17	**L'Essential** 6a

SECTEUR CONCERTO

SE	18	**Rêves d'Enfants** 5c
SE	19	**Le Fou du Roi** 6c
SE	20	**Night** 6c
SE	21	**Day** 6b+
SE	22	**Senoritas** 6a
SE	23	**Symphonie Fantastique** 6c
SE	24	**Les Amants de la Déroute** 6b
SE	25	**Bonzäi** 5c
SE	26	**Marie** 5c

SECTEUR INITIATION

SE	27	**L'Oeil** 4a
SE	28	**La Pomme** 3b
SE	29	**Jeudi** 4c
SE	30	**L'Encore** 5c
SE	31	**Eh Hop** 4c-5b. (A number of routes a few metres apart vary in grade by the margin indicated.)
SE	32	**Les Vieux Croutons** 3b
SE	33	**Les Jeunes Loups** 3c

SE (1 - 7) Seynes, Secteur Top Secret

SE (8 - 17) Seynes, Secteur Diable Par la Queue

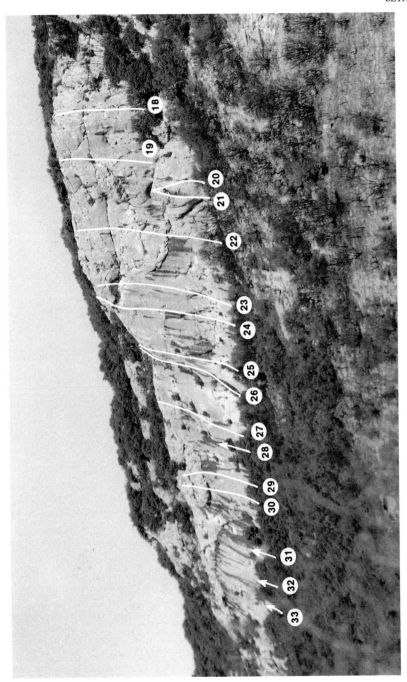

SE (18 - 33) Seynes, Secteurs Concerto & Initiation

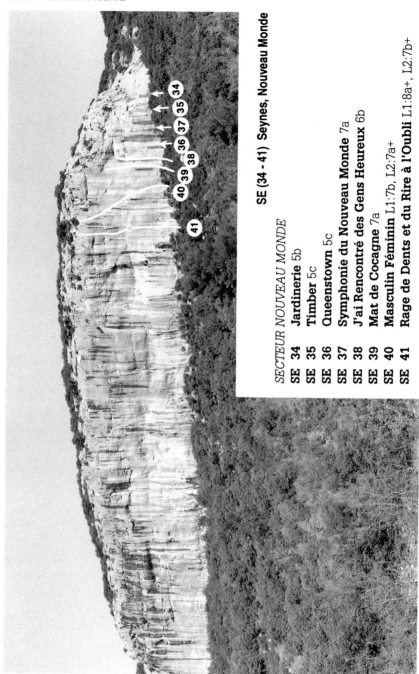

SE (34 - 41) Seynes, Nouveau Monde

SECTEUR NOUVEAU MONDE

SE	34	**Jardinerie** 5b
SE	35	**Timber** 5c
SE	36	**Queenstown** 5c
SE	37	**Symphonie du Nouveau Monde** 7a
SE	38	**J'ai Rencontré des Gens Heureux** 6b
SE	39	**Mat de Cocagne** 7a
SE	40	**Masculin Féminin** L1:7b, L2:7a+
SE	41	**Rage de Dents et du Rire à l'Oubli** L1:8a+, L2:7b+

HORTUS

Map Ref: *Michelin Motoring Atlas, page 156, C2.*

Area Maps: IGN 2742e, L=(3167.2, 719.8-720.9). MICH 80.17 and 83.7.

Guidebook: *Falaise de l'Hortus*, a topo guide.

Climate/Climbing Season: Precipitation (rain/snow) 900mm on 70 days of the year. Climbing possible all year round.

Restrictions: None

Rock and Protection: Limestone, blocky and loose in places although generally sound. Insitu protection variable from poor and old to reasonable on the more popular routes. In addition to quick draws carry a small rack of gear.

Situation: Some 20km N of Montpellier and 3km E of St Martin de Londres, Montagnes d'Hortus is opposite the Pic St Loup above the col de Fambétou. Département Hérault (No.34).

Access: The Autoroute du Soleil A7 is forsaken to travel W at Orange and the autoroute A9 followed passing Nîmes to Montpellier. From here drive N for 25km on the D986 to St Martin de Londres. Take the D122 E gradually rising up the small

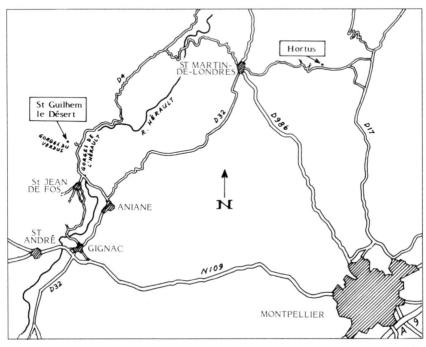

pass of the col de Fambétou between the mountain masses of Pic St Loup to the S and Montagne d'Hortus to the N. Just over the summit of the pass a forestry track leads off up to the L - signed Piste Forestière. Follow this until, with the cliffs just visible through the trees up to the L, a widening in the track provides parking space below the centralmost part of the cliff. A track leads directly up through the bushes and steep scree to the crag (15 minutes).

Camping etc: Camping at St Martin de Londres (April to September) or Montpellier. Water and limited supplies available at St Martin de Londres. There is a climbing shop in the Rue de Palais, Montpellier.

Crag Facts: This large cliff is split into two main buttresses by a tree-filled descent gully. The L-hand buttress is the largest and dominates the view from the forestry track car park. The most recognisable feature on the L-hand buttress being the large right-angled corner formed by a prominent square pillar (towards the R third of the buttress). This is the point of arrival at the crag and from here the path traverses beneath either to the R or the L. However, the lesser R-hand buttress is equally significant in climbing terms and is mainly comprised of the best and soundest rock. The crags face due S and are reasonably sheltered from the wind despite their prominent position; they are a noted winter climbing venue. Many of the older routes are poorly equipped with old gear and it is recommended that these are given a wide berth, but quite a few routes have now been re-bolted. There are some 60 routes to be found from 90m to 130m in length, varying in difficulty from 5b to 7a.

CRAG CHAT

Finding and negotiating the correct route out of Montpellier can be a nightmarish experience. It would be better to make a stop elsewhere for buying any necessary supplies. However, once in the mountain region beyond, a radically different environment unfolds.

At Hortus there is little sign of any human habitation at all. This is a pleasantly wild region with only wooded hillocks to break up the flat plains below. The sweetly scented air remains clean and pure and even in climbing terms this remains a relatively quiet area. Eagles circle the mountains here and falcons swoop from the rocks.

The crag is best viewed from some large boulders, which provide a break in the wooded slopes, a few minutes descent beneath the parking area. The sheer scale of the crag is impressive. Yet, possibly due to its south-facing aspect, it appears attractive rather than menacing. One of the most prominent lines rises from a cave at a point where the approach path meets the crag. The large dièdre above formed by a prominent pillar gives a long route of about E1 in standard. The rock looks alarming but is generally not too bad. Many of the better climbs will be found by walking a few hundred metres more to the R to the smaller but more solid R-hand

RIGHT BUTTRESS

LEFT BUTTRESS

HO (1 - 2) Hortus

HO (2) Hortus, R-hand Buttress

First pitch of Pilier de Gauche, La Bissone, Saint Guilhelm le Desert

Climber on La Fissure Gobbi (5c), L'Aiguille, Face Sud, Mortain

crag. A variety of climbs exist here from the long and steep to shorter slabby routes on its R end.

HIT LIST (From L to R)

LEFT BUTTRESS
HO 1   Central Dièdre 100m, L1:6b, L2:6b. Abseil descent necessary.

RIGHT BUTTRESS
HO 2   LA CAGNE 90m, L1:4b, L2:5c, L3:5b. SELECTED ROUTE (see below).

SELECTED ROUTE AT HORTUS: La Cagne (HO 2)

LA CAGNE: 90m, L1:4b, L2:5c, L3:5b. (British grading - Hard Very Severe, 3c, 4c/5a, 4c.)

Location: The R-hand buttress, Hortus.

First Ascent: Unknown

Route Facts: Start some 30m R of the large tree-filled gully beneath a diagonal line of corner cracks leading from bottom R to top L.
L1, 35m, 4b. Climb the corner chimney crack to reach a stance and two-bolt belay by a bush.
L2, 30m, 5c. Climb the very steep corner above to a stance by a jammed block. Insitu pegs and sling thread constitute the belay.
L3, 25m, 5b. Continue up the corner then move left. Climb straight up through the bulges and final overhang to belay on the terrace.

Descent: Scramble through the bushes for a little way then walk L along the terrace to the great chimney. Descend a little to an abseil point and then make one 45m abseil. Easy scrambling leads to the base of the chimney and the path.

ROUTE CHAT

Placed near the L edge of the R-hand buttress this diagonal corner ramp forms a line of weakness that cannot be missed. A deservedly popular classic. Even so, first acquaintance does not reveal the full extent of its character. Only by coming to grips with each of its three pitches does the true steepness and quality emerge.

There is some loose rock to be found, but in many ways this adds another dimension to the route. Handle it with care and all will be well. Insitu bolts, although generally good, are quite spaced in places, up to 10m apart. However, there is ample opportunity to place natural protection and many will wish to do so. To assess the overall difficulty of the route is not easy, it seems to hover somewhere between Very Severe and Hard Very Severe. I finally plumped for HVS because of the unexpected steepness and sustained nature of the climbing.

The first pitch has a hint of epic looseness about it, but this is mainly illusory. The concrete-like backfill in the chimney actually proves quite sound. For the first half of the pitch, which is not technically too difficult, insitu gear is best described as scrappy. Inexplicably, new bolts blossom somewhere around the half-way mark.

Above the stance the corner rears to almost overhanging proportions. Those with wide bridging capacity and a long reach will be best accommodated here. The persistent approach does pay for suitably large jugs arrive just when you most need them. A long, tiring, sustained pitch of excellent quality.

The next pitch although appearing even more impressive is easier. One which despite its overhanging nature, can be climbed in short sections, after which it is perfectly feasible to stand in balance and rest. Again the rock does look alarming in places and requires some care. Thankfully most of the genuinely loose material has long since been disposed of. Finally at the end of this steep and spectacular pitch a roof juts out horizontally above your head. To reach the terrace above you have to climb it. A fitting climax to a splendid route - fortunately the holds are enormous.

SAINT GUILHEM LE DÉSERT

Map Ref: *Michelin Motoring Atlas, page 156, A2.*

Area Maps: IGN 2643e, L=(3150.0-3150.5, 696.2-697.8). MICH 83.6.

Guidebook: *Falaises de St-Guilhem-le-Désert,* a topo guide by P.Pages and R.Pierre-Auguste.

Climate/Climbing Season: Precipitation (rain) 900mm on 70 days of the year. Climbing possible all year round.

Restrictions: None

Rock and Protection: Limestone of variable quality, many of the stratified cliffs hold ledges strewn with blocky debris, some bands (particularly the lower ones) are quite shattered, others are of good quality. On the most popular routes gear is insitu and of reasonable quality, a mixture of old pegs and newer bolts. In addition to quick draws and a few long slings carry a small selection of Rocks and Friends.

Situation: Some 45km W of Montpellier these cliffs take the form of a horseshoe gorge. Gorge du Verdus, emanating from the medieval village of Saint Guilhem le Désert. Département Hérault (No.34).

Access: Take the D109 from Montpellier and quit this in 30km to take the D32 through Gignac to Aniane. Continue on the D27 to the Pont du Diable (preserved old stone arch bridge) cross the River Hérault (new bridge) and turn N following the D4 above the river to reach the village of Saint Guilhem le Désert in a further 5km. Turn L in the village and pass the central village car park to find a smaller park at the end of the track. From here access into the gorge is made by crossing the stream to gain the track and following this past a football field to continue along the path by the stream (25 minutes to the head of the gorge).

Camping etc: Wild camping in the gorge or on the football pitch (out of season). Saint Guilhem is very tourist orientated and there are a number of cafés and restaurants. Water is available from the toilet block opposite the central car park or from the spring at the head of the gorge. Shops are small and limited.

Crag Facts: The cliffs here are huge and impressive and the village and surrounding area intriguing. The Achilles heel is unfortunately the often loose nature of the rock. Fortunately this does not prevail on all the climbs but one should be selective. Working in a clockwise manner around the cirque of cliffs the most distinguished areas are: La Bissonne with its twin pillar face standing sentinel-like at the mouth of the gorge (facing generally NE and N), the massive Lune en Bulle forming the southern flank (facing N), a cluster of many cliffs at the head of the gorge, Dièdre Infranchissable just right of the stream at the head of the gorge and the massive Falaise Sud forming the northern flank. Then come perhaps the three most popular cliffs, S-facing and solid, situated closest to the village - the slabby wall of Dalle Grise, and near the edge of the village beneath the ruined castle - Dièdre Gris and Le Château. Altogether there are some 70 routes from 40m to 200m in length and ranging from 3c to 7a.

CRAG CHAT

The jumble of tiny medieval tiny houses, narrow streets and the eleventh-century cathedral set in wild surroundings and looked over by a ruined castle - Le Château - make Saint Guilhem one of the showpiece attractions of this area of France. The village, hanging above the main valley and river of l'Hérault, whose waters teem with trout, guards the entrance to a remarkable natural gorge. Starting virtually above the village itself a great horseshoe of cliffs forms a virtually impenetrable natural barrier.

From the head of the gorge issues a spring of cool, crystal-clear water feeding terraces and vineyards, which once must have been of considerable economic value. Today this area is virtually neglected and extensively overgrown. Full of wild flowers and wildlife it is a delightful area in which to camp. Beware, however, of sampling the water below the spring - I was just putting my lips to the stream when I spotted a water snake immediately beneath the surface.

SELECTED ROUTE

GD (1) Saint Guilhem Le Désert, La Bissonne & L side of the gorge

The cirque of cliffs that form the gorge above Saint Guilhem le Désert is, outside the high Alps, as impressive as any in France. Amazingly underdeveloped when compared with the cliffs of the SE this can in part be explained by its generally loose nature. However, this should not put you off a visit for there is much worthy climbing to be had.

The lesser crags of Dalle Grise, Dièdre Gris and Le Château may not look as impressive as the rest but offer a variety of climbs from 20m to 40m in length. Mainly they are equipped with modern bolts and offer climbing in the modern sport idiom. They are quickly accessible and face S.

The larger faces present a much more serious proposition. There are a number of

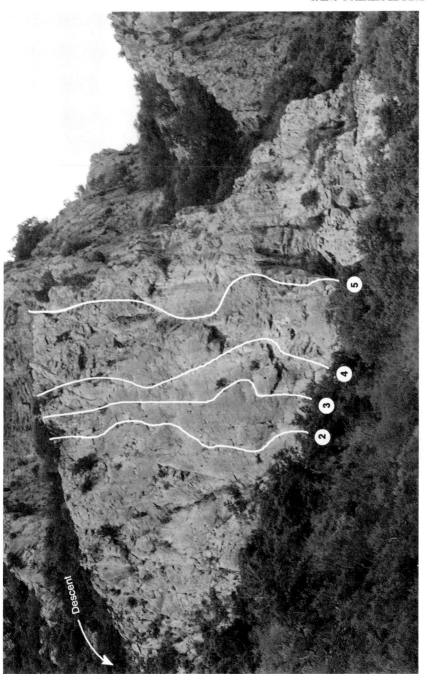

GD (2 - 5) Saint Guilhem Le Désert, Dalle Grise

DESCENT

ABSEIL
DESCENT

230

GD (6 - 13) Saint Guilhem Le Désert, Diedre Gris & Le Château

worthy routes but reliable information should be sought before launching off. On many routes retreat would be tricky, so find out both the state of the rock and the protection throughout the length of the route.

HIT LIST (From L to R)

LA BISSONNE

GD 1   PILIER DE GAUCHE 170m, L1:4b, L2:5b, L3:5c, L4:5c, L5:6a, L6:4b, L7:5a. SELECTED ROUTE (see below).

DALLE GRISE

GD 2   Voie Pericou 6a
GD 3   Karamel Sphitophage 6c
GD 4   Fissure à Satan 6b
GD 5   Un Dimance à la Campagne 6a

DIÈDRE GRIS AND LE CHÂTEAU

GD 6   La Rampe L1:3b, L2:4b
GD 7   Dièdre Nord L1:3b, L2:4b
GD 8   L'Y L1:4b, L2:4c
GD 9   Le Dièdre Gris L1:4b
GD 10   Spit Prélude 6c
GD 11   Le Paroi Jaune 6b
GD 12   Le Pezouillet 6b
GD 13   Fissure du Château L1:3b, L2:3b, L3:5b

SELECTED CLIMB AT SAINT GUILHEM LE DÉSERT: Pilier de Gauche (GD 1)

PILIER DE GAUCHE: 170m, L1:4b, L2:5b, L3:5c, L4:5c, L5:6a, L6:4b, L7:5a. (British grading - E1/E2, 3c, 4c, 5a, 5a, 5b, 3c, 4b.)

Location: NE face of La Bissonne.

First Ascent: D.Marcais, Y.Gilles, circa 1950s.

Access: From the car park take the track into the gorge. In a little way, at the end of a small field and prior to reaching the football field, take a path bearing L along by the wire fence. Continue on the well defined path (shortcuts not advised) which zigzags steeply up the hillside until it levels off to traverse directly beneath the foot of the buttress (30 minutes).

Route Facts: Start beneath the obvious crescent beneath the overhangs some

30m L of the lowest point of the buttress. The rock is rather loose for the first two pitches.

L1, 25m, 4b. Climb the wall to a large block-strewn ledge. Follow the curving line beneath the overhangs R to a 3-bolt belay.

L2, 25m, 5b. Move right and step down to a bolt on the edge. From this move right slightly then climb straight up the wall finding the occasional bolt runner. Reach a ledge and belay - 2 bolts and 2 pegs.

L3, 35m, 5c. The rock improves from now on. Leave the ledge and climb up diagonally L across the wall (bolt runners) to gain a ledge and stance below the corner (3 insitu pegs and possible stance). Move left into the groove up the front face of the pillar. Climb this which steepens and forms a narrowing groove ramp. Finally climb its R edge to gain a large horizontal ledge and 2-bolt belay.

L4, 25m, 5c. Step L (L again of a bolt which has been misplaced) and pull onto the wall. Move up into the corner (bolt on R wall) and continue to the roof. Move R onto the arête, keep traversing R beneath the overhang then move up and back L to gain a ledge. Bolt belay.

L5, 25m, 6a. Crux. Move up diagonally left through very steep ground. Continue in the same line to peg runners and continue, still steeply, to a ledge. One bolt, 2-peg belay.

L6, 20m, 4b. Step R onto the shattered pillar and keep traversing R (bolt runner). Climb more directly past a further bolt to continue diagonally R to a ledge and stance. Two bushes and 2-bolt belay.

L7, 15m, 5a. From the bush step R and climb the cleft (bolt runner) then continue easily to the top.

Descent: This is easy. Follow the track L then down to meet the horizontal section of the approach path.

ROUTE CHAT

The great sentinel of rock known as La Bissonne, some 150m high and incredibly steep, provides the most aesthetic single buttress in the whole cirque. Its NE face forms a bold and striking nose, which is split by a deep groove from mid-height upwards, effectively forming two huge hanging pillars. Beautifully coloured by the morning light the obvious challenge, rising from dark shadows cast by the banded overhangs, is the majestic Pilier Gauche.

Its first ascent, a remarkable lead for the 1950s and doubly so considering the sparsity of cracks for peg protection, was solved by the ingenious and bold route described here. It gives a long and absorbing climb of sustained interest. The crux pitch is placed very near the top of the pillar and this coupled with its length and continual exposure provides a real "big route" feel.

Today chiefly protected by a mixture of modern bolts and older pegs, the route lies somewhere between the adventure and sport climbing categories. There is little opportunity to place natural gear and in places, particularly on the crux pitch, the climbing feels distinctly runout. These factors coupled with obvious difficulties of making an abseil retreat, make it a serious proposition.

Try not to be put off by the first ledge which is littered with blocky debris fallen from the overhangs above. Take care too not to snag any loose blocks with the rope. Test the holds and treat the rock with respect and grit your teeth until the end of the second pitch. From thereon the rock is much better and the climbing infinitely more enjoyable.

LE CAROUX, GORGE D'HÉRIC

Map Ref: *Michelin Motoring Atlas, page 155, E3.*

Area Maps: IGN 2543w, L=(3142.0-3144.0, 649.4-651.0). MICH 83.4.

Guidebook: *Escalades au Caroux* by G.Pistre, a CAF guide. A useful map *Caroux Rochers d'Escalades* is also published by the CAF. *Le Topo du Massif du Caroux* by Pascal Cendon.

Climate/Climbing Season: Precipitation (rain/snow) 800mm-1,100mm on 90 days of the year. The area is most popular from April to October inclusive.

Restrictions: None, although wild camping is not encouraged.

Rock and Protection: Gneiss of excellent quality (comparable to Glen Nevis in Scotland). Generally regular protection pegs are in place, these are usually good although a small rack of gear is recommended. There are only a handful of modern sport climbs with bolts.

Situation: Some 70km W of

Montpellier, 20km W of Bédarieux and just N of d'Olargues, this deep gorge cuts into the upland region of Le Caroux effectively forming its SW terminus. Département Hérault (No.34).

Access: The autoroute A9 can be quit at Béziers and the D909 followed N towards Bédarieux. Turn L to join the D908 before Bédarieux (D909A) to join the D908 and proceed W through Lamalou and St Martin to turn off at the small village of Mons. Continue through the village to find a car park at the base of the Gorges d'Héric (a small fee is charged). A surfaced track (cars prohibited) leads from here rising all the way up the gorge to the tiny hamlet of Héric in 4km, now deserted apart from café and *gîte* (allow 1 hour). The numerous crags lie on either side of this track and the approach time from the track can vary from a few seconds to hours for cliffs high on the hillside.

Camping etc: There is camping at Olargues and limited shops here and at Lamalou. The car park at the base of the gorge has a snacks café, and bivouacking appears to be allowed.

Crag Facts: Logically singling out the deep cut and impressive Les Gorges d'Héric from the rest of the Massif du Caroux still leaves an extensive area with many separate crags. Therefore only the low-lying crags on either side of the gorge will be detailed. They are selected for their ease of access, simplicity of identification and climbing variety. The first buttress reached on the track up the gorge (about 10 minutes from the car park) lies on the R-hand side (looking up the gorge) - Beylot Ferrand. Concrete steps lead from the track down to a small concrete footbridge spanning the river - the Pont des Soupiers - and just above this is the crag. Note that a constructed footpath leads from the bridge under the crag and zigzags up the hillside through the trees to access some of the higher crags. Some 100m along the track the distinctively topped Tête de Braque can be seen up to the L. The foot of this is reached in about 10 minutes from the track. Descent from its summit is effected by the chimney-gully to its R. Although this can be done solo it is probably best to make a short abseil down the upper section. Continuing up the gorge, just before the track crosses the river at the first bridge, Le Rocher Marre can be seen with its toe in the stream bed on the R (reached in about 15 minutes from the car park). Immediately before and above the second bridge, Georges Vergues stands on the R. This consists of two walls one above the other, the higher wall which provides traditional climbing can be reached easily by walking in from the R. The clean lower wall has recently been bolted and is an attractive proposition for those who prefer sport climbing. In the Gorge d'Héric there are a few harder sports climbs but much of the climbing lies in the adventure category. The route names are generally written on the rock at the start of the climbs. There are around 25 separate crags accessible from the gorge and some 200 routes from 25m to 150m in length, ranging from 3b to 7b in difficulty.

CRAG CHAT

Rising in an area of France noted for its great beauty and quiet charm, the upland shoulder of Le Caroux stretches for 4km at an altitude of over 1,000 metres. A huge volcanic shoulder of a mountain, holding a myriad of crags and buttresses that together form Haut Languedoc's climbing centrepiece. The dark attractive rock here is gneiss, it casts a powerful spell over the landscape making it refreshingly different from that associated with the more frequent limestone. Deciduous trees line the road and softening the hills with their graceful canopy.

The mountain massif is brought to an abrupt end in the SW by the intriguing Gorge d'Héric. This tree-filled valley with frequent crags outcropping on both flanks, has a character strongly resembling Borrowdale in the English Lake District.

I walked its length to the hamlet of d'Héric one fine October day. The autumnal colours of red and gold, the falling leaves and the harvest of sweet chestnuts, falling for all to enjoy, provided a subtlety to the landscape I realised I had missed since I had left my Lakeland home some time ago. Arriving at the dark, neatly constructed, dry stone walls of the upland hamlet I had to blink twice to realise that this was not Watendlath or Wasdale Head but d'Héric. Sadly all now seems deserted, the pastures empty, the mountain folk gone. Only a part-time café operates during the summer months - pleasant enough but no substitute for a working community.

In the Gorge d'Héric crags abound. They range in accessibility from the roadside attractions of Beylot Ferrand, above the Pont des Soupiers, Le Rocher Marre and Georges Vergues rising 100m in height, to the more distant rock faces. Even higher above are the tall Alpine-looking faces and ridges collectively known as Les Aiguilles. Further along the track, up to the R, the attractive crags of yet another massive area can be observed. This is Le Cirque de Farrières; the first dominant buttress (L - side of the cirque) is Le Pouce and below this stands the unmistakably fine swallow tailed pinnacle of Roc des Hirondelles. Both mark the start of this extensive area and are reached in about 40 minutes from the track. Many crags and much climbing all in a serene setting of considerably beauty.

CX (1 - 9) Le Caroux, Gorge D'Héric, Beylot Ferrand

HIT LIST

BEYLOT FERRAND (From R to L)

CX 1   **Voie des Toits** 5c
CX 2   **ZZ Stop** 6c+
CX 3   **Flip Matinal** 6b
CX 4   **Voie de la Niche** 5c
CX 5   **Tendre Baiser** 6b/c
CX 6   **Cabou Vilain** 6b
CX 7   **Le Tendon Gaston** 6c
CX 8   **Bas le Pet** 6a
CX 9   **Début Sans Fin** 5a

CX (10 - 13) Le Caroux, Gorge D'Héric, Tête de Braque

TÊTE DE BRAQUE

CX 10   **Pilier Rouge** 70m, L1:5b, L2:6b, L3:4b
CX 11   **Voie de l'Horlagger** 100m, L1:5b, L2:5a
CX 12   **La Directe** 100m, L1:4b, L2:5b
CX 13   **Voie Normale** 150m, 4b. The quality trade route up the R edge of the
             buttress.

DESCENT PATH TO
PONT DES SOUPIERS →

CIOCH BLOCK

SELECTED ROUTE

GORGE TRACK

(above): **CX (14, L4) Le Caroux, Gorge D'Héric, 'Le Rocher Marre' - climber moving R on the Cioch-like block**

(left) : **CX (14) Le Caroux, Gorge D'Héric, Le Rocher Marre**

ACCESS TO
UPPER TIER

LE ROCHER MARRE

CX 14   **LE ROCHER MARRE** 100m, L1:3b, L2:3b, L3:3c, L4:4b, L5:3c.
SELECTED ROUTE (see below).

GEORGES VERGUES

CX 15   **La Classique** 50m, L1:4b, L2:4b, L3:4b, L4:4b

CX 16   **Normale** 50m, L1:5b, L2:5a

CX 17   **Joe Dalton** 20m, 6b

CX 18   **Sherpa** 20m, 7a

CX 19   **La Dièdre** 90m, L1:5c, L2:5b

CX 20   **Voie Directe** 50m, 6a

CX 21   **Super Directe** 50m, 6a+

CX 22   **La Fissure** 50m, 5c

SELECTED CLIMB AT GORGE D'HÉRIC: Le Rocher Marre (CX 14)

LE ROCHER MARRE: 100m, L1:3b, L2:3b, L3:3c, L4:4b, L5:3c. (British grading - Very difficult, 2c, 2c, 3a, 3c, 3a.)

Location: Front face of Le Rocher Marre (route and crag name one and the same), the E side of Gorge d'Héric.

First Ascent: Unknown.

Access: From the car park pass beyond the café to take the surfaced track leading up the gorge (passing the locked barrier preventing vehicular access). The track drops down into the gorge to follow on just above the river (note at this point a few concrete steps lead down to a concrete bridge known as the Pond des Soupiers - this is written in the concrete deck). Continue along the track until just before the first bridge. Taking the track across the river a path leads across the rocks of Le Rocher Marre, rising straight from the bed of the stream (15 minutes).

Route Facts: From the stream bed scramble up the first easy rocks to a ledge below a prominent V-groove.

L1, 30m, 3b. Climb the V-groove to a white overhanging barrier. Move over this and up to a stance.

L2, 30m, 3b. Follow a short blocky chimney, then take a ramp and groove leading L up the rocks above. Keep L beneath the overhanging prow and gain a stance below a short wall and above the tree-filled gully.

CX (15 - 22) Le Caroux, Gorge D'Héric, Georges Vergues

L3, 10m, 3c. Climb the steep wall above on good holds with excellent insitu peg protection in the cracks. Walk across the ledge until below the large (Cioch-like) obelisk.

L4, 15m, 4b. Gain the V-notch in the face of the obelisk which is gained by an awkward and strenuous pull. Climb to the roof and make some exposed moves out R. Climb the red wall on the side of the obelisk to its top. Ledge and tree belay.

L5, 15m, 3c. Move up from the belay to step from a block and climb the little wall above to a ledge.

Easy scrambling now leads in about 100m towards the summit of the rock. Just before this is reached a path moves L and over a shoulder to descend (perhaps 10m) to a constructed path passing behind the summit block. The crag now visible just up to the L is very popular and forms a logical extension to the climbing day.

Descent: Follow the path down to the R (facing uphill). It zigzags down through the woods to cross the stream by the Pont des Soupiers and gain the surfaced track.

ROUTE CHAT

I first spotted this route when climbing Le Pilier Rouge on the Tête de Braque on the opposite side of the gorge. I had mistakenly identified the grade of Le Pilier as British Severe and persuaded Dave Birkett to rise from his sick bed (he was recovering from a severe throat infection) to have a go. Actually the real grade turned out to be British E2/3 5c and making moves above a band of overhangs with a single 9mm rope stretching away horizontally, whilst carrying rucksack and full camera gear did little to endear me to the topo guide that had duped me onto the route.

Despite the unfolding epic, I did manage to observe the attractive and obviously popular Le Rocher Marre on the opposite side of the valley.

Arriving at the summit of the Tête de Braque buttress I pointed out Le Rocher Marre to Dave and despite his illness he agreed to make an ascent. It proved a perfect climb to unwind in the evening sunshine. An entertaining outing of impeccable character.

The route equates remarkably with the exposed character of Little Chamonix on Shepherds' Crag in Borrowdale though Le Rocher Marre is much longer and the actual physical composition of the climbing quite different. The gneiss is sound throughout and offers a plentiful supply of positive holds and protection. Numerous white veins of quartz run through it and combine in the sunshine with the crystals of mica to flash like diamonds. However, should it rain, the general angle of the face still makes it a climbable proposition. This despite the varying friction as its skin alternates from dry prune-wrinkled to face-lift smooth.

A distinctive series of grooves lead to an upper wall, with an airy position high above a tree-filled side gully. The wall, although obviously short, looks tough from

242

below. Unbelievably, a ladder of jugs take you up it to the foot of the main feature of the climb: a great obelisk of rock resembling the Cioch on Sron na Ciche in the Black Cuillin of Skye. This gives remarkable climbing which, before you set off on it, again looks way beyond its actual grade. A long route, constantly interesting and full of pleasant surprises.

VINGRAU

Map Ref: *Michelin Motoring Atlas, page 177, E2.*

Area Maps: IGN 2447e, L=(3061.6-3064.0, 637.5). MICH 86.9.

Guidebook: *Escalades Sur Les Falaises Des Vingrau* by Jean Gaillarde.

Climate/Climbing Season: Precipitation (rain/snow) 500mm on 60 days of the year, maximum in October and March. The crag faces W and is considered to be a reliable winter climbing venue although it can be windy. During summer there is little or no shade and it can be very hot in the afternoon.

Restrictions: Whilst wild camping may be possible thieving is an acute problem here. Any money left in your vehicle stands to be stolen.

Rock & Protection: The hard grey limestone is of excellent quality and tends to be very rough. With sharp-edged pockets and flakes in abundance the climbing can be a finger painful

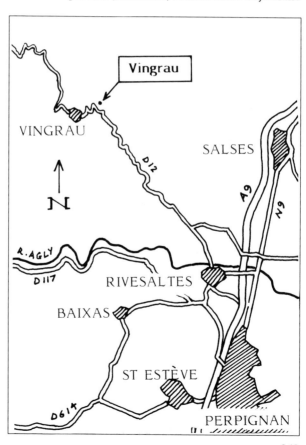

CAR PARK

LES TETES
REDUITES

LES PLAISIRS
DEMODES

L'INDIEN

PILIER DES
ANABOLISANTS

ECOLE
D'ARTIF

PETITE
ECOLE

V-D-P

NIRVANA
CHROME

ANGEL-HYPNOSE

JARDIN DES TROPIQUES

PARTIE DU PARKING

DORYP

VN Vingrau, looking along the length of the crag

experience. The southern half of the escarpment detailed here is mainly (but not entirely) bolt-protected and sport climbing is the order of the day. Further N, as the crags increase in height, towards and beyond the classic face of Petit Dru, many of the routes remain adventure climbs and a selection of nuts should be carried.

Situation: The most southerly of France's Mediterranean crags, some 20km NNW of Perpignan and 2km NE of the village of Vingrau. Département Pyrénees-Orientales (No.66).

Access: Heading S on the A9 leave the motorway at the Rivesaltes junction. It is probably easiest to drive through Rivesaltes (it can be bypassed utilising the D12, but this is poorly signed). Following the signs for Rivesaltes, immediately join the N9 and keep S for 1km before turning off to Rivesaltes, reached in a further 3.5km. Leave it N following the D12 towards Tuchan (Vingrau is reached before Tuchan but wasn't signed at the time of writing). The road rises to a col, the Pas

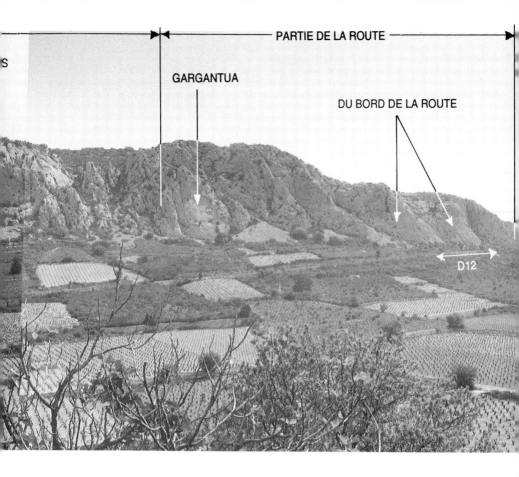

de L'Escale, before beginning to fall to Vingrau. In a short distance the road passes directly below the end of the band of crags up to the R. Park on the verge here for the crags directly above - the road must not be restricted and parking may not be possible because of other vehicles (upwards of 15 seconds to reach the crags) - or at a small car park where the road does a hairpin bend some few hundred metres beyond (15 minutes to Pilier des Anabolisants from there).

Camping etc: A number of *gîtes* can be found in the village but the nearest campsite would appear to be at Estagel some 15km to the SW. Supplies available in Vingrau along with a café and restaurant.

Crag Facts: First appearances from the road are deceptive. The crag looks quite minor in nature for it isn't easy to view beyond the slabs and lesser buttresses forming this, the southern and lowest end. In fact this long escarpment, the precipitous W face of La Serre, stretches for over 1km. Only the S half of the crag will be detailed here. These mainly sport climbs are all reached within 20 minutes from either the road or the car park. From R to L (S to N), the most southerly end of the chain - those crags strung out directly above the road - is known as Partie de la Route. It consists of Secteur Sous la Route, Secteur du Bord de la Route, Gargantua. The next section, above and R of the car park, is known as Partie du Parking and comprises six *secteurs:* Doryphores, Jardin des Tropiques, Angel-Hypnose, Nirvanachrome, V-D-P, and Petite École. Above the car park are five more *secteurs* offering excellent climbing: École d'Artif, Pilier des Anabolisants, L'Indien, Les Plaisirs Démodés, Les Têtes Réduites. Detailed description of the extensive crags stretching N from here is beyond the scope of this book. However, proceeding N along the path from the car park a climbing refuge will be found - perched on the col - and above it towers the great classic buttress of Petit Dru. Nuts are required here and multi-pitch routes reach 120m in length, with many routes between 4a and 6a in standard. Taking the escarpment as a whole there are some 150 routes, 20m to 120m in length, ranging in difficulty between 3b and 8a. There is a wide spread of interest throughout the grades and enough here for several days.

CRAG CHAT

Although located in the hills some distance from the coast, this crag's southerly location means plenty of sunshine. The slabs and walls of Partie de la Route are the most popular in the evening when the locals arrive to park their cars in the verge immediately below the climbs. From slabs to cracks, it is a most pleasant location in which to climb.

Accessible from the car park the V-shaped face of V-D-P (Voie des Parisiens) is the most continuous of the area with some dozen routes varying in difficulty between 5c and 7b. The more traditional routes here are some 80m high and up to three pitches in length: they require nuts for protection. Over to the L the stubby but grossly overhanging pillar of École d'Artif provides the hardest, finger-wrecking, climbs of the area with two 8as and a 7b/c.

Immediately to its L the clean ivory tower of Pilier des Anabolisants is one of the most enjoyable buttresses of the region. Some nine routes range in difficulty from 5c to 7a. Don't be tempted to pass the abseil chain after one pitch, for above it the climbing is not of the same quality - pegs of dubious worth offer protection. The classic route, L'Emmental 5c (British Hard Very Severe 5a), takes the right side of the pillar. Appropriately named after a Swiss cheese, the extensively pocketed rock is a pure delight to climb, its rough nature defying all attempts to polish it.

Placed as the last stop before Spain, near the Mediterranean end of Pyrenees, this rugged escarpment, the W face of La Serre, is undeniably a charming area of considerable character. Unfortunately my experiences at Vingrau were rather soured by a break-in to the camper-van parked in the car park, immediately below Pilier des Anabolisants. This was from a vehicle in sight throughout the climbing day - so be warned.

VN (1 - 7) Vingrau, Partie de la Route, Secteur du Bord de la Route

VN (8 - 17) Vingrau, Patrie de la Route, Secteur du Bord de la Route (L-side)

VN (GARG) Vingrau, Partie de la Route, Gargantua, Pitches and grades as indicated - routes unnamed on this buttress

VN (18 - 43) Vingrau, Partie du Parking, Dalle Dess Doryphores, Le Jardin des Tropiques, Angel-Hypnose, Nirvanachrome, V-D-P, Petite École

HIT LIST (From R to L)

BORD DE LA ROUTE (Routes reach 40m in length)

VN	1	Mes Couilles le Temps se Brouille 6b				
VN	2	Insomniaque 6b				
VN	3	La Cague Mouille 6a				
VN	4	Supercramps 6c				
VN	5	Noctambule 5c				
VN	6	La Voie des Cerdans 5c				
VN	7	Amicalement Votre 6a+				
VN	8	La Galette 5b				
VN	9	Balade Pour une Petite Mort 6b				
VN	10	Bouducon le Pied-Main 6b				
VN	11	Petit Navire 6b+				
VN	12	Vidéoscop 6b				
VN	13	Diable en Boite 6a+				
VN	14	La Fissure 6a	VN	16	Les Tetons 6a	
VN	15	Les Nénés 6b+	VN	17	Désirée 7a	

GARGANTUA

There are a number of worthwhile unnamed routes on this cliff, their line and grading have been marked directly onto the photograph - VN (GARG). Those climbing to the first ledge are around 10m in length, those starting from the ledge (reached by scrambling from the L) are up to 50m in length.

DORYPHORES (Routes up to 50m - rock superb)

VN 18   **No Name** 4b
VN 19   **Éstivanodrome** 6b
VN 20   **Tronche de Crise** 6a
VN 21   **Oh Blond!** 6b
VN 22   **Les Doryphores** 5c
VN 23   **Grassette Insecticide** 5c
VN 24   **Pény Céline** 6b
VN 25   **T'as le Sang pour les Caves** 6c

LE JARDIN DES TROPIQUES

VN 26   **Milan-Pécheur** 6c+
VN 27   **La Buche** 7a
VN 28   **No Name** 6b
VN 29   **Le Fil à la Patte** 5b
VN 30   **Appollon Sous les Tropiques** 6c

VN (44 - 56) Vingrau, École D'Artif, Pilier des Anabolisants, L'Indien, Les Plaisirs Démodés, Les Têtes Reduites

ANGEL-HYPNOSE
VN 31 **Bétadia** L1:5b, L2:4c
VN 32 **Angel-Hypnose** L1:6b, L2:6c
VN 33 **Diadème** 4c
VN 34 **Cheiroptère** L1:6b, L2:4c

NIRVANACHROME (A steep pillar of tremendous rock giving routes of some 40m)
VN 35 **Nirvanachrome** 6b
VN 36 **SOS** 6c
VN 37 **Fredastouille** 6c+

V-D-P (Voie-des-Parisiens, a classic face with routes up to 3 pitches.)
VN 38 **Sacré Coup de Martea** L1:7b, L2:7a
VN 39 **VDZ** L1:5b, L2:6b, L3:6a
VN 40 **VDP** L1:5b, L2:6a, L3:6c
VN 41 **Sysiphe** L1:6a, L2:6a, L3:5c +AO
VN 42 **Grand Duc and Voie Cola** L1:6c+, L2:6b

PETITE ÉCOLE
There are a number of unnamed pitches on this little slabby wall. Positioned either side of the route indicated they vary in difficulty from 3b to 6b.

VN 43   **No Name** 5c

ÉCOLE D'ARTIF
VN 44   **En Moulinette** 8a
VN 45   **Soupir pour Mieux Dormir** 8a
VN 46   **L'Infini à la Portée des Caniches** 7c

PILIER DES ANABOLISANTS
(One of the best bits)
VN 47   **L'Emmental** 5c
VN 48   **Thé Rosé** 6b
VN 49   **Les Anabolisants** 6b
VN 50   **Canderelle** 6c
VN 51   **Chronos** 7a
VN 52   **Dianabole** 6a+

INDIEN (Routes on the lower wall reach 30m, those above the first ledge up to 50m)
VN 53   **Rèves Psychédeliques** 6b+
VN 54   **Bison Futé** 6a
VN 55   **L'Indien** L1:5b, L2:4a, L3:5c
VN 56   **Giovani** 5b

LES PLAISIRS DÉMODÉS
VN 57   **La Déportation** L1:5c, L2:5c
VN 58   **La Mirandalle** 6c

LES TÊTES REDUITES
The unnamed routes on this wall reach 30m, pitch direction and grade have been indicated on the photograph.

VN (47) Vingrau, Pilier des Anabolisants, climber on 'L'Emmental' (5c)

PÈNE HAUTE

Map Ref: *Michelin Motoring Atlas, page 169, D3.*

Area Maps: IGN 1847w, L=(3080.3, 443). MICH 85.19.

Guidebook: *Fuges Verticales*

Climate/Climbing Season: Precipitation (rain/snow) 1,000mm-1,300mm on 120 to 130 days of the year. Climbing extends from April to November.

Restrictions: None

Rock and Protection: Immaculate pocketed limestone, fully bolted. Only quick draws need be carried.

Situation: On the edge of the Pyrenees roughly half-way between the Mediterranean and the Atlantic, 14km S of Lannemezan and 5km NE of Sarrancolin. Département Hautes-Pyrénées (No.65).

Access: Leave the D929 at Sarrancolin to wind along tight narrow streets (through the village on the E of the main road) turning L (N) to find a small surfaced track rising very steeply out of the village up the hillside. This zigzags up for a seemingly endless distance eventually entering pine woods and deteriorating to an unsurfaced forestry track. Follow the signs for Col d'Estivère, a level meadow area marks the summit of the track, which is reached in 8km from Sarrancolin. Ample parking either side of the track. The main crag faces due S and is reached by following the path (N) of the track which bears L diagonally up the hillside to enter woods and first traverse L then rise directly to the crag (15 minutes).

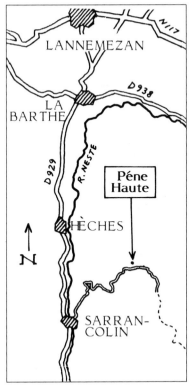

Camping etc: Wild camping in the pleasant meadows is permissible (but should be done on the edge of the wood on the S of the track and in such a way as to minimise loss of grazing - a precious commodity at this altitude).

Crag Facts: This magnificent wall drops from the summit plateau of Pène Haute providing pure sport climbing. The main wall covered here faces due S and despite the altitude (some 1,450m) it is generally too hot to climb here between 0900 and 1500 hours in the summer months. Round the nose to the R the E face (not detailed) offers respite from the sun and a further selection of routes. Access is usually blocked by snow from December to March for the Col d'Estivère lies at an altitude of 1,217m. The long, straight face changes character, and slight direction, roughly in its centre. The crag is exceptionally steep but the L half does offer some easier climbs and is slightly more broken. The R half varies from vertical/slightly impending to impressively overhanging. Presently there are some 60 routes from 50m to 100m in length and varying in difficulty from 5a to 8b. Names of the existing routes are written on the rock at the base of the climb. Massive scope for hard development remains.

CRAG CHAT

The long approach drive from the floor of the valley may seem tedious at the time but perseverance is handsomely rewarded. No rock climber could be disappointed with this extraordinarily fine crag. The rock is superb, clean, hard and flaky, frequently pocketed with *gouttes d'eau*; it compares with the best in France. All the routes are steep or overhanging and well equipped. This and the short approach slot it firmly in the sport climbing category.

A sport climbing crag placed high in superlative mountain scenery. In the meadows surrounding the col a shepherd watched over his sheep and the jingling of their bells could be heard high on the face. Alpine gentians carpet the ground by the path. Beech woods stand beneath the crag, pine forests stretch beyond and snow-capped mountains fill the horizon.

Although most of the climbs here are in the upper spectrum of difficulty there are a number of easier routes and the crag is a popular venue with local climbers. Lizards may run up and down the bottom section of the wall with consummate ease but the R half of the crag especially is extremely difficult. At roughly the half-way stage the crag changes nature slightly and its L half offers a number of easier climbs within the 5a to 6a bracket. Although invariably all the routes are steeper than they actually look when viewing head on, hidden pockets and flake holds turn up with reassuring frequency. Whatever your standard this crag should be a must for those looking to experience the full flavour of French rock climbing.

HIT LIST (From L to R)

PT	1	**Vive la Mariée** 15m, 5b
PT	2	**Beep Beep** 15m, 6a
PT	3	**Es Bouarat** 20m, 6b
PT	4	**Goûte à Tout** 25m, L1:6b, L2:6a
PT	5	**M'Enfin** 15m, 6c
PT	6	**Chico** 15m, 6a
PT	7	**Petit Clic ou Grande Claque** 20m, 7b

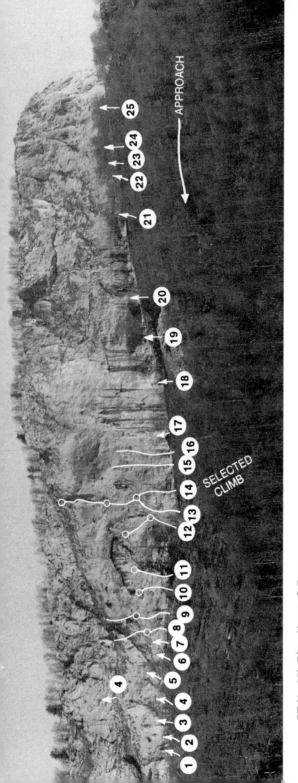

APPROACH

PT (1 - 25) Pène Haute, S Face

PT	8	**L'Amie Dalle** 45m, L1:6b, L2:6c
PT	9	**Vide Ordure** 45m, L1:6a, L2:6c
PT	10	**Charlotte aux Pommes** 30m, 6c+
PT	11	**Vos Gueules les Moulinettes** 20m, 7b
PT	12	**Les Mickeys** 40m, L1:4c, L2:5c
PT	13	**Les Charlots** 25m, 6a+
PT	14	**DANSE DU SANGLIER** 60m, L1:6c, L2:6c, L3:6b/c.
		SELECTED ROUTE (see p. 259).
PT	15	**Café con Lèche** 30m, 7b

PT	16	**Combat de Rue** 20m, 7c
PT	17	**Mamie à Tope** 20m, 7c+
PT	18	**Vol du Sphynx** 25m, 7c
PT	19	**Homard Galactique** 20m, 8b
PT	20	**Yi-King** 20m, 8a/b
PT	21	**Hang Ten** 25m, 7a/b
PT	22	**Tac Tic** 15m, 6b
PT	23	**Chic Choc** 25m, 6a
PT	24	**Fil à Surplomb** 20m, 6a/b
PT	25	**Vas-Y Toi** 20m, 7b/c

PT (14) Pène Haute, climbers on the 2nd pitch of 'Danse du Sanglier' (6c)

SELECTED CLIMB AT PÈNE HAUTE: Danse du Sanglier (PT 14)

DANSE DU SANGLIER: 60m, L1:6c, L2:6c, L3:6b/c. (British grading - E3, 6a, 6a, 6a.)

Location: Just left of centre, S face of Pène Haute.

First Ascent: Unknown

Route Facts: About 30m L of the point at which the approach path joins the crag the wall turns slightly and eases in angle. Start on the L side of a small shallow cave-like alcove. The name is written on rock and there is an obvious line of bolts.

L1, 25m, 6c. Climb up the initial wall then steeply through the bulge to reach the upper wall. Continue up this (crescent-shaped overlap to the L) until it impends and becomes riddled with *gouttes d'eau*. Climb with sustained difficulty until it is possible to pull onto the easier angled wall above and make a final couple of strenuous reaches to gain the belay ledge (insitu bolts and chain).

L2, 20m, 6c. Continue up pocketed wall following the line of bolts which starts easily and gradually increased in difficulty.

L3, 15m, 6b/c. This leads on to the diagonal weakness.

Descent: Abseil

ROUTE CHAT

This route virtually defines the L edge of the overhanging R half of the cliff. Just to its left the rock becomes slabbier and a number of popular easier routes (mainly one-pitch and beginning at a British technical grade of 4c) emanate from here. A remarkable climb, it owes its existence, as do the majority of sports climbs, to the scattering of *gouttes d'eau* which provide the means to climb an otherwise blank wall. There is no striking natural weakness, but identification is easy enough as it is marked by a recess at ground level.

It starts steeply and strenuously on big holds. This soon changes to delicacy, in turn relenting to strenuous finger climbing up a gently overhanging steep and heavily pocketed section. This is the crux. A crux which lasts to the belay stance some 5m above. The reach for the last large flake at the stance is both extremely strenuous and long.

I noted in my diary "Perhaps the finest pitch I've led in France." It seemed that good at the time. In the unbearably hot afternoon sun most climbers abseil off from here but a further two pitches of sustained difficulty and excellent climbing complete this vertical dance.

PT (13) Pène Haute, 'Les Charlots' (6a+)

CÉOU

Map Ref: *Michelin Motoring Atlas, page 124, A4.*

Area Maps: IGN 2037w. MICH 75.17.

Guidebook: *Escalades au Céou*, a topo guide by Francis Thibaudeau.

Climate/Climbing Season: Precipitation (rain/snow) 800mm on 115 days of the year. Climbing usual between April and November inclusive.

Restrictions: None

Rock and Protection: Rough pocketed limestone, completely bolted, only quick draws need be carried.

Situation: Just S of the River Dordogne 15km SW of Sarlat la Canéda and 60km E of Bergerac, 2km SE of Castlenaud in the small subsidiary valley of Céou. Département Dordogne (No.24).

Access: From Sarlat la Canéda proceed SW along the D57 to cross the Dordogne by a magnificent stone arched bridge and enter the tiny village of Castlenaud. Continue along the D57 until a small but surfaced road turns off L to cross the small river of Céou and proceed along it to a campsite. This is situated directly beneath the crag which lies on the hillside to the E. If staying at the campsite (highly recommended) a path proceeds through the farm building and field on the opposite side of the road to the camping field and up through the woods. First it bears diagonally L until (junction with alternative approach) it climbs more directly to arrive at the foot of the crag underneath the "Bastion" W face. If not staying at the campsite a lane leading L off the road (some 250 metres before campsite) provides parking in the verge (take care not to block tractor-access to fields). Walk up the track to gain the wood then follow the path diagonally R. This joins the previous approach as indicated (both approaches 15 minutes).

Camping etc: There is an excellent campsite directly below the crag. Limited supplies available at Castlenaud.

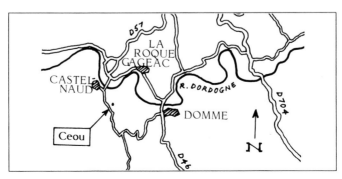

Crag Facts: Set in a line above the wooded hillside forming the E side of the subsidiary valley formed by the River Céou which feeds the Dordogne. The rock and nature of climbing here closely resembles that of Buoux in Provence. Generally the rocks face W. A few buttresses lie to the L from the point where the path arrives at the crag though most are situated to the R. The latter constitutes the main area and the sections are named here from L to R starting at the point of arrival: Bastion Face Ouest, Bastion Dalles Sud-Ouest, Falaise des Corbeaux, Grande Falaise, Mur Gris, La Cathédrale, Petit Fronton, Le Ventre, Grand Fronton, Fronton Sud and finally the small but grossly overhanging barrel-shaped buttress on the far R end, the Falaise du Conte. Some 140 routes from 40m to 50m in length range in difficulty from 3c to 7c+. This is purely a sport climbing crag and the names of the routes are painted on the rock at their base.

CRAG CHAT

The Dordogne river valley is of course one of the most famous scenic attractions in France. Prehistoric cave paintings, fine wines et al. complement the splendour of this majestic river which sweeps from the high Le Mont Dore due W to join the Atlantic near Bordeaux. Adjacent to the river, reached by an elegant seven-arch stone bridge and overlooked by a fairy tale turreted castle, the tiny village of Castlenaud typifies the massive appeal of this classic region. The crag and campsite lie within easy walking distance of its small cafés and restaurants.

Although nowhere near as extensive, as high, or as famous, as Buoux, it is remarkably similar. The rock is virtually identical, with the same gritty texture and honeycomb pocketing. The situation is aesthetically appealing. Prehistoric cave dwellings abound and nearby the museum at Les Eyzies and the cave paintings of Font de Gaume and La Mouthe (to mention only two of the many) are of world importance.

A fine setting, the excellent campsite immediately below and a variety of superb sport climbs make this a viable venue for three to four days' intense climbing activity. Indeed, unless all you want to do is to tick the very hardest free climbs in Europe, this miniature Buoux has a lot going for it. There are many hard routes just stopping short of the magical grade 8 but the easier and mid-grade climber will find more of interest here. A Parisian climber I met on the crag reckoned it to be only 7 hours drive from Paris and a viable weekend crag for him but even so the crag never seems overcrowded.

CU (17) Céou, La Cathédrale, with climber on 'La Couleur Tombée du Ciel'

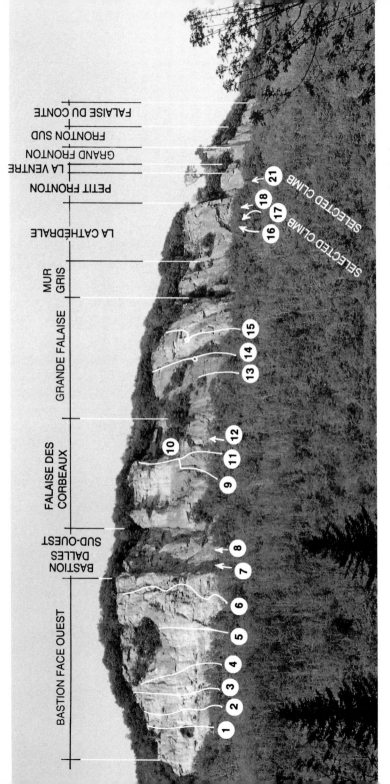

FALAISE DU CONTE
FRONTON SUD
GRAND FRONTON
LA VENTRE
PETIT FRONTON

LA CATHÉDRALE

MUR GRIS

GRANDE FALAISE

FALAISE DES CORBEAUX

BASTION DALLES SUD-OUEST

BASTION FACE OUEST

SELECTED CLIMB

SELECTED CLIMB

CU (1 - 34) Céou R-side, viewed from the campsite. From L to R - Bastion Face Ouest to Falaise du Conte

HIT LIST (From L to R)

BASTION FACE OUEST

CU 1   **L'Obscénité** 6a+
CU 2   **Les Temps Modernes**, 6c
CU 3   **Dévers Pépère** 7a
CU 4   **Tentative de Coup de Pub** 6c
CU 5   **Le Génie d'Albert** 6c
CU 6   **Voie Normale** L1:4c, L1:5c

BASTION DALLES SUD-OUEST

CU 7   **La Classique** 5b, 5b
CU 8   **Impression de Voyage** 6a, 6b

FALAISE DES CORBEAUX

CU 9   **Les Cristalliers** 5a
CU 10   **Nelson Mandela** 5b
CU 11   **Barbouilleur d'Étoiles** 7b
CU 12   **Cristal Qui Songe** 6b

GRANDE FALAISE

CU 13   **Pacific** 7c
CU 14   **L'Espoir du Futur** L1:6c, L2:7b
CU 15   **Le Fil à Plomb** L1:6a, L2:5b

LA CATHÉDRALE

CU 16   **Et Mourir de Plaisir** 8a
CU 17   **LA COULEUR TOMBÉE DU CIEL** 20m, 7a/b. SELECTED ROUTE (see p. 266).
CU 18   **La Sorcellerie** 8a

PETIT FRONTON

CU 19   **Sika Vertical** 6a
CU 20   **Éthique en Tac** 6a
CU 21   **HEURE D'AUTOMNE** 15m, 6a+. SELECTED ROUTE (see p. 266).
CU 22   **Duel au Soleil** 6b

LE VENTRE

CU 23   **Bébinou** 7a

GRAND FRONTON

CU 24   **La Kuter** 7a+

CU 25 **Une Porte sur L'Été** 7b+
CU 26 **Les Fleurs du Mâle** 7a. A superb and long pitch.

FRONTON SUD
CU 27 **Canaillou** 6c
CU 28 **La Voie Lactée** 5b
CU 29 **Floraline** 5a
CU 30 **L'Oubliée** 5a

FALAISE DU CONTE
CU 31 **N'en Jetez Plus** 6c
CU 32 **La Tape à l'Oeil** 6a+
CU 33 **Le Piano du Pauvre** 7c+
CU 34 **Métamorphose du Vampire** 7a+

SELECTED CLIMBS AT CÉOU: La Couleur Tombée du Ciel (CU 17), Heure d'Automne (CU 21)

LA COULEUR TOMBÉE DU CIEL: 20m, 7a/b. (British grading - E5, 6b.)
Location: The right arch of La Nef, La Cathédrale area, Céou.
First Ascent: Unknown
Route Facts: Start just right of the large cave up R rib of the arch.

L1, 20m, 7a/b. Gain a standing position in the square-cut post hole with difficulty. Follow the arch curving L to the centre of the cave then move up to a lower-off point.
Descent: Lower off.

HEURE D'AUTOMNE: 15m, 6a. (British grading - E1, 5a/b.)
Location: Front pillar of Petit Fronton, Céou.
First Ascent: Unknown
Route Facts: Start a few metres right of a large elongated cave at the base of the pillar.

L1, 15m, 6a. Climb the line of bolts up the front face of the pillar to a lower-off point.
Descent: Lower off.

ROUTE CHAT

A friendly crag, not in the least intimidating, where a pleasant atmosphere

CU (20) Céou, Petit Fronton, climber on "Ethique En Tac' (6a). The rope on the R is on 'Heure d'Automne

prevails. The majority of the climbs are climbed in one pitch to a lower-off point, although care should be exercised on the longer routes - on Grand Fronton for example - to ensure your rope is long enough to reach the ground. Generally steep in nature there is an even spread of routes throughout the range of difficulty and climbers of quite disparate abilities and fitness can have an equally satisfying time here. The two routes singled out are selected to illustrate the best of their respective grades.

La Cathédrale area of Céou is well named and unmistakable. Roughly in the centre of the cliffs, reached by walking R from the approach path, a large dome-shaped cave rises from walled ruins to dominate the scene. The R rib of the arch constitutes the challenging line taken by La Couleur Tombée du Ciel.

A very difficult fingery start, technically the crux, enables one first to reach then to stand in a rectangular hole in the pillar. This post hole once supported the timbers of the now ruinous (prehistoric?) buildings beneath. From here the climbing becomes very strenuous - best not to linger. A steady supply of jugs take you, feet dangling, across the arch until at its apex a difficult move and a long reach is necessary to gain the lower-off point. Short but explosive climbing taking a most aesthetic natural line.

Seventy metres to the R can be found a distinct lozenge-shaped cave running up the crag and R of this an attractive pillar. A line of bolts immediately R of the cave is Ethique et Tac (6a) - enjoyable climbing - but R again lies Heure d'Automne. The climbing here may be relatively short but will not be found wanting in either character or technical interest. The banded nature of the rock resembles the bulging shape of the Michelin Man. The bolts, however, are regularly spaced and this is a good route on which to push your grade. Even before gaining the most bulging third band it will be discovered that the climbing is much more interesting than first appearances may have suggested.

CHAUDEFOUR VALLEY, LA RANCUNE

Map Ref: *Michelin Motoring Atlas, page 112, C3.*

Area Maps: IGN 2433e. MICH 73.13.

Guidebook: *Topo Guide du Mont Sancy.*

Climate/Climbing Season: Precipitation (rain/snow) 1,900mm on 160 days of the year. The area is usually snowbound for 4 to 5 months of the year, generally climbing is possible between late May and October inclusive.

Restrictions: Situated in Parc Regional des Volcans, no wild camping.

Rock and Protection: Volcanic, a dark andesite resembling the characteristics of a medium-grained granite, generally of excellent quality and giving good friction. Mostly the insitu gear is good, extensive re-bolting has recently been carried out, but a small selection of Rocks and Friends can be useful.

Situation: Some 30km SW of Clermont Ferrand, 6km SE of Mont Doré, La Vallée de Chaudefour lies 2km ENE of Puy de Sancy. Département Puy de Dôme (No.63).

Access: The Chaudefour Valley lies on the E side of the mountain pass Col de la Croix St Robert (altitude 1,426m). Although only 6km distance from the ski resort of Le Mont Doré this is in effect on the other side of the mountain. If approaching from the E (Clermont Ferrand) it is best to continue along the autoroute N9 to Issoire to avoid extensive negotiation of mountain passes. From here follow the D996 to Chambon turn L and rise up the D637 to join the D36. Continue along this for 1km in the direction of the pass Col de la Croix St Robert to find a car park on the opposite side of the road (S) to the restaurant Le Burron. Parking advised here. Continue up the track to its end, cross the footbridge, and follow the path up the valley. La Rancune can be seen up on the hillside to the R. Follow a path across the fields and steeply up through the woods to circumnavigate the obelisk below its N face (bear R) until the shoulder below the W face (that facing the hillside) is reached (allow 1 hour). Vehicular access along the track is restricted and shouldn't be attempted - although it is physically possible to drive to the head (this reduces the approach to half an hour) it is illegal and an on-the-spot parking fine will be imposed.

Camping etc: Nearest camping and limited supplies are available at St Victor la Rivière.

Crag Facts: This remarkable obelisk of rock is situated at an altitude of 1,200m on the flanks of Puy du Sancy above the Chaudefour Valley. It can be snowbound for 4 to 5 months of the year. Seen from below are its E end and S face, the W face abuts with the hillside behind and the formidable N face lies out of sight. There is climbing on all four faces, the W face and the Voie Normale providing the easiest and shortest way to the summit, the S face (reaching a vertical

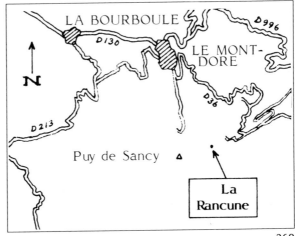

height of perhaps 100m) holds the majority of quality climbs. The E end looks challenging but the rock on the overhanging N face looks rather loose and denatured. There are around 20 routes from 50m to 100m in length and varying in difficulty from 6a to 7b. Traditionally peg-protection was employed but bolts, some old, some new, have now mainly replaced these.

CRAG CHAT

This mighty rectangular pillar of rock appears as a slim finger when viewed end-on and as a huge up-ended tilting paving slab when seen obliquely. How ever viewed, this super Napes Needle presents a striking feature which rises some 100m from the steep sloping flanks of the tree-filled Chaudefour Valley. There are no easy ways to the summit and its ascent became a prized objective. It was first conquered in the 1940s by the Voie Normale up its lesser, but still impressive, slender W face.

The whole upland area SW of Clermont Ferrand is quite remarkable. Known as the Parc Regional des Volcans it was originally formed by extensive volcanic activity. Now silent, the hollowed tops of these once fiery cones today cradle lakes, known as crater lakes. The dark andesitic rocks form a number of dominant features associated with their formation. La Rancune is part of the hardened magma core of such a volcano. Tougher than the surrounding rocks it has resisted the forces of erosion to stand independently. As such it offers excellent rock for climbing, being both sound and reliable.

To photograph and climb La Rancune I have visited the region twice. Once in April when the Chaudefour Valley was white and its trees bare. Though the roads were passable snow swirled vigorously even at valley level and chill winds dulled any ambition to climb. The tooth itself, stark and black, stood in savage contrast to the hillside beneath.

Such was the magnetism of the challenge we returned again in early October to stroll towards the tooth in perfect sunshine. Leaves were falling and the beech, rowan, silver birch and hazel, blazed yellow, red and gold to contrast wonderfully their autumnal colouring against the green of the Chaudefour meadows. High against a blue sky La Dent de la Rancune beckoned.

HIT LIST (From L to R)

LR 1 **VOIE NORMALE** 50m, L1:6a, L2:6a + a point of aid. SELECTED ROUTE (see p. 273).

LR 2 **Le 2nd Souffle** L1:6c, L2:6b+

LR 3 **La Classique de la Face Sud** L1:5b, L2:6b, L3:5b

LR 4 **Voie de la Demi-Lune** L1:7a, L2:6b, L3:6b

LR 5 **India Song** L1:6a, L2:7a, L3:5c

LR 6 **Voie Bobo** L1:6a, L2:5b, L3:5b

LR (1 - 6) La Rancune,from L to R, W and S Faces

LR (1) La Rancune, W Face, climber on the belay ledge of La Voie Normale' (6a)

SELECTED CLIMB LA RANCUNE: La Voie Normale (LR 1)

LA VOIE NORMALE: 50m, L1:6a, L2:6a + a point of aid. (British grading - E1, 5b, 5b using a point of insitu aid on 2nd pitch.)

Location: The west (uphill) edge of La Rancune, Chaudefour Valley.

First Ascent: Circa 1940s

Route Facts: Start beneath the W edge from the shoulder formed by the pinnacle and hillside behind.

L1, 20m, 6a. Climb the R edge of the pillar, taking a groove to reach parallel overhanging cracks where the edge impends. Step L and pull onto the narrow glacis above with difficulty. Continue to reach the large belay ledge in a few more metres.

L2, 30m, 6a. From R edge of ledge climb corner to top of blocks. Continue up the edge to gain the overhanging crack. Climb this with a point of aid (insitu aid and protection - possible belay at this point). Move L across the slab to a bolt in the centre of the face, then climb up and back R into a corner. Follow up this to regain the R edge of the pillar. Continue more easily to the top.

Descent: One 50m abseil, insitu bolt, down the W face reaches the shoulder.

ROUTE CHAT

Bathed in afternoon sunshine with the rough granitic rock hot to touch Martin Bagness and I climbed the W face. As the climb progressed the S face joined the black N face to become cast in shadow. Like a spotlight on centre stage this isolated the Voie Normale as a line in space, dramatically heightened its already considerable exposure and slender precariousness.

The name, Voie Normale, is rather deceptive. This may be the regular route up this extraordinary obelisk of rock but its ascent is no pushover. If a point of aid is used on the second pitch it still gives a climb of full value British E1, 5b. If this isn't used it would be at least British 6a. If more aid is used and I suspect this is the way this route is most often climbed - it would still be HVS.

Immediately you begin to climb exposure is intense. Below the start there sweeps some 40m of slabs which in fact may be climbed at around a technical grade of 5b (British 4c), to give an additional pitch up the S face to the shoulder. The edge is followed until moves left enable an insecure pull utilising fingerholds in a thin diagonal crack to gain a glacis (just to the right are twin cracks but this is not the way). If a small selection of nuts is carried the insitu bolt can be effectively backed-up with a higher runner. The large ledge stance lies just above.

The impact of the long second pitch provides the crux of the route. Just reaching the overhanging crack on the R edge of the pillar is imposing enough even utilising a point of aid. It can be dispensed with, but neither of us succeeded in this; it must be minimum of British 6a and possibly harder. Above the interest does not diminish and steep sustained, often delicate, climbing leads first L into the centre of the face and then back R to a corner groove. This emerges onto the R edge of the wall yet again. A fine exposed finish is made to gain the slabby W end of the summit. Sensibly the ropes can be left here, ready to make the abseil, whilst the summit ridge is traversed.

A very fine climb in its own right but I must admit that we topped out and strolled along the summit ridge, to admire the view and reach the actual summit, very much with the feeling that "...going to the right place at the right time, with the right people is all that really matters. What one does is purely incidental." (A remark made by Colin Kirkus to Alf Bridge on the summit of Sgurr Alasdair in the Black Cuillin of Skye, Scottish Highlands, from the Scottish Mountaineering Club guidebook *Rock Climbs in Skye.*)

Petite the area may be, unspectacular perhaps, but it is this region of France, Normandy and Brittany, that has the strongest Celtic links with Britain. With its cider production, endless golden beaches, and comparably high rainfall figures (to Cornwall not Glencoe that is), it is impossible not to feel at home here. Four crags and six selected climbs are described and it is possible to hop off the Brittany cross-channel ferry at Caen and be climbing at Clécy within the hour. Its other crags, especially Pen Hir and Le Cube in Brittany, lend themselves well to a shared climbing/family holiday.

CLÉCY

Map Ref: *Michelin Motoring Atlas, page 32, A3.*

Area Maps: IGN 1514e. MICH 55.1.

Guidebook: *Escalade à Clécy*

Climate/Climbing Season: Precipitation (rain/snow) 700mm on 120 days of the year. Climbing possible between April and October inclusive.

Restrictions: No wild camping.

Rock and Protection: The rock is a dark agglomerate of good quality. All routes are well bolted and strictly speaking only quick draws are necessary. Nut placements abound, however, and a small selection may be worth carrying.

Situation: Normandy, some 32km SSW of Caen, above the N bank of the River Orne, 2km S of the village of Clécy. Département Calvados (No.14).

Access: From Caen follow the D562 S through Thury-Harcourt to turn off L into the village of Clécy after a further 10km. Drive through the village and cross the bridge, over the Orne, to the E. Enter the hamlet of Le Vey and immediately turn R. This road continues to pass the campsite then becomes a track. Follow the track to a large parking area beneath the viaduct crossing the river - park here, do not continue under the viaduct and along the track. A path scrambles up the bank of the viaduct and then continues along the railway track before bearing R into the wood. Traverse this path which contours beneath the crag in a few hundred metres (15 minutes). Alternatively if staying at the campsite cross the road

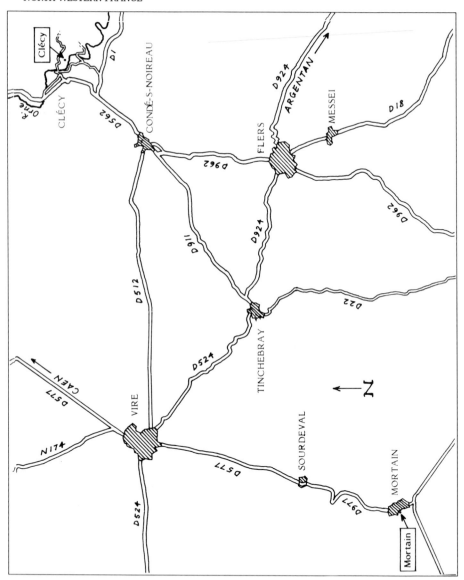

opposite to find a path running parallel to the track at a higher level. In a short way this crosses the railway track and continues through the woods to join the previous approach (25 minutes).

Camping etc: There is a municipal campsite very near the crag as already described (open April to October). Supplies available in Clécy.

Crag Facts: This popular and conveniently sited crag rises from the woods above the River Orne. The main crag of the region, it is commonly referred to just as Clécy but its full title is actually Les Rochers des Parcs. The latter title differentiates it from the lesser 'L'Aiguillette' to be found some way downstream the Orne from the hamlet of Le Vey. Although Normandy isn't noted for a particularly hot, dry climate, it equates pretty well with southern England, the crag faces S and dries very quickly. Basically the crag offers one in-line face but this is broken by ledges and gullies into some 12 different *secteurs*. For easy of identification the following have been singled out: the first wall, seen above the path traversing from L to R beneath the cliff, is known as Les Plaques, followed by Délices du Diable and Tobogan (the R wall of the rectangular bay). Slanting up at right angles to the path the popular Beaujolaise has numerous routes. The headwall of Grands Surplombs stands above the lower wall of Pagode. Carrying on to pass the central point of the cliff, rising from the trees just above the path from the lowest rocks of all, is Reposante. Next comes Essaim, then some way right appearing as a separate little buttress, split from Essaim by the steep chimney of Couloir Lemeilleur, is Secteur Chartreuse. There is a good spread of interest with many routes of medium difficulty - this is considered to be one of the most important crags in this north-western region of France. Although the crag rises from the trees the routes themselves are clean and of good quality. Some 60 routes from 30m to 60m in length range in difficulty from 3b to 7b. Names of the routes are written on the rock.

CRAG CHAT

Normandy is a green attractive region with a character that feels closer to the cider and cheese counties of England than one associated with an area of France. Perhaps it's something to do with the climate - it does tend to rain here rather a lot. Clécy is little more than half an hour's drive from the ferry at Caen, making it the most convenient crag in France for those travelling across the Channel. There is a strong case for taking the Portsmouth-Caen crossing rather than the more usual Dover-Calais. Although this crossing is longer, surprisingly the cost is the same (excluding the cost of a cabin - which in any case is minimal for the most basic unit available). The sailing time of around six hours allows time to relax or sleep after the drive to the ferry terminal and within an hour of waking you can be cragging in France.

Rising steeply from oak woods above the River Orne this popular crag is strongly reminiscent of Shepherd's Crag in the Lake District or Tremadog in North Wales. The rock, however, is quite different from either. Very dark in colour it is an agglomerate matrix consisting of a tough cement holding together a mix of flattened pebbles and white quartz-like nodules of silica. Despite first appearances it is solid and compact, making for a good climbing rock.

The crag itself consists of a number of walls and buttresses interspaced with many ledges, and is split by cracks, frequent corners, chimneys and gullies. The angle varies from stepped overhangs to gently leaning slabby walls. Individually the climbs generally offer a kaleidoscope of problems and situations despite their brevity.

HIT LIST (From L to R)

SECTEUR LES PLAQUES
CY 1 La Dalle du Bout du Monde 6a/b

SECTEUR DÉLICES DU DIABLE
CY 2 Maurice 4b. (6a Direct)
CY 3 Le Premier Pilier 5b
CY 4 Les Délices du Diable 6b

SECTEUR TOBOGAN
CY 5 La Rallye 67 6b
CY 6 Le COB 5a
CY 7 Les Coin de Bois 6a
CY 8 La Souris par la Dalle 4c
CY 9 Le Tobogan L1:3c, L2:4c

SECTEUR BEAUJOLAISE
CY 10 La Source 5c
CY 11 La Beaujolaise 5b

SECTEURS PAGODE & GRANDS SURPLOMBS
CY 12 La Pagode 6a
CY 13 Les Grands Surplombs 6b+
CY 14 La Couronne 3c. A popular route reached by traversing in from the L.

SECTEUR REPOSANTE
CY 15 La Reposante L1:3b, L2:3b, L3:3b
CY 16 LA VÉRONIQUE 60m, L1:5c, L2:5c. SELECTED ROUTE (see p. 283).

SECTEUR ESSAIM
CY 17 L'Essaim 4c

SECTEUR CHARTREUSE
CY 18 LA CHARTREUSE 30m, 4c. SELECTED ROUTE (see p. 283).

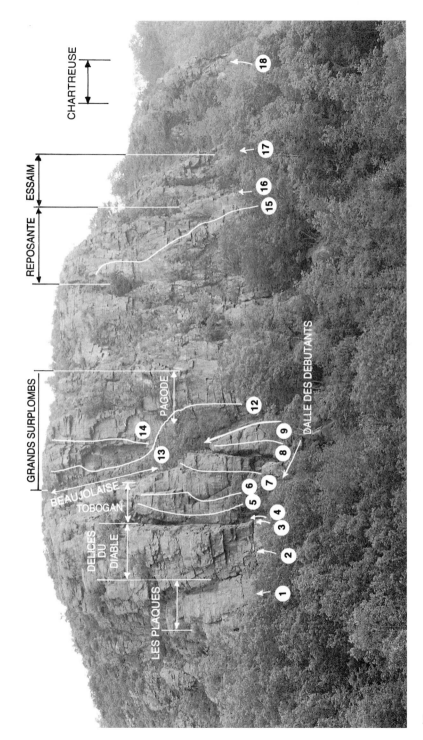

CY (1 - 18) Clécy, Les Rochers des Parcs. From L to R - Secteur Les Plaques to Secteur Chartreuse

CY (12 - 14)   Clécy, Les Rochers des Parcs, - Secteurs 'La Pagode' (6b) & 'Grands Surplombs' (6c)

CY (18) Clécy,, Les Rochers des Parcs - approaching the overhang on 'La Chartreuse' (4c)

281

CY (16) Clécy, Les Rocher des Parcs, climber on the 1st pitch of
'La Véronique' (5c)

SELECTED CLIMBS AT CLÉCY: La Véronique (CY 16), La Chartreuse (CY 18)

LA VÉRONIQUE: 60m, L1:5c, L2:5c. (British grading - Hard Very Severe, 5a, 5a.)

Location: To be found a little over half-way along the crag on the Secteur Reposante, Les Rochers des Parcs, Clécy.

First Ascent: Unknown

Route Facts: Start directly beneath the obvious V-groove.

L1, 25m, 5c. Climb the groove to the notched roof. Move through this and continue in the steep and steepening groove line to its top. Possible belay here but usual to arrange a runner and make a traverse R along a horizontal foot traverse to a 2-bolt belay beneath another imposing corner.

L2, 35m, 5c. Climb the impending open-book corner directly above. Possible belay. Continue directly up the wall above to move through the final overlaps and gain the top of the crag.

Descent: Two abseils. The first to the mid-stance and the second to the ground from here.

LA CHARTREUSE: 30m, 4c. (British grading - Mild Very Severe, 4a/b.)

Location: Near the far R end of the crag on a separate buttress known as Secteur Chartreuse, Les Rochers des Parcs, Clécy.

First Ascent: Unknown

Route Facts: Start at the mid-point of the pillar.

L1, 30m, 4c. Follow the line of bolts weaving up the centre of the pillar to stand beneath the capping roof. Pull up a rib, holds on the edge, to enter a niche in the centre of the overhangs. Continue more easily to the top.

Descent: Abseil recommended although it is possible to descend the steep (and tricky looking) Couloir Lemeilleur to the L.

ROUTE CHAT

Viewing the crag from the viaduct is a sound measure before taking the path up through the woods. Even so, because of the density of the wood beneath the crag and the rather broken complex nature of the face, it is helpful to walk along the length of the crag before beginning to climb. Having done this the logical route to start is Chartreuse - taking its own isolated buttress located almost at the far R end of the crag.

The line is simple enough, taking the front face of the buttress centrally from toe to tip. The climbing is constantly interesting and quite technical. Indeed if it were not for the frequency of the insitu bolt protection - I counted eight clips excluding one placed 2m off the ground - guaranteeing leader safety throughout it could easily be one or even two overall grades harder.

Even so, the climbing is exciting enough with a series of technical moves taking you up to the impressive top overhang. Perfect protection allows you to work out the moves with some composure though it still constitutes a difficult and strenuous crux. A remarkably absorbing and satisfying climb, longer and more demanding than would first be imagined. Keep a watchful eye out for falling stones when belaying below the Couloir Lemeilleur as this is frequently used in descent (not recommended unless by abseil).

La Véronique gives two remarkably sustained and interesting pitches. A hanging system of corner grooves constitutes the first pitch and rising just above the path at probably the lowest point of the rocks it is immediately recognisable. Even the initial slight groove leading to the first overhang proves no giveaway. Above, difficulties steadily increase with altitude. The groove is very steep indeed and at the top impends even further providing a perfect crescendo to this immaculate exercise in technical bridging.

Having completed this pitch it is possible to belay directly above though if the runners are arranged carefully, reaching the stance and two-bolt belay across the foot traverse to the R is the best option. Above this the gently overhanging open-book corner takes on classic proportions. A strenuous and demanding start to a very fine pitch of some length, for above it continues up an open and exposed wall, passing a number of overlaps and tricky sections before finally reaching the top. Insitu bolt-protection is good throughout but a few tapes serve to supplement it. In fact the rock is very conducive to placing nut runners and if you have not yet acclimatised to bolt-protected climbing *à la Français*, it is perfectly feasible to place "natural" protection. If La Véronique looks slightly daunting, another classic route begins just to its L. La Reposante (the name of this *secteur*) is climbed in three pitches at French 4b - equivalent to British Hard Severe, 3c.

MORTAIN

Map Ref: *Michelin Motoring Atlas, page 31, E4.*

Area Maps: IGN 1415w. MICH 59.9.

Guidebook: *Escalades sur le Gres Armoricain,* topo guide.

Climate/Climbing Season: Precipitation (rain/snow) 1,500mm on 150 days of the year. Climbing usual between April and October.

Restrictions: No wild camping.

Rock and Protection: Quartzite of impeccable quality. Recently bolted - only quick draws need be carried.

Situation: In Normandy some 80km SW of Caen and 32km ESE of Avranches. Département Manche (No.50).

Access: In Mortain follow the road sign La Petite Cascade which leads down to a large car park by the side of the distinguished Château (town hall). Walk downhill passing the front of the Château until a tiny lane leads off R at the break in the wall (signed La Petite Cascade). Follow this descending (crags above to the R and factory at the bottom to the L) to cross a small footbridge and follow a short lane to a field and picnic area directly beneath the dominant tower of L'Aiguille - the rocks are collectively known as Le Site de L'Aiguille (10 minutes).

Camping etc: The municipal campsite, a small walled field full of character if a little short on facilities, is sited behind the car park. British and French flags fly at the opening but otherwise the site is very well concealed. It is actually perched on top of the crags situated above the descent lane - pull onto the wall and you can look down and across to L'Aiguille. All facilities available in Mortain.

Crag Facts: The small crags at Mortain are collectively named Le Site de L'Aiguille named after the distinctive central tower. Descending down the lane from the main road they appear in order as: Donjon Pic Blanc - the first slender buttress (warning sign Chute de Pierres), Les Dalles du Donjon, Divin Enfant and then Babydalle (the most major of those above the path). Across the stream and taking the lane leading along from the factory there is a landscaped garden lawn area dominated by the distinct cubic tower of L'Aiguille (the front main face due S). This marks the R end of another group of crags, proceeding from R to L: L'Aiguille (itself), L'Envers de L'Aiguille, Dièdre au Bivouac and Mystères de l'Est. To the R of the field/picnic area its the imaginatively named blocky ridge of Charmoz Grépon. The path signed La Petite Cascade weaves up a tiny valley following a small stream to arrive at the waterfall. To its L are some steep cliffs which at the time of writing showed signs of development but had no bolts insitu. Some 75 routes from 25m to 30m in length range in difficulty from 5a to 7a.

CRAG CHAT

A compact rather secluded climbing area with a pleasant atmosphere. Possibly produced by long-past quarrying activities, the great rectangular tower standing independently at the heart of the area - L'Aiguille - provides the main challenge and provides the justification for further development.

Climbing began in the 1940s, reputedly by Alpinists taking exile in Normandy during the war years. Lionel Terray and René Desmaison both climbed here. One can but smile at their imaginative naming of the blocky profile of the Charmoz Grépon - there is indeed a resemblance to its Alpine namesake.

The white quartzite here is a revelation. It has all the plus qualities of Gogarth in North Wales, sharp positive holds, hidden flakes and cracks, and that distinctively coke-crunchy texture, without any of its looseness. It dries instantaneously, a distinct advantage in this, one of the wettest regions of France. There is enough of interest, at quiet Mortain, to provide perhaps two full climbing days.

HIT LIST (From R to L)

LE PIC BLANC
MN 1 **À C— la F...** 6c
MN 2 **À Fond la Caisse** 7b

LES DALLES DU DONJON
MN 3 **Venise Retour** 5c

DIVIN ENFANT
MN 4 **Le Divin Enfant** 6a
MN 5 **Le Proton Fou** 7c
MN 6 **L'Anniversaire du Prince** 6a
MN 7 **Prima Vista** 6c

BABYDALLE
MN 8 **Moi Tarzan** 6b
MN 9 **Premier Amour** 6b
MN 10 **Babydalle** 6c
MN 11 **L'Apothicaire** 4b
MN 12 **Le Nom de la Rose** 5b
MN 13 **Dangeur Travaux** 4c
MN 14 **Paulo Gai** 6a

L'AIGUILLE FACE EST
MN 15 **L'Arête du Grand Couloir** 5c
MN 16 **Les Choucas** 6a

L'AIGUILLE FACE SUD
MN 17 **L'Arête des Aigles** 6b+
MN 18 **La Pompischpratz** 6c.
MN 19 **LA FISSURE GOBBI** 30m, 5c. SELECTED ROUTE (see p.289).
MN 20 **Belzebuth, Dieu des Mouches** 6c+
MN 21 **La Henri 11** 6b

L'ENVERS DE L'AIGUILLE   (The wall behind the pinnacle)
MN 22 **La Directe** 4b

MN (8 - 14) Mortain, Secteur Babydalle

MN (15 - 22) Mortain, L'Aiguille & L'Envers de L'Aiguille

DIÊDRE AU BIVOUAC
MN 23 **Dièdre au Bivouac** 4b
MN 24 **L'Envers Fait les Vôtres** 6b

MYSTÈRES DE L'EST
MN 25 **Les Mystères de l'Est** 4c

SELECTED CLIMB AT MORTAIN: La Fissure Gobbi (MN 19)

LA FISSURE GOBBI: 30m, 5c. (British grading - E1, 5a+.)

Location: L'Aiguille S Face, Mortain, Normandy.

First Ascent: Circa 1940s

Route Facts: The central crack.

L1, 30m, 5c. Climb the impending groove to enter the wide crack. Follow it to the top.

Descent: Abseil

ROUTE CHAT

Once seen the line must be climbed. A wide vertical crack splitting a shining white tower of perfect quartzite. In the old days it must have been protected with wooden wedges and the odd peg, later large nuts may have served, today it is all bolt-protected. Just go for the clip and relax to enjoy the actual climbing.

In actual execution the bolts feel quite spaced. However, a little adventure adds extra spice, and in any case in the event of a fall you would be very unfortunate to come to any harm. The climb is deceptive. At first sighting it looks stunningly impressive. As you uncoil your ropes directly beneath, a foreshortening effect helps to diminish the apparent difficulties. Starting up the route puts it back into proper perspective. Very steep and challenging throughout, there are no easy sections - only bits that are harder than the rest.

Sharp flakes and fingerholds appear when they are most needed and careful examination of the inside of the crack often reveals hidden finger cracks. Not an easy route to give a precise British grade but I found it more E1 than HVS and certainly at the upper end of British 5a. However difficult you may or may not find it, it is indisputably the easiest and most obvious line up this S face.

Other good routes abound. The R arête is taken by L'Arête des Aigles 6b+ (British E3, 5c) with the bold crux right at the top. The centre of the E face (that to the R) is taken by Les Choucas 6a (British E2, 5b) with the hardest section again at the top - an excellent wall climb with interesting moves over the overhang.

MN (19) Mortain, L'Aiguille - starting 'La Fissure Gobbi' (5c)

LE CUBE

Map Ref: *Michelin Motoring Atlas, page 26, B3.*

Area Maps: IGN 0417e. L=(1097.7, 103.2). MICH 58.4.

Guidebook: *Rochers de L'Impératrice Plougastel,* a CAF topo guide.

Climate/Climbing Season: Precipitation (rain/snow) 1,000mm on 150 days of the year. Climbing possible all year round.

Restrictions: No wild camping, access is approved by the landowner but one should keep a low profile.

Rock and Protection: Quartzite of excellent quality. Insitu modern bolts now protect all the routes and only quick draws need be carried. Nuts, however, could be placed to reduce the distance between the insitu protection.

Situation: Just SW of the Albert Louppe Bridge 8km S of Brest and 1.8km WNW of Plougastel, Brittany. Département Finistère (No.29).

Access: Le Cube is visible from Brest looking S over the bay of Brest, just above the Albert Louppe Bridge spanning the River Elorn. From Brest head towards Plougastel over the bridge on the D33 to take the second road on the R (after passing a triangular junction which feeds the first road on the R). This extremely

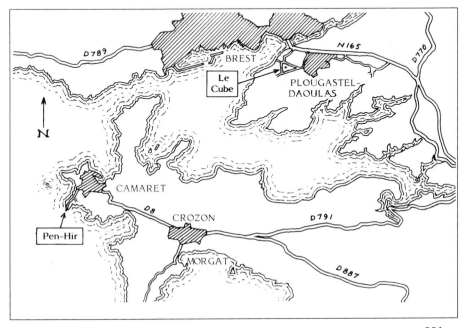

narrow road is found at the point where the main highway becomes two-lane. It is difficult to see as it is set back slightly and appears more like a private drive but it is directly opposite a bus stop on the far side of the main road. Having turned R follow the road to a parking space directly below Le Cube - do not block any access to the nearby houses. Walk up the drive towards a fine house (alternatively there is a path through the woods to the left) then take a footpath L through a boulder field to the base of Le Cube (5 minutes).

Camping etc: Camping in Plougastel (April to September) or a municipal campsite open all year at Brest-St-Marc (by the D33). Supermarkets in Brest but no climbing shop.

Crag Facts: Le Cube is one of a number of small rock outcrops in the vicinity of Plougastel. Just to its S, and reached from the hamlet of the same name, is Roch Nivelin. Including both localities there are some 20 routes from 18m to 30m in length ranging in difficulty from 2 to 6b. The main face of Le Cube faces N and it can be cold here midwinter. Another important crag nearby on the other side of the D33, on the road to Le Passage, is L'Impératrice and this sports some 60 routes from 30m to 45m in length and ranging from 3b to 6b in difficulty. The names and grades of some of the routes are painted on the rock.

CRAG CHAT (by Ian Dunn)

Le Cube fell out of a sugar bowl - honestly. A more perfect lump of granular quartzite would be hard to find. On my first visit here you had to back-up the rusting pegs (the sea salt atmosphere here is highly corrosive to insitu gear) with wires. Today the protection has improved tremendously and a quick call here for a workout is a pleasant start to any French holiday.

HIT LIST (From L to R)

LC 1 **Le Dièdre Vert** 4b. The obvious corner groove. Note there are a number of bolted lines to the L but their grades are not known by the writer.

LC 2 **Depot de Bilan** 6a. Note direct variation is graded 6a+.

LC 3 **BISKOAZ KEMEND ALL** 17m, 5c. SELECTED ROUTE (see below).

LC 4 **LA FACE** 18m, 6b. SELECTED ROUTE (see below).

LC 5 **Prise de Tête** 6c

LC (1 - 5) Le Cube, Brittany

SELECTED CLIMBS AT LE CUBE: Biskoaz Kemend All (LC 3), La Face (LC 4)

BISKOAZ KEMEND ALL: 17m, 5c. (British grading - Hard Very Severe, 5a.)

LA FACE: 18m, 6b. (British grading - E3, 5c.)

First Ascents: Unknown

Location: N face of Le Cube, Brittany.

Route Facts: Both routes are on the front face of Le Cube, the former taking the central crackline and the latter taking the wall to the R. Both climbs are well protected on positive holds, sustained and strenuous at their respective grades. For Biskoaz Kemend All start at the foot of the central crackline and climb it directly to the summit. La Face starts 4m R of the central crackline - and just L of the route

LC (3) Le Cube, Claudie Dunn climbing 'Biskoaz Kemend All' (5c).
Photo: Ian & Claudie Dunn collection

Prise de Tête 6c (British grading - E3, 6a) - climb the wall directly till a move L at the top brings you to the belay of Biskoaz Kemend All.

Descent: Scramble down the S side of Le Cube - there are some short beginners' routes here well protected and often used for the instruction of children.

ROUTE CHAT (by Ian Dunn)

The two routes described are the best, but all the routes are worth doing on this N face. The central crackline gives the French phenomenon - the bolt-protected crack climb! It is steep and continuous and it maintains a good standard throughout. The only criticism is the amount of ancient ironmongery left behind, it's a pity it wasn't purely nut-protected.

La Face is a fine climb, it would be so in Dovedale (English Peak District) or at Buoux. What makes it so good? Well it is direct, sustained, the protection is good without being over generous. Moves are very interesting on small, sharp holds a bit similar to the routes on Rubicon Wall (English Peak District) but at a more amenable standard and with better protection.

The first time I did this route I had no idea of the grade. It would have been easy to top rope it first, something that can be done with any of the routes here. However, as there was a selection of pegs and bolts leading up the wall I tried it totally *à vue,* taking care to progress carefully, checking the protection and making sure I was not leading myself into any blind alleys.

As I moved up the wall working out the moves and clipping the insitu gear, occasionally backing it up with the odd nut, I really started to enjoy myself. To climb a route with no prior knowledge at all, except that it has been ascended, is one of the purest forms of climbing. It would only have been purer to solo the route, though that would have been a much more gripping affair.

When I reached the top I had the inner glow that you have after doing a superb climb. Perhaps I had just tasted the sweetness of Le Cube. The route is now well bolted and you do not need gear other than a rack of quick draws.

NW of Brest about 20km along the coast road between Melon and Tremazan there are various area worth visiting for bouldering. The excellent granite is very like that in Cornwall and is there for those wishing to explore, investigate and enjoy it for themselves.

POINTE DE PEN-HIR

Map Ref: *Michelin Motoring Atlas, page 26, B4.*

Area Maps: IGN 0417e. L=(1086.5, 84). MICH 58.3.

Guidebook: None

Climate/Climbing Season: Precipitation (rain/snow) 750mm on 130 days of the year. Climbing can reasonably be expected all year round.

Restrictions: There are no access restrictions but there are very large tides in this area (15m) and care must be exercised on routes beginning near sea level.

Rock and Protection: Quartzite, generally of good quality. Most routes are now bolt-protected but nuts may occasionally be useful.

Situation: The distinctive peninsula S of Brest, Brittany. Département Finistère (No.29).

Access: The crag is to be found just W of the cross at Pointe de Pen-Hir, some 4km W of Camaret - leave Camaret on the road to Tas de Pois. From the large stone cross monument (Croix-de-Lorraine) above the cliff descend a path to the S of the headland. Scrambling leads N beneath the main buttress (10 minutes).

Camping etc: Camaret and Crozon are small villages and provide all daily basic requirements. Supermarkets in Brest. Camping at Crozon. There are no local climbing shops - so don't forget your boots.

Crag Facts: The sea cliff is often compared to Gogarth (North Wales) in quality and character. Generally the cliff faces W and is open to the full fury of the sea. Cracks tend to weep after prolonged rain, otherwise the crag dries quickly. The climate of Brittany is very similar to that of Cornwall. Some 130 routes from 40m to 80m in length range in difficulty from 2 to 7a. The main cliffs are found directly beneath the large stone cross. By following the approach path there will be found first a buttress seamed by cracks. There are numerous enjoyable and popular routes at a reasonable standard (British grading - D to VS). L of this area the crag turns direction and plunges into the sea to become steeper and more continuous. The routes L of Aphrodite (Selected Route) are usually approached by abseil. Opposite the Croix-de-Lorraine on the next headland, following a scrambly path over the crest of the ridge and down the other side, can be found a slabby buttress. This is a very popular wall, approximately 30m in height, with around six routes of medium difficulty starting from a large ledge. Below the ledge a steeper wall falls directly into the sea. This offers (fully bolt-protected) a very fine pitch of perhaps British E1 standard.

CRAG CHAT

Pointe de Pen-Hir is a popular tourist resort and compares with Land's End in Cornwall. However, once on the cliffs below, sunny and hot in the afternoon, you have the feeling of being on a big crag far away from the madding crowds. The cliffs are extremely impressive and fall sheer into the sea. As with Cornwall the high corrosive action of the saltwater destroys insitu gear in double quick time.

The following routes selected from the main cliff are all of outstanding quality, though their exact line is uncertain (with the exception of Aphrodite - the Selected Route) and to avoid confusion they have not been specifically delineated on the photo-topo. However, the area is extremely popular at weekends and the friendly locals will, I'm sure, be happy to indicate their location.

HIT LIST

PH 1 **APHRODITE** 45m, L1:5b, L2:6b. SELECTED ROUTE (see below).
Le Soleil-Rouge 4c
Le Bocal 5c
Super-Bocal 6a
Fil-d'Ariane 6b

SELECTED CLIMB AT POINTE DE PEN-HIR: Aphrodite (PH 1)

APHRODITE: 45m, L1:5b, L2:6b. (British grading - E4, 4c, 5c.)

First Ascent: Unknown

Location: Main Buttress, Pen-Hir, Brittany.

Route Facts: Taking the slim groove up the arête on the front of the buttress overlooking the sea. It can be viewed from the edge of the cliffs just to the N some 30m away and it is advisable to do so before descending to climb the route. The main pitch is sustained with one technical move low down and a strenuous upper section. It is now protected by bolts throughout although Friends could supplement these.

L1, 20m, 5b. Start up slabs below the main line of the arête, follow the slabs until a short groove can be climbed leading to good belay ledge beneath the main pitch. (This pitch can easily be bypassed by making a simple rock scramble diagonally from the R to the foot of the 2nd pitch - this allows the route to be climbed whatever the state of the tide.)

L2, 25m, 6b. Climb directly into the groove and follow it to the top of the buttress.

PH Pointe de Pen-Hir, the main cliffs below Croix-de-Lorraine

PH (1) Pointe de Pen-Hir, a climber coils the rope above the impressive hanging groove of Aphrodite. Photo: Ian & Claudie Dunn collection 299

**PH (2) Pointe de Pen-Hir, the slabby buttress on the next headland
beyond Croix-de-Lorraine**

ROUTE CHAT (by Ian Dunn)

Pointe de Pen-Hir is a popular tourist spot in the Land's End vein. However, once you descend to the foot of the crags, you have the feeling of being on a big crag away from the crowds, the cliffs are very impressive, falling straight into the sea - another Gogarth. Aphrodite was the only route I knew anything about on this large cliff having spied a picture of a youthful Jean-Claude Droyer on it in an ancient copy of *Alpirando* (November 1979 issue). In reality the route looked much bigger than the picture, why does that always happen? The line was obvious and we descended to do it.

The ascent up the belay ledges beneath the arête was mainly straightforward with only the short groove presenting any difficulty. A comfortable belay ledge with gulls visiting regularly to keep me company. Or were they just laughing at our feeble attempts to defy gravity?

Above, the going looked hard; the buttress overhangs in two directions and progress was to be via a layback/jam crack up the groove in the corner. At least with the traditional British rack of gear I would be able to protect myself, though plugging in the Friends and nuts proved strenuous until an awkward move at about one-third height led to a semi-rest. *(Ian led the route in 1983: it is now fully bolt-protected - BB.)*

Tightening forearms made me think that success may be slipping away. A good shake of the arms, a good nut, and up I went. The next 8m looked as formidable as the first section. Soon I started to pump out when I made the classic fumble, the wrong sized nut. Unwilling to join the seagulls even for a brief flight, in a last burst of effort I made it to the final easier groove.

A perfect hand and body jam enabled me to stop shaking and gain my composure before pulling over the top. The watching holidaymakers, who had a perfect view, greeted me excitedly and explained how French hero Patrick Edlinger would have free soloed the route without ropes etc., etc. Top French rock climbers have a status and popularity akin to our top footballers and are well known. Even so, if they weren't climbers they couldn't have known for sure.

There are many other routes to do in this area but as there is no guidebook and the situation with regards to fixed equipment and sea cliffs has not been solved, be careful and do what climbers are traditionally good at, exploring.

CICERONE GUIDES

Cicerone publish a wide range of reliable guides to walking and climbing abroad

FRANCE
TOUR OF MONT BLANC
CHAMONIX MONT BLANC - A Walking Guide
TOUR OF THE OISANS: GR54
WALKING THE FRENCH ALPS: GR5
THE CORSICAN HIGH LEVEL ROUTE: GR20
THE WAY OF ST JAMES: GR65
THE PYRENEAN TRAIL: GR10
THE RLS (Stevenson) TRAIL
TOUR OF THE QUEYRAS
ROCK CLIMBS IN THE VERDON
WALKS IN VOLCANO COUNTRY (Auvergne)
WALKING THE FRENCH GORGES (Provence)
FRENCH ROCK

FRANCE / SPAIN
WALKS AND CLIMBS IN THE PYRENEES
ROCK CLIMBS IN THE PYRENEES

SPAIN
WALKS & CLIMBS IN THE PICOS DE EUROPA
WALKING IN MALLORCA
BIRDWATCHING IN MALLORCA
COSTA BLANCA CLIMBS
ANDALUSIAN ROCK CLIMBS

FRANCE / SWITZERLAND
THE JURA - Walking the High Route and
  Winter Ski Traverses
CHAMONIX TO ZERMATT The Walker's Haute
Route

SWITZERLAND
WALKING IN THE BERNESE ALPS
CENTRAL SWITZERLAND
WALKS IN THE ENGADINE
WALKING IN TICINO
THE VALAIS - A Walking Guide
THE ALPINE PASS ROUTE

GERMANY / AUSTRIA
THE KALKALPEN TRAVERSE
KLETTERSTEIG - Scrambles
WALKING IN THE BLACK FOREST
MOUNTAIN WALKING IN AUSTRIA
WALKING IN THE SALZKAMMERGUT
KING LUDWIG WAY
HUT-TO-HUT IN THE STUBAI ALPS

ITALY & SLOVENIA
ALTA VIA - High Level Walkis in the Dolomites
VIA FERRATA - Scrambles in the Dolomites
ITALIAN ROCK - Rock Climbs in Northern Italy
CLASSIC CLIMBS IN THE DOLOMITES
WALKING IN THE DOLOMITES
THE JULIAN ALPS

MEDITERRANEAN COUNTRIES
THE MOUNTAINS OF GREECE
CRETE: Off the beaten track
TREKS & CLIMBS JORDAN
THE ATLAS MOUNTAINS
WALKS & CLIMBS IN THE ALA DAG (Turkey)

OTHER COUNTRIES
ADVENTURE TREKS - W. N. AMERICA
ADVENTURE TREKS - NEPAL
ANNAPURNA TREKKERS GUIDE
CLASSIC TRAMPS IN NEW ZEALAND
TREKKING IN THE CAUCAUSUS

GENERAL OUTDOOR BOOKS
THE HILL WALKERS MANUAL
FIRST AID FOR HILLWALKERS
MOUNTAIN WEATHER
MOUNTAINEERING LITERATURE
THE ADVENTURE ALTERNATIVE
MODERN ALPINE CLIMBING
ROPE TECHNIQUES IN MOUNTAINEERING
MODERN SNOW & ICE TECHNIQUES
LIMESTONE -100 BEST CLIMBS IN BRITAIN

CANOEING
SNOWDONIA WILD WATER, SEA & SURF
WILDWATER CANOEING
CANOEIST'S GUIDE TO THE NORTH EAST

CARTOON BOOKS
ON FOOT & FINGER
ON MORE FEET & FINGERS
LAUGHS ALONG THE PENNINE WAY

*Also a full range of guidebooks
to walking, scrambling, ice-climbing,
rock climbing, and other adventurous
pursuits in Britain and abroad*

---

*Other guides are constantly being added to the Cicerone List.
Available from bookshops, outdoor equipment shops or direct (send for price list)
from CICERONE, 2 POLICE SQUARE, MILNTHORPE, CUMBRIA, LA7 7PY*

Printed in Hong Kong by Vimnice Printing Press Co Ltd.